Charles Seale-Hayne Library
University of Plymouth
(01752) 588 588

AUDITORY PROCESSING OF COMPLEX SOUNDS

Edited by
Willliam A. Yost, PhD
Parmly Hearing Institute
Loyola University, Chicago, Illinois

Charles S. Watson, PhD
Department of Speech and Hearing Sciences
Indiana University, Bloomington, Indiana

LEA LAWRENCE ERLBAUM ASSOCIATES, PUBLISHERS
1987   Hillsdale, New Jersey   London

Lawrence Erlbaum Associates, Inc., Publishers
365 Broadway
Hillsdale, New Jersey 07642

Library of Congress Cataloging-in-Publication Data

Auditory processing of complex sounds.

"With the support of the AFOSR the Sarasota Workshop
on Auditory Processing of Complex Sounds was held in
April 1986"—Pref.
Includes bibliographies and indexes.
1. Auditory perception—Congresses. 2. Psychoacoustics
—Congresses. I. Yost, William A. II. Watson,
Charles S. III. United States. Air Force. Office of
Scientific Research. IV. Sarasota Workshop on Auditory
Processing of Complex Sounds (1986)
QP465.A93 A93 1986 152.1'5 86-29135
ISBN 0-89859-981-4

Printed in the United States of America
10 9 8 7 6 5 4 3 2 1

TABLE OF CONTENTS

iii

CONTRIBUTORS:

Paul J. Abbas
Dept. of Speech Pathology-
Audiology
University of Iowa
Iowa City IA 52242

P.E. Barta
Dept. of Biomedical
Engineering
Johns Hopkins University
School of Medicine
Baltimore MD 21205

Leslie R. Bernstein
Dept. of Psychology
University of Florida
Gainesville FL 32610

Jens Blauert
Ruhr-Universitat,
Lehrstuhl AEA
Postfach 102148
4630 Bochum 1
Fed. Republic of Germany

Brian P. Callaghan
Boys Town National
Institute for Communication
Disorders
555 N. 30th St.
Omaha NE 68131

Robert P. Carlyon
MRC Institute of Hearing
Research
University Park
Nottingham England NG7 2RD

Nelson Cowan
Dept. of Psychology
210 McAlester Hall
University of Missouri
Columbia MO 65211

Pierre Divenyi
Speech & Hearing Facility
VA Medical Center
Martinez CA 94553

Raymond H. Dye, Jr.
Parmly Hearing Institute
Loyola University
6525 N. Sheridan Rd.
Chicago IL 60626

Deborah A. Fantini
Dept. of Psychology
University of Minnesota
75 E. River Rd.
Minneapolis MN 54455

Glen R. Farley
Boys Town National
Institute for Communication
Disorders
555 N. 30th St.
Omaha NE 68131

Lawrence L. Feth
University of Kansas
Depts. of Speech, Language,
Hearing
3129 Tomahawk Drive
Lawrence KS 66045

C. Craig Formby
University of Florida
Depts. of Communicative
Disorders/ Neurology
Box J-174/ J.H. Miller
Health Center
Gainesville FL 32610

Robert H. Gilkey
Central Institute for the
Deaf
818 S. Euclid
St. Louis MO 63110

David M. Green
Dept. of Psychology
University of Florida
Gainesville FL 32605

Steven Greenberg
Dept. of Neurophysiology
University of Wisconsin
Madison WI 53706

Joseph W. Hall
School of Medicine
Division of
Otolaryngology
Head and Neck Surgery
The University of North
Carolina
Chapel Hill NC 27514

Patrick J. Harder
Parmly Hearing Institute
Loyola University
6525 N. Sheridan Rd.
Chicago IL 60626

William M. Hartmann
Physics Dept.
Michigan State University
East Lansing MI 48824

J.W. Horst
Institute of Audiology
University Hospital
P.O. Box 30.001, Groningen
The Netherlands

Tammo Houtgast
Institute for Perception
Soesterberg, Kampweg 5
Postbus 23
The Netherlands

Stewart H. Hulse
Dept. of Psychology
Johns Hopkins University
Baltimore MD 21218

Eric Javel
Boys Town National
Institute for Communication
Disorders
555 N. 30th St.
Omaha NE 68131

Gerald Kidd, Jr.
Boston University
Dept. of Communication
Disorders
48 Cummington St.
Boston MA 02215

Michael Kubovy
Dept. of Psychology
Rutgers State University of
New Jersey
Psychology Building/Busch
Campus
New Brunswick NJ 08903

Marjorie R. Leek
Dept. of Communication
Disorders
University of Minnesota
Minneaplois MN 55455

James D. Miller
Central Institute for the
Deaf
818 S. Euclid
St. Louis MO 63110

Brian C.J. Moore
University of Cambridge
Psychological Lab
Downing St.
Cambridge CB2 3EB
England

Donna L. Neff
Boys Town National
Institute for Communication
Disorders
555 N. 30th St.
Omaha NE 68131

Roy D. Patterson
MRC Applied Psychology
Dept.
15 Chaucer Rd.
Cambridge
England CB2 2EF

David B. Pisoni
Dept. of Psychology
Indiana University
Bloomington IN 47405

William S. Rhode
Dept. of Neurophysiology
University of Wisconsin
Madison WI 53706

Virginia Richards
Dept. Psychology
University of Florida
Gainesville FL   32610

Donald A. Robin
Dept. of Speech Pathology-
Audiology
University of Iowa
Iowa City IA   52242

Fred L. Royer
Dept. of Speech Pathology-
Audiology
University of Iowa
Iowa City IA   52242

Murray B. Sachs
Dept. of Biomedical
Engineering
Johns Hopkins School of
Medicine
Baltimore MD   21209

Robert D. Sorkin
Psychological Sciences
Building
Pierce Hall
Indiana University
West Lafayette IN   47907

Liza J. Stover
University of Kansas
Depts. of Speech, Language,
Hearing
3129 Tomahawk Drive
Lawrence KS   66045

Enrst Terhardt
Tech. Univ Muenchen
Arcisstr 21, D-8000
Muenchen 2
Fed. Republic of Germany

Neal F. Viemeister
Dept. of Psychology
University of Minnesota
75 E. River Rd.
Minneapolis MN   54455

Raymond L. Winslow
Institute for Biomedical
Computing
Washington University
St. Louis MO   63110

Charles S. Watson
Dept. of Speech and
Hearing Sciences
Indiana University
Bloomington IN   47405

William A. Yost
Parmly Hearing Institute
Loyola University
6525 N. Sheridan Rd.
Chicago IL   60626

Preface

This book is the result of a workshop on the processing of complex sounds held in Sarasota Florida in April 1986. The workshop was supported by the Air Force Office of Scientific Research (AFOSR), Life Sciences, and was chaired by the editors of this book. A series of recent events led to the workshop and to publication of this book. In 1982, Dr. John Tangney of AFOSR asked the Committee on Hearing, Bioacoustics and Biomechanics (CHABA) of the National Academy of Sciences to survey recent developments and trends in the biological and behavioral study of the auditory system. The result of the request from AFOSR was a 1983 Symposium on _Basic Research in Hearing_ organized by CHABA and sponsored by the AFOSR (Dolan and Yost, J. Acoust. Soc. Am. 78, No.1 Part 2, 1985). After reviewing the proceedings of the CHABA Symposium and considering its program goals, AFOSR began a program of support for research on complex auditory perception. The support by the AFOSR, the discussions at the CHABA Symposium, and the increase volume of research on the topic of auditory processing of complex sounds stimulated us to organize a meeting on this topic. With the support of the AFOSR the Sarasota Workshop on Auditory Processing of Complex Sounds was held in April, 1986.

Although the chapters in this book include most of the topics presented at the workshop, the book is not a "proceedings." We did not organize the workshop with the intent of publishing a book. The topics were chosen from the many excellent submitted papers in order to sample as diverse a cross-section of research as possible and yet provide continuity to the three day meeting. The quality and quantity of abstracts submitted for inclusion in the workshop and the enthusiastic and insightful discussions at the meeting convinced us and the participants that a timely publication devoted to these topics would be a useful contribution. Therefore, following the workshop the authors prepared chapters in camera-ready form in order to produce a book in a short period of time. The chapters are not just transcriptions of the presentations given at the workshop, but were written as brief papers on the topic of the author's interest. Authors were encouraged to provide some background and to make sure the germinal references on their topic were included in the bibliography.

Assistance for this project has come from many sources. The Workshop and the book would not be possible without the foresight and dedicated support of John

Preface

Tangney as a Program Director in the Life Sciences
Division of AFOSR. The staff at the Sarasota Sheraton
Hotel provided a pleasant environment in which to meet.
Lawrence Erlbaum Press has been very helpful in assisting
us in getting the book out quickly. The staff of the
Parmly Hearing Institute at Loyola University, especially
Marilyn Larson, Beth Langer, Ned Avejic, and Scott
Stubenvoll have been invaluable, as has the staff of the
Department of Speech and Hearing Sciences at Indiana
University, especially Janet Farmer. Most importantly we
want to thank the authors of the chapters and the
participants and observers at the Workshop. Without their
stimulating ideas, high quality research, and good-
natured acceptance of our deadlines and ultimatums, there
would be no book.

We hope this book captures some of the excitement we
felt at the workshop as we discussed this new era in the
study of auditory processing. All of the important
contributions that are being made to understanding
auditory processing of complex sounds could not be
included in this single volume. However, the chapters do
touch base with many of the lines of research and theory
on complex sound and its perception, and they should
provide both food for thought and a broad introduction to
the literature on a topic that we are sure will be
studied intensely during the next couple of decades.

WAY
CSW

Introduction: Auditory Processing of Complex Sounds

William A. Yost
Parmly Hearing Institute
Loyola University
Chicago, Illinois

Charles S. Watson
Department of Speech and Hearing Sciences
Indiana University
Bloomington, Indiana

This Introduction provides a general overview of some of the major concepts that appear throughout the chapters of the book. It is not an exhaustive coverage of the subjects discussed in the individual chapters, although it does attempt to highlight some of the new directions taken by the authors in their study of auditory processing of complex sounds.

This workshop brought together investigators with a remarkable diversity of approaches to the general problem of how humans (and nonhumans) process (or "hear," or "perceive") complex sounds. The only common denominator at the onset was that each had responded to an announcement (mailed or published in a journal), asking for contributed papers for a "workshop on complex sound perception." Surprisingly, this yielded a range of topics, research paradigms, and theoretical perspectives with some well-defined themes.

We anticipated that "complexity" would mean different things to different people, but the range of meanings that can be inferred from these twenty-eight papers is actually relatively small. In general, "simple sounds" are considered to be the individual pure tones or noise bursts that have served as the stimuli in most studies of the auditory system since Helmholtz. "Complex stimuli" mean those that vary systemically in either their spectrum, or in time, or both. While most of the contributors created complex stimuli to test particular hypotheses about auditory processing, a few dealt with natural or environmental sounds, speech, birdsongs, or music.

Many of the authors avoided the need to discuss physical criteria for stimulus "complexity," and instead opted for distinctions based on mechanisms of processing.

1

"Simple processing" in the spectral domain was equated by most authors with a critical band (CB) model, and in the temporal domain with the time constant of a simple temporal integrator. "Complex processing" was shown to require a considerable variety of mechanisms beyond these traditional workhorses of auditory theory, including spectral-shape and temporal-pattern detectors, and even more elaborate analyzers (hardware, software, or both) whose operation in many cases requires knowledge of the sources of complex sounds.

In general, the contributions can be divided into: (1) spectral processing, (2) temporal processing, (3) pitch, (4) speech, (5) physiological processing, and (6) perceptual organization; including "object" or event perception and central mechanisms. These a posteriori categories cannot, of course, capture the scope of numerous papers that treated more than one of these topics as, for example, several that dealt with stimuli varying both in spectrum and in time. The papers have been grouped into these six categories, but the reader is warned not to expect discussions of spectral processing to be confined to papers in the section bearing that name, and so forth.

The chapters that deal with spectral aspects of complex processing generally agree, as observed above, that considerably more elaborate frequency analysis can be demonstrated in psychoacoustic experiments than is predictable from a "bare-boned" critical-band filter bank. It should be stressed that none of these "failures of critical band theory" in fact provide evidence against the CB as an initial stage in frequency analysis. Several lines of investigation, however, demonstrate that when it is to the advantage of the listener to do so, he or she can simultaneously process energy arriving in several critical bands. That ability is demonstrated in two types of experiments. In one, a broad-band spectral array itself is treated as the meaningful event (i.e., a "signal"), rather than just one part of the spectrum (that associated with the output of a single auditory filter). Studies of "profile analysis" or spectral shape discrimination and its derivatives are examples of this approach. In the other, it is shown that temporal correlations among the noise levels across critical bands can reduce the masking efficiency of a critical-band masker (co-modulation release from masking or CMR). In both cases, mechanisms are implied which are simultaneously sensitive to the relative levels in each

2

of a number of adjacent auditory channels. Common sense would have predicted at least one of these findings; vowel identification obviously requires recognition of spectral shape.

Some of the chapters discuss the nature of the physiological code that might subserve spectral pattern processing. The consensus seems to be that rate codes _and_ temporal codes are both used by the central nervous system to process complex spectral patterns. These lines of research (both psychophysical and physiological) promise to establish the limits within which such spectral-shape- or profile-based recognition can operate.

Many sounds of everyday life may be described as temporal sequence of stimuli. If very similar (highly correlated) sounds occur in close temporal proximity, then under many circumstances, the auditory system is most sensitive to the first arriving information rather than to the pattern of the events. Studies of the precedence effect have provided insights into the mechanisms that govern the influence of the first acoustic wavefront. When the sequence of sounds is made up of different or uncorrelated acoustic events, the temporal pattern may lead to a variety of perceptions. Often times one part of a temporal pattern may be "heard out" from the background of the rest of the sound. In many contexts the last acoustic events are the most salient. The analogy to the foreground/background concepts of stream segregation (as derived from Gestalt Theory) is one theoretical approach to describe the dominance or saliency of certain aspects of a complex temporal pattern. Several computational schemes also provide insights into how to model discrimination among different sequences of sound. A variety of lines of research show the major role played by temporal modulation in our perception of complex sounds. The abundance of useful information available in the temporal code of the auditory nerve provides a physiological argument favoring temporal modulation as a variable around which many perceptions of complex sounds appear to be organized.

There are only so many words that can be used to describe a sound. One of the most common is "pitch." Although there is some disagreement about the precise definition of pitch, a variety of complex sounds are capable of producing sensations listeners refer to has having that perceptual attribute. Many authors consider

3

pitch to be a major organizing feature for our
perceptions of complex sounds. Models based only on
auditory neural tuning or only on neural temporal
periodicity, have failed to provide adequate descriptions
of the pitch evoked by many complex sounds. Thus, the
debate concerning whether complex pitch is spectrally or
temporally based continues. Much of the research in this
book suggests that the extraction of pitch from complex
stimuli is not an "either-or" question. In both spectral
shape processing and pitch processing neural tuning <u>and</u>
temporal coding must be considered. In addition, although
the auditory nerve contains a wealth of temporal and
spectral information, central mechanisms are probably
required to fully process the peripheral neural code in a
manner adequate to account for complex pitch perception.

If a complex sound contains short term spectral
changes then these might give rise to pitches which
listeners could use in processing these sounds. The work
on stream segregation, spectral shape discrimination, and
tonal pattern recognition suggest the need to consider
possible long-term and short-term spectral cues that may
be used to detect, discriminate, or identify many complex
sounds.

Most of the chapters generally conclude, not only
that the peripheral mechanisms of auditory tuning and
simple temporal integration are inadequate to explain the
hearing of complex sounds, but also that some fairly
elaborate central processing must be involved. A few
papers explicitly deal with selective attention, short-
term memory capacity, and other such cognitive
constructs. It is clear that the "passive" auditory
system is in fact very dynamic and can effectively be
"programmed" to look like quite a variety of acoustic
information processing devices. If we are to cope with
such practical issues as auditory code learning (speech
or non-speech), it is essential that we learn some of the
primary limitations within which the central processor
functions. How long can a sound be, if it is to be
accurately recalled, or recognized later? How much of a
complex sound must be processed "categorically," if any?
Within what parameters must selective auditory attention
function? Are there two auditory modes, one for speech
and one for non-speech? Or, do we process very familiar
sounds (e.g. speech in our native tongue) differently
from novel sounds? Several papers made efforts to deal
with these issues, but it is clear that a great deal

remains to be done before we will understand the actual auditory processing that occurs at a cocktail party.

One fascinating line of thought carries on from the tradition of Gestalt Psychology. Certain organizing principles seem to be used when we hear a novel complex sound. Sometimes a portion of a total waveform "stands out", i.e. seems to be closer. That is an instance of auditory Gestalt perception. Those chapters concerned with Gestalt theory suggest a number of possible organizing rules for processing novel sounds. Certainly, frequency similarity is one of the potent determinants of forming a "figure" from the "background." It appears that musicians may be ahead of basic scientists in understanding some of these organizing axioms. Many of these concepts appear to be applicable whether we use speech and human communication, complex non-speech sounds, music, or an animal model, such as songbirds, as our tool for understanding auditory processing.

In general, the chapters in this book do two things. They provide many examples of why tuning and/or simple temporal integration are not sufficient mechanisms to account for the perception of complex sounds. They also review a variety of recent experimental findings that should be considered when models or theories of perceptual organization are proposed to describe auditory perception of complex sounds. These chapters provide a few answers and many, many questions. It is the latter, that indicates a rich future for the study of hearing.

THE DETECTION OF SPECTRAL SHAPE CHANGE

Leslie R. Bernstein, Virginia Richards, and David M. Green
Psychology Department, University of Florida, Gainesville, Florida, 32611, U.S.A.

Introduction

We describe several experiments involving the detection of a change in the spectral shape of a complex auditory signal, what we call profile-analysis. All of the experiments are discrimination tasks involving a broadband "standard" spectrum and some alteration of that spectrum produced by adding a "signal" to the standard. For all of the experiments described here, we used a standard composed of a set of equal-amplitude sinusoidal components. The spectrum of the standard was, therefore, essentially flat. In different experiments, various waveforms were added to this standard to create changes in its spectral shape, and the ability to detect such changes was measured. In the first experiments, we describe how the relative phase among the components of the standard waveform influences the detection of a signal. The results are very simple. Phase seems to play no important role. The detection of a change in spectral shape appears to depend only on changes in the power spectrum of the signal and is independent of the temporal waveform. Next, we describe how the detection of an increment in a single component depends on the frequency of that component. These results provide the basic data to evaluate complex changes in the whole spectrum, such as a sinusoidal ripple in the amplitudes of the components over the entire spectrum. Our data indicate that there is a sizable discrepancy between the ability to detect changes occurring over the entire spectrum and the ability to detect changes in single components.

Procedure

We used a two-alternative, forced-choice procedure to evaluate the detectability of the change in spectral shape. In one interval, the listener heard the "stardard" sound; in the other interval, the listener heard the "standard plus signal". The signal component was always added at a fixed phase relation to the standard component, generally in-phase. An adaptive

6

two-down, one-up rule was used to estimate 70.7 % correct detection. The thresholds reported are the signal amplitude re the component of the standard to which the signal is added. A threshold of 0 dB means that the signal and standard components are equal in amplitude. Typically, the average threshold was based on at least 12 runs of 50 trials. Each sound was generated digitially and presented for about 100 msec.

The standard spectrum was composed of a sum of sinusoidal components. Except for one experiment where the number of components is varied, there were 21 components extending in frequency from 200 to 5000 Hz. The ratio of the frequencies between sucessive components was constant; that is, the frequencies were spaced equally on a logarithmic scale. Because distance along the basilar membrane is proportional to the logarithm of frequency, our components provided a roughly uniform stimulus over the linear receptor surface of the cochlea.

One final experimental feature must be clearly understood. Because we are interested in the detection of a change in spectral shape, we must ensure that the observer is not simply discriminating a change in intensity at a single frequency region. To do this, we randomly varied the overall level of the sound on each and every presentation. The level of the sound was chosen from a rectangular distribution of intensity covering a range of 20 or 40 dB in 1 dB steps. The median level was about 50 to 60 dB SPL. Thus, while the "flat" standard might be presented at 71 dB, the altered spectrum, the "signal plus standard", might be presented at 34 dB on a given trial of the forced-choice procedure. The observer's task was to detect the sound with the altered spectral shape despite the difference in overall level.

Effects of phase

In most of the experiments concerning profile analysis, the phase of each component of the multitonal complex has been chosen at random and the same waveform (except for random variation of level) is presented during each "non-signal" interval. Therefore, the logical possibility exists that observers might recognize some aspect or aspects of the temporal waveform. If this were true, then discrimination could

7

be based on some alteration of the temporal waveform during the "signal" interval rather than by a change in the spectral shape of the stimulus per se.

Green and Mason (1985) investigated this possibility directly with the following experimental manipulations. Multicomponent complexes were generated which consisted of 5, 11, 21, or 43 components spaced logarithmically. In all cases, the frequency of the lowest component was 200 Hz, the highest was 5 kHz. The overall level of the complex was varied randomly over a 40 dB range across presentations with a median level of 45 dB SPL per component. The signal consisted of an increment to the 1-kHz, central component of the complex.

In what Green and Mason termed the "fixed-phase" condition, four different complexes were generated for each number of components (5, 11, 21, and 43) by randomly selecting the phases of each component. Note that for these fixed-phase conditions, the same waveform (except for random variation of overall level) occurred during each non-signal interval.

In what Green and Mason called the "random-phase" conditions, 88 different phase-randomizations of the multicomponent complex were generated. On each interval of each trial, one of the 88 waveforms was selected at random (with replacement) for presentation. Thus, the temporal waveforms generally differed on each presentation. The amplitude spectra, however, were identical.

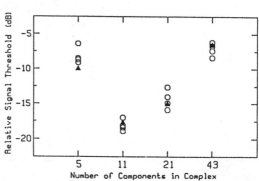

Figure 1. Signal threshold (dB) as a function of the number of components in the complex. Open circles: data obtained for each of the four phase-randomizations when the phase of each component was fixed throughout a block of trials ("fixed-phase" condition). Filled triangles: data from the "random-phase" condition in which the phases of the components were chosen at random on each presentation.

The results are presented in Figure 1. For each value of component number, the open circles represent

8

the thresholds obtained for each of the four
randomizations in the fixed-phase condition. The
triangles represent the data obtained in the random-
phase conditions. The results indicate that changing
the phase of the individual components and thus the
characteristics of the temporal waveform has little, if
any, effect on discrimination even if the waveform is
chosen at random on each and every presentation. These
data are consistent with those obtained by Green,
Mason, and Kidd (1984) who generated waveforms
utilizing a procedure similar to the fixed-phase
condition described above.

The inability of changes in the phase of the
individual components, and thus changes in the
characteristics of the temporal waveform, to affect
discrimination supports the view that, in these tasks,
observers are, indeed, basing their judgements on
changes in spectral shape.

The form of the function relating threshold to the
number of components in the complex is one that has
been replicated many times in our laboratory. In
general, as the number of components and thus the
density of the profile is increased from 3 to 11 or 21
performance improves. An intuitive explanation for
this result is that as the number of components which
compose the profile is increased, additional
independent bands or channels contribute to an estimate
of the "level" of the profile.

Further increases in the density of the profile
lead to decrements in performance and this trend is,
for the most part, explained by simple masking. When
the components are spaced so closely such that several
components fall within the "critical band" of the
signal, the addition of the signal produces a smaller
relative increase in intensity and thus becomes more
difficult to detect. In future publications we will
present a more detailed analysis of these effects.

Frequency Effects

The results discussed above suggest that detection
of an increment to a single component of a multi-
component complex is based on changes in spectral
shape. The phase relation among the components appears

9

to have little, if any, effect on performance.

In exploring the nature of this process, one fundamental question is whether the frequency of the component which is incremented (the frequency region where the change in the power spectrum occurs) greatly influences the ability to detect a change in spectral shape.

This question also bears on that of how the auditory system codes intensity. There are, at least, two different mechanisms that have been proposed as the basis for detecting changes in the intensity of sinusoidal components. One is what we will call the "rate" model. It assumes that changes in acoustic intensity are coded as changes in the rate at which fibers of the eighth nerve fire. One limitation of this model is the fact that the firing rates of practically all auditory fibers saturate as the intensity of the stimulus is increased (Kiang 1965; Sachs and Abbas, 1974; Evans and Palmer, 1980). The dynamic range of firing rate for many fibers is only about 20 to 30 dB. On the other hand, it is possible that there is some residual information in small changes of rate even at the highest stimulus levels where the amount of change produced by increasing the intensity of the stimulus is small. There is also the question of how one should regard saturation when one considers the entire population of fibers which may respond to a given stimulus in that different populations of fibers may saturate at different intensities.

A second view of intensity coding stresses the temporal characteristics of neural discharges. Sachs and Young (1979) and Young and Sachs(1979) have demonstrated that "neural spectograms" based on neural synchrony measures preserve the shape of speech spectra better than those based on firing rate. We were, therefore, particularly interested in how well observers could detect a change in spectral shape at very high frequencies. At the highest frequencies, above 2000 Hz, neural synchrony deteriorates and, if that code were used to signal changes in spectral shape, then the ability to detect such alterations in the acoustic spectrum should also deteriorate.

In one previous study, Green and Mason (1985), we

10

made some measurements of how the locus in frequency affects the ability to detect a change in a complex spectrum. Our results suggested that the mid-frequency region, 500 to 2000 Hz, yielded the best performanace but variability among the different observers was sizable. Also, those data may have been contaminated by the listeners having received substantial prior practice with signals which were in the middle of the range.

The results of our most extensive experiment (Green, Onsan, and Forrest, 1986) on this issue are shown in Figure 2. The standard spectrum is a complex of 21-components, all equal in amplitude and equally spaced in logarithmic frequency. The overall level of the standard was varied over a 20-dB range with a median level of 40 dB SPL per component. The signal, whose frequency is plotted along the abscissa of the figure, was an increment in the intensity of a single component. The ordinate, like that of Fig. 1, is the signal level re the component level to which it was added. The results show that best detection occurs in a frequency range of 300 to 3000 Hz, with only a mild deterioration occurring at the higher and lower frequencies. If detection of an increment in this task were mediated by changes in neural synchrony, one would expect to observe considerably poorer performance at the highest frequencies as compared to the middle and low frequencies. This did not occur.

Figure 2. Signal threshold (dB) as a function of the frequency of the signal. Twenty-one-component complexes were employed. The signal was added in-phase to the corresponding component in the complex.

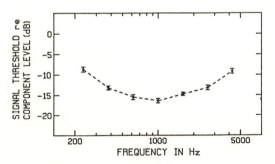

One other result from this recent study also deserves mention. The experiment described immediately above was repeated with one important exception. The median level of the standard was 60 rather than 40 dB SPL. This higher intensity level would be expected to produce firing rates at or close to saturation in nearly all fibers. Despite this fact, the thresholds obtained were, in almost all cases, <u>lower</u> than those obtained at the lower intensity level.

In conclusion, these two results do not afford a determination of the underlying neural code which mediates the detection of a change of spectral shape in our experiments.

Complex Spectral Changes

The experiments described above involve changes in the intensity of a single component of the multi-component profile (a "bump" in the spectrum). We now turn our attention to more complicated manipulations, experiments in which the intensities of several components of the spectrum were altered simultaneously. A primary goal of these experiments was to determine whether listeners' ability to detect these complex changes could be predicted on the basis of their sensitivity to changes in the intensity of a single component in the profile.

Figure 3. Three different frequencies, k, using sinusoidal variation. The signal amplitude at each component frequency is given by Eq. 1 and is added to the standard with a relative amplitude about 1/5 the standard amplitude.

Once again, a flat, "standard" composed of logarithmically spaced components ranging from 200 to 5000 Hz was used. The signal, however had an amplitude-spectrum that varied sinusoidally. The amplitude of the ith component, a[i], was given by

a[i] = sin(2 * pi * k * i/M)   i=1,M   Eq. 1

where k represents the "frequency" of the variation and M is the number of components presented. We refer to this variation in amplitude as a "sinusoidally rippled" spectrum, and to k as the "ripple frequency". Figure 3 illustrates the result of in-phase addition of the

"standard" and the "signal" of for case M=21. The
three values of k are as indicated. Cosinusoidally
rippled amplitude spectra have also been examined.
Such signals are generated as described above, except
that the sine term of Eq. 1 is replaced by cosine.

Two points deserve note. The first is that k, the
frequency of the ripple, is restricted by the number of
components. This value must be smaller than one half
the number of components (k < M/2). Second, changing
the value of k does not alter the signal's root-mean-
square (RMS) amplitude. All values of k produce the
same a[i]'s, only their order is changed.

Thresholds were measured as the RMS amplitude of
the signal re the RMS amplitude of the standard.
Values of k ranged from 1 to 10. Thresholds were
virtually constant for all values of k (ripple
frequency) and type of varialtion (sine or cosine),
with an average of -24.5 dB across all conditions
(Green, Onsan and Forrest, 1986).

These data define a modulation transfer function
(MTF). Interestingly, this function is flat rather
than exhibiting the low-pass characteristic that is
typically observed in sensory psychophysics. Because k
may not exceed 10 for this 21-component complex, we
were unable to investigate higher ripple frequencies
and thus to assess more completely the form of the MTF.
Undoubtedly, thresholds would increase if the ripple
frequency were sufficiently large. We are currently
examining the effect of greater ripple frequencies by
using profiles composed of a greater number of
components. These data will allow us to describe more
fully the MTF i.e., the relation between the frequency
of the ripple and detectability.

Finally, let us compare the rippled specrtum
thresholds with predictions based on the ability to
discriminate a bump in the spectrum; data obtained
using increments to a single component of the profile.
Because the ability to detect an increment in a single
component of a 21 component spectrum is, to a first
approximation, independent of the frequency of the
signal (Fig. 2), one may predict the threshold for
these 21 component rippled spectra. If we assume that
the information concerning changes in the intensity of
each of the signal's 21 channels is processed

13

independently and that d' is proportional to pressure, then the optimal combination is the one in which the squared d' for the complex stimulus is equal to the sum of the squared d's associated with the each of the channels (Green and Swets, 1966). This leads to the expectation that the detectability will be improved by the square root of 21.

The process is as follows. The detection of a bump in a flat profile leads to thresholds of about -16 dB. This translates to a pressure of 0.16 relative to the standard. Thus, we would expect that the average pressure per component for a 21 component signal to be $0.16/\sqrt{21}$ or 0.035 (relative to the standard) which is equivalent to an RMS amplitude of -29 dB. This value is 4.5 dB smaller than the mean of -24.5 dB observed. Thus, performance on the complex spectral shape discrimination task is poorer than expected based on the data collected using changes in the intensity of a single component in the spectrum.

One could argue, of course, that there are less than 21 independent estimates of the spectrum. This is certainly possible, but two points argue against it. The first is that only six or seven independent channels across the 200 to 5000 Hz range are needed in order to acheive the level of performance found in using the rippled spectra. Second, if the different components are not processed independently, then increasing the ripple frequency would be expected to produce increases in discrimination thresholds. Rather, we find that ripple frequency does not affect threshold levels over the range of values tested, and that the thresholds obtained using complex, rippled spectra fall short of those expected based on the results of discrimination of changes in a single component of the profile.

Acknowledgement

This research was supported in part, by grants from the National Institutes of Health and the Air Force Office of Scientific Research. Dr. Richards was supported, in part, by an NIH post-doctoral fellowship.

References

Evans, E. F. and Palmer, A. R. (1980). Relationship

14

between the dynamic range of cochlear nerve fibres and their spontaneous activity. Experimental Brain Research, 40, 115-118.

Green, D. M. and Mason, C. R. (1985). Auditory profile analysis: Frequency, phase, and Weber's Law. Journal of the Acoustical Society of America, 77, 1155-1161.

Green, D. M., Mason, C.R. and Kidd, G., (1984). "Profile analysis: Critical bands and duration," J. Acoust. Soc. Am. 75, 1163 - 1167.

Green, D. M., Onsan, Z. A. and Forrest, T. G. (1986). Frequency effects in profile analysis. Paper in preparation for the Journal of the Acoustical Society of America.

Green, D. M. and Swets, J. A. Signal detection theory and psychophysics. New York: Wiley, 1966 (Reprinted by R. E. Krieger, Huntington, N. Y., 1974.)

Kiang, N. Y.-S. (1965). Discharge patterns of single fibers in the cat's auditory nerve. Research Monograph 35, Cambridge, MA: MIT Press.

Sachs, M. B. and Abbas, P. J. (1974). Rate versus level functions for auditory-nerve fibers in cats: Tone-burst stimuli. Journal of the Acoustical Society of America, 56, 1835-1847.

Sachs, M. B., and Young, E. D. (1979). Encoding of steady-state vowels in the auditory nerve: Representation in terms of discharge rate. Journal of the Acoustical Society of America 66, 470-479.

Young, E. D. and Sachs, M. B., (1979). Representation of steady-state vowels in the temporal aspects of the discharge patterns of populations of auditory-nerver fibers. Journal of the Acoustical Society of America, 66, 1381-1403.

Additional Reference

Green, D. M. Profile Analysis:Auditory Intensity Discrimination. In Press, Oxford University Press, 1986.

Auditory discrimination of complex sounds: The effects
of amplitude perturbation on spectral shape
discrimination.

Gerald Kidd, Jr.
Department of Communication Disorders, Boston University,
48 Cummington Street, Boston, Massachusetts 02215

     This paper describes some of the conditions
limiting performance in spectral shape discrimination
experiments. Specifically examined is the relationship
between detection of an alteration in a broadband
reference spectrum, the effects of "random perturbation"
in amplitude of the reference spectrum and the information available to the observer in sequential stimulus
presentations. The experimental results help illustrate
the complexities of devising a comprehensive model of
"auditory profile analysis".

INTRODUCTION
     The work described in this paper is based on a
series of experiments performed during the past four
years dealing with the perception of complex sounds.
The author's collaborators on portions of this work were
David M. Green, Thomas E. Hanna and Christine R. Mason.
     From infancy, human listeners learn to identify a
vast number of complex, nonspeech sounds based on their
characteristic patterns of time-varying acoustic energy.
Thus, we are able to detect, locate, attend to, and
derive information from a multitude of sound sources in
our environment.
     As a result of the availability of electronic sound
production equipment over one-half century ago, the
study of auditory perception has focused on relating
observer's perceptions to simple acoustic signals. Pure
tones, and to some degree, bands of random noise, are
readily characterized by the perceptual correlates of
intensity, frequency and duration; that is, loudness,
pitch and apparent duration. Further, it is relatively
easy to vary the physical properties of these signals in
a well-defined manner and expect that detectability or
discriminability will also vary in an orderly and
meaningful way.
     An important goal of current research in audition
is to relate the theories and models developed over the

16

past half-century using simple acoustic signals to listener's auditory behavior in the complex, time-varying acoustic environment we live in. This is now a realistic goal because the technical tools have become available for generating complex sounds of arbitrary composition quickly and accurately. Just as the advent of modern electronics expanded and shaped auditory research early in the century, so has the availability of low-cost digital computers allowed the synthesis of virtually any physically realizable waveform. Thus, it is possible to devise a whole new class of experiments that would have been difficult, if not impossible, twenty years ago.

As the technical limitations on research in complex sound perception disappear, fundamental questions remain about what should be measured, how we should measure it and why it is important. Which aspects of complex acoustic signals have meaningful perceptual correlates? Which physical properties of sounds may be varied to produce orderly detection or discrimination functions that teach us something about perception of complex sounds in the "real world"?

EXPERIMENTAL RESULTS AND DISCUSSION

The experiments described in this paper were designed to measure the discriminability of complex sounds on the basis of spectral shape. Spectral shape discrimination, per se, received relatively little attention until a recent series of papers by Green and his colleagues from Harvard University (Spiegel et al., 1981; Spiegel and Green, 1982; Green et al., 1983; Green and Kidd, 1983; Green, 1983; Green et al., 1984; Mason et al., 1984; Green and Mason, 1985; Kidd, Mason and Green, 1986). The basic paradigm requires that the listener detect an alteration (such as an intensity increment or decrement) to a broadband spectrum. While such a measurement would seem to be a minor variant on the traditional tone-in-noise masking experiment, one important improvisation was added by Spiegel et al. (1981). They limited the usefulness of choosing the more intense sound of each pair by randomly "roving" the overall level of each sound from interval to interval of every 2AFC trial. They used the term "profile analysis" to describe the process whereby changes in spectral shape were discriminable. The first figure is a schematic of common reference and comparison stimuli that are used in spectral shape discrimination experi-

ments. In this figure, two complex, multitone spectra
are shown. The spectrum on the left is the reference
spectrum and is composed of 21 equal-amplitude tones
equally spaced in logarithmic frequency from 200 to 5000
Hz. The spectrum on the right is the comparison
spectrum and is identical to that on the left, except
that a signal has been added. The signal is a 1000 Hz
sinusoid added in-phase to the 1000 Hz component of the
reference spectrum. The result of the addition of the
signal is an increment in the amplitude of a part of the
reference spectrum. The listener may discriminate
between the two sounds on the basis of a qualitative cue
that reflects an alteration in the shape of the reference spectrum. To assure that discrimination is based
on spectral shape, however, a within-trial random rove
of the overall level of the sounds is employed. Thus,
as shown in Figure 1, the nonsignal stimulus may have a
greater overall SPL than the sound containing the signal
limiting the usefulness of overall level as a cue in
discrimination. All of the experimental results described in this paper were obtained using a 40-dB within-
trial random rove of overall level. If the listener
were to attend to the output of a single critical band
centered on the 1000 Hz component, that level would
contain little useful information. In this procedure,
the level of any given sound is chosen randomly from a
rectangular distribution of levels (cf. Mason et al.,
1984).

The procedure of randomly roving the value of a
reference sound to limit the information available for
discrimination has been widely used in auditory
psychophysics. For example, Harris (1952) used a
"roving standard" frequency to measure the effects of

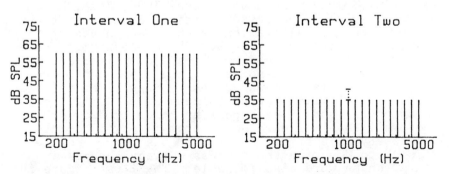

Figure 1. Multitone spectra used in spectral shape
    discrimination experiments.

interstimulus interval in a frequency discrimination
task. He found that roving the frequency of the standard
prevented the development of a long-term reference in
memory that could be used to overcome the effects of
ISI. The following is a small sample of studies
reporting similar or related findings employing a roving
or uncertain standard: Creelman (1960) and Green (1961)
for detection of signals of random frequency; Jesteadt
(1971) for frequency and intensity discrimination; Kidd
and Neff (1984) for frequency discrimination using a
roving standard and random interstimulus interval;
Berliner and Durlach (1973) for intensity discrimination;
Boggs and Sorkin (1982) and Sorkin (1984) for frequency
discrimination of tone sequences or tonal patterns;
Sorkin et al. (1982) for discrimination of temporal
jitter; Watson and Kelly (1981) for various aspects of
word-length tonal patterns; and Hanna (1985) for the
discriminability of samples of frozen noise.

Recently, we have applied the roving standard
procedure to spectral shape discrimination in a new way.
In this application, the shape of the reference spectrum
is randomly "roved" in a manner limiting certain aspects
of the discrimination task. The way spectral shape is
"roved" in this procedure is to introduce a quantifiable
"perturbation" in amplitude of components of the broadband reference spectrum. Figure 2 is a schematic of the
random amplitude perturbation. This figure shows the
21-component reference spectrum seen in the previous
figure. In this case, however, the amplitudes of the
tonal components of the multitone spectrum have been
"perturbed" by a gaussian weight. In the digital signal
generation procedure, the amplitude of any given
component is chosen randomly from a normal distribution
having an expected mean of 0 dB (that is, a "flat"
spectrum having no amplitude perturbation) and a standard deviation that is the independent variable. In all
cases, the 1000 Hz component to which the signal is
added, is "unperturbed", that is, at 0 dB relative level
perturbation. The dashed line and normal curve seen in
the figure indicate the expected mean and standard
deviation of the distribution, respectively.

Since the observer's task is to detect an alteration in the reference spectrum, the degree of amplitude
perturbation and the way in which it is employed in the
two-alternative forced-choice discrimination task, limit
discriminability. There are three ways that we have
presented stimuli that have been perturbed in this
manner. First, the stimuli are FIXED across a block of

19

trials. That is, a single irregular or perturbed reference spectrum is presented in every trial during a block of trials. The comparison stimuli are identical in spectral shape to the reference stimuli except for the addition of the intensity increment forming the signal. Thus, in the FIXED condition, the observer may use the accumulated information about the "sound" of the reference spectrum obtained during the block of trials. Further, it is possible to compare directly the two sounds within each trial. The primary limitation on discriminability imposed by this procedure is the degree of perturbation of the spectra, that is, the size of the standard deviation of the distribution.

A second condition is one in which the sound spectra are "perturbed between trials" (PBT). In this case, we generate a pool of reference spectra - usually about 100 in number - and store them on disk. Each member of this pool of 21-tone waveforms is a different set of samples from the same normal distribution of amplitudes. For the PBT condition, a different waveform from this pool is presented on every trial. The two sounds within each trial are identical in spectral shape except for the addition of the signal increment. Thus the listeners may compare directly the two sounds presented on any given trial, but, since the reference spectra are different on different trials, the information accumulated across trials is limited.

The third condition is one in which the spectra are "perturbed within trials" (PWT). In this case, every

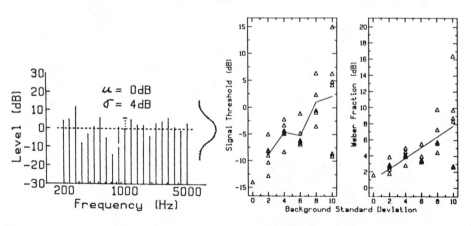

Figure 2. "Perturbed" multitone spectrum.

*Figure 3. Results from FIXED condition.

stimulus presentation is a different waveform chosen
from the pool of waveforms. One of the two sounds in
each trial is incremented by the addition of the
signal - just as in the other conditions. This procedure places limitations on both the direct comparison
of sounds within any given trial and on the accumulation
of information throughout a block of trials.

Figure 3 shows the results from a FIXED amplitude
perturbation experiment. The abscissa in both panels
is the standard deviation of the distribution of
amplitudes in decibels. The ordinate in the left panel
is signal threshold expressed as the ratio of the signal
tone to the corresponding tone in the background in
decibels. The same data are plotted in the right panel
with the quantitiy on the ordinate being one way of
expressing the Weber fraction in decibels, that is,
$10 \log ((\Delta I + I)/I)$. The triangles at each standard
deviation are six different samples of the reference
spectrum chosen from the same distribution. The single
triangle at a standard deviation of 0 dB represents the
threshold for a "flat" reference spectrum. Each triangle represents six estimates per subject obtained
using a 50-trial adaptive tracking procedure and averaged across three experienced observers. It is apparent
that, as the standard deviation of the reference spectrum increases, the average thresholds and the disper-
sion of thresholds about the mean both increase. A
straight-line fit to the thresholds in the right panel
has a slope of about 0.6, and the range of thresholds in
the same panel increases from about 3 dB at a standard
deviation of 2 to about 14 dB at a standard deviaton of
10. Part of this effect is attributable simply to
masking. That is, as the standard deviation of the
background increases, it becomes more likely that a tone
near in frequency to the signal tone will be at a level
that will mask the signal increment. Beyond that,
however, we believe that the differences in thresholds
reflect genuine differences in discriminability across
specific randomly perturbed spectra resulting from the
patterns of peaks and valleys in the spectra.

Figure 4 shows the results from a PBT condition.
The abscissa is interstimulus interval and the ordinate
is relative signal threshold. The two functions plotted
are for standard deviation's of 3 dB (filled circles)
and 6 dB (open circles). Each point is the average
threshold estimate across three observers derived from
an adaptive tracking procedure. The point of this study
was to examine conditions in which judgments of spectral

shape were made successively, rather than simultaneously.
The distinction between successive and simultaneous
comparisons was elaborated by Green et al. (1983) in a
paper contrasting spectral shape discrimination with
intensity discrimination. The results of the experiments
shown in Figure 4 indicate that, under certain conditions, listeners may rely upon successive comparisons
of spectral shape as the principal means for discrimination. This conclusion is drawn from the increase in
threshold as interstimulus interval is increased. This
effect of ISI shown in Figure 4 is generally not seen
for FIXED or PWT conditions.

At the opposite extreme from the FIXED condition is
the condition in which the amplitudes of the multitone
complexes are perturbed within trials (PWT). Figure 5
is a plot of the results from a PWT experiment. The
axes are the same as in Figure 3. That is, the abscissa
is the standard deviation of the reference spectra, the
left panel ordinate is relative signal threshold in dB
and the right panel ordinate is the Weber fraction in dB.
Each stimulus on every interval was chosen from a pool
of 100 stored waveforms for each standard deviation.
The data points are intersubject averages for six estimates per observer for three observers. The most
striking thing about these results is the rapid threshold increase as a function of the standard deviation of
the reference spectrum. The slope of the straight line
fit in the right panel is about 1.7.

While it may seem quite reasonable that the PWT
condition should have devastating effects on spectral
shape discrimination, there are some puzzling aspects of
these results. Consider a very simple model of the

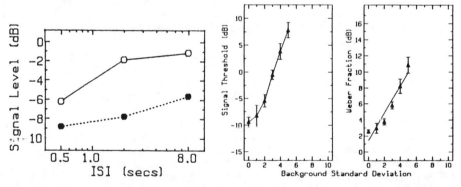

Figure 4. Results from the *Figure 5. Results from the
    PBT condition.   PWT condition.

comparison between components of the complex spectra.
Let's assume that the detectability of the signal
increment results from a simultaneous comparison of the
level of the critical band containing the signal and one
other critical band containing any other component of
the reference spectrum. Using straight-forward signal
detection arguments, it can be shown that the relationship between the standard deviation of the within-trial
amplitude perturbation and the Weber fraction in decibels should have a slope of about 0.4 (Kidd et al., 1986)
- a prediction which was supported by the results of a
"control" experiment. Although at present there does
not seem to be an easy way to reconcile these radically
different estimates, the solution must be related to the
manner in which information from different frequency
channels is combined. Durlach et al. (1986) have
recently proposed a model for the discrimination of
broadband sounds in which randomly roving the overall
level of sounds introduces a strong correlation between
different frequency channels or critical bands. It is
possible that a "decorrelation" introduced by the PWT
condition multiplied by the number of bands would
account, at least in part, for the observed result. Any
conclusions, however, must await further experimentation
and more quantitative analyses of these results.

The apparent failure of conventional models of
frequency analysis or masking to account for spectral
shape discrimination results suggests a re-examination
and, possibly, a re-interpretation of certain classical
studies. One such project, which is only partially
completed, deals with the detection of a tonal increment
to a bandlimited noise. In each interval of the two-
interval two-alternative forced choice task, the listener
hears a tone embedded in a band of random noise. The
"signal" is an intensity increment to the tone which is
added in one of the two intervals and is varied adaptively as in previous experiments. The main experimental variables are the bandwidth of the noise and the
level of the tonal "pedestal" relative to the spectrum
level of the noise. At very low pedestal levels, the
listener's task is just the usual tone-in-noise detection
task with the exception that the sounds are roved in
level from interval to interval of each trial - just as
in other spectral shape discrimination tasks. At
relatively high pedestal levels, however, the listener
hears a tone in each interval and must judge something
about the "spectral shape" of the tone/noise ensemble
to choose the correct alternative. Figure 6 shows some

preliminary results from this experiment. These data
are the intersubject means from three observers, but the
number of estimates per subject varies considerably for
different points. The upper curve is for a pedestal
level (relative to the spectrum level of the noise) of
0 dB. The lower curve is for the average of pedestal
levels of 24 dB and 36 dB. Note that the thresholds
are signal level relative to the level of the pedestal.
In a sense, these results help tie together the traditional "critical band masking experiment" and spectral
shape discrimination experiments. Perhaps the most
interesting finding to date from the spectral shape
studies has been that adding additional energy to the
background or reference spectrum, well outside the critical band centered on the signal, improves the detectability of the signal intensity increment. This result
is also seen in Figure 6 (filled circles) when the
reference spectrum is noise.
Figure 6, together with unpublished results from a
number of intermediate pedestal levels, suggests that
some tone-in-noise masking
experiments might be evaluated in terms of discriminating differences in spectral shape, or for roving
narrowband stimuli, differences in waveshape rather
than in terms of the energy
in successive sound presentations. (Work supported by
NIH/NINCDS and Office of
Naval Research.)

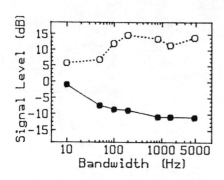

Figure 6. Results of the
roving level tone-
in-noise experiment.

REFERENCES

Berliner, J.E., and Durlach, N.I. (1973). Intensity
    perception IV. Resolution in roving-level discrim-
    ination, JASA, 53, 1270-1287.
Boggs, G.J., and Sorkin, R.D. (1982). Context coding in
    auditory memory for pitch, JASA, 71, S38.
Creelman, C.D. (1960). Detection of signals of uncertain
    frequency, JASA, 32, 805-810.
Green, D.M. (1982). Detection of auditory sinusoids of
    uncertain frequency, JASA, 33, 897-903.

Green, D.M. (1983). Profile analysis: A different view of auditory intensity discrimination, Am. Psych., 38, 133-142.

Green, D.M., and Kidd, G.Jr. (1983). Further studies of auditory profile analysis, JASA, 73, 1260-1265.

Green, D.M., and Mason, C.R. (1985). Auditory profile analysis: Frequency, phase and Weber's law, JASA, 77, 1155-1161.

Green, D.M., Kidd, G.Jr., and Picardi, M.C. (1983). Successive versus simultaneous comparisons in auditory intensity discrimination, JASA, 73, 639-643.

Green, D.M., Mason, C.R., and Kidd, G.Jr. (1984). Profile analysis: Critical bands and duration, JASA, 75, 1163-1167.

Hanna, T.E. (1984). Discrimination of reproducible noise as a function of bandwidth and duration, Percept. and Psychophys., 36, 409-416.

Harris, J.D. (1952). The decline of pitch discrimination with time, J. Exp. Psych., 43, 93-99.

Jesteadt, W. (1971). Memory for the pitch and loudness of pure tones, Doctoral Thesis, Univ. of Pittsburg.

Kidd, G.Jr., Mason, C.R., and Green, D.M. (1986). Auditory profile analysis of irregular sound spectra, JASA, 79, 1045-1053.

Kidd, G.Jr., and Neff, DL. (1984). Frequency discrimination for conditions of roving standard and random interstimulus interval, JASA, 75, S21.

Mason, C.R., Kidd, G.Jr., Hanna, T.E., and Green, D.M. (1984). Profile analysis and level variation, Hear. Res., 13, 269-275.

Sorkin, R.D. (1984). Discrimination of binary tone sequences, JASA, 75, S21.

Sorkin, R.D., Boggs, G.J., and Brady, S.L. (1982). Discrimination of temporal jitter in patterned sequences of tones, J. Exp. Psych., 8, 46-57.

Spiegel, M.F., and Green, D.M. (1982). Signal and masker uncertainty with noise maskers of varying duration, bandwidth and center frequency, JASA, 71, 1204-1210.

Spiegel, M.F., Picardi, M.C., and Green, D.M. (1981). Signal and masker uncertainty in intensity discrimination, JASA, 70, 1015-1019.

Watson, C.W., and Kelly, W.J. (1981). The role of stimulus uncertainty in discrimination of auditory patterns, in: Auditory and Visual Pattern Recognition, D.J. Getty and J.H. Howard, eds., Lawrence Erlbaum, N.J.

* Reprinted by permission from the Journal of the Acoustical Society of America.

Spectral and Temporal Comparisons in Auditory Masking

Robert H. Gilkey
Signal Detection Laboratory
Central Institute for the Deaf
St. Louis, MO 63110

The critical band as it relates to simultaneous tone-in-noise masking is reevaluated in light of the results from two experiments. The first measures the detectability of a 500 Hz tone masked by white Gaussian noise when the overall level of the stimulus is randomized from interval to interval and trial to trial. The results indicate that subjects can use information that is outside the critical band centered at the signal frequency, or outside the temporal interval that contains the signal, to overcome the performance decrement caused by randomizing level. The second experiment investigates the detectability of a 500 Hz tone masked by reproducible noise. A multiple channel model, fit to the data, suggests that subjects compare information in different spectral/temporal regions of the stimulus in order to determine the presence of the signal.

INTRODUCTION

The concept of the critical band evolved from the work of Fletcher (1940), who investigated the detectability of pure tone signals as a function of the bandwidth of a simultaneous white Gaussian noise masker. He found that detectability decreased as the bandwidth of the masker increased, until a "critical bandwidth" was reached. Further increases in bandwidth did not affect detectability, even though the total masker energy increased. The results can be explained by assuming that the system has fixed bandwidth (approximately one critical band wide) internal filters, centered at each signal frequency, that limit the bandwidth of the effective masker. Thus, increases in the bandwidth of the external masker beyond the critical bandwidth do not change the energy in the effective masker. These basic results have been replicated in numerous studies since Fletcher's initial work (e.g., Weber, 1977), and the concept of the critical band has become a cornerstone of psychophysical thought on hearing. Despite an awareness that in isolation the critical band would be inadequate to explain such complex phenomena as speech and music perception, it has been assumed that the critical band could provide a front end for these complicated processes. Moreover, for simple situations, like masking, critical band theory is typically considered to be adequate in and of itself. That is, the system has been modeled as a single filter followed by a simple detector (e.g., an energy detector). Similar constructs have also been applied in the temporal domain. Although the results are less consistent, in general the subject in a masking task has been seen as processing information over a single fixed integration window, that roughly corresponds to the interval that contains the signal when it is present (e.g., Robinson and Trahiotis, 1972).

A number of more recent results suggest that even for masking tasks, critical band theory may be an oversimplification. Experiments measuring frequency selectivity in nonsimultaneous masking tasks suggest interactions among frequency regions that cannot be explained by critical band theory (e.g., Houtgast, 1972). Studies of simultaneous masking where the masker is an inharmonic tone complex whose level is randomized from trial to trial suggest that performance is augmented by the addition of information in frequency regions well outside of a single critical band (e.g., Green, 1983). Similarly, detection in certain amplitude-modulated noises suggests that performance improves as the bandwidth of the noise is increased beyond a critical bandwidth (e.g., Hall et al., 1984). Despite these results, it has still been thought that for simple stimulus configurations like those used by Fletcher, with simultaneous masking of a pure tone by an unmodulated band-limited white Gaussian noise, the critical band is an adequate construct to explain the results. That is, subjects ignore the portions of the noise that are outside the critical band and temporal interval that contains the signal. In contrast, the current chapter describes the results from two experiments that suggest that even for very simple simultaneous noise masking tasks, critical band theory may be inadequate.

EXPERIMENT 1

Experiment 1, like the Profile Analysis experiments of Green (1983), randomizes the overall level of the stimulus from trial to trial, in an attempt to force the

27

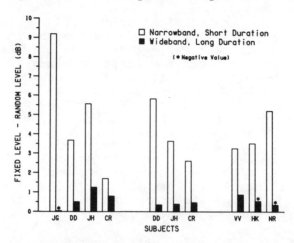

Figure 1. Effect of randomizing overall level for the
NBSD masker and the WBLD masker. Left two groups of
bars are for monaural presentation and the right
group is for binaural presentation.

subjects away from a strategy based on energy detection
in a single critical band, and into a discrimination
based on spectral shape. Here, the background (i.e.,
the masker) is a noise, rather than a tone complex. A
two-interval, forced choice adaptive staircase technique
was used to obtain the threshold of a 50 msec, 500 Hz
sinusoid, masked by white Gaussian noise maskers. For
reasons not addressed in this chapter, both monaural and
binaural (diotic) stimulus configurations were employed.
With each stimulus configuration both wide-band
long-duration (WBLD) maskers and narrow-band
short-duration (NBSD) maskers were investigated. The
bandwidth of the WBLD maskers was 100 to 2000 Hz; the
duration was 300 ms for binaural presentations and 654
ms for monaural presentations. The bandwidth of the NBSD
maskers was 50 Hz, centered at 500 Hz; the duration was
56 ms for both monaural and binaural presentations.
Detection was investigated under a fixed level condition
in which the overall level of the stimulus was fixed,
and a random level condition in which overall level was
randomized, from interval to interval and trial to
trial, over a 30 dB range (binaural presentations) or a
40 dB range (monaural presentations).

Figure 1 shows the difference in threshold
attenuation between the fixed and the random level

28

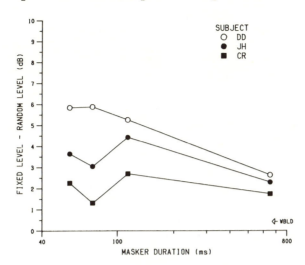

Figure 2. Effect of randomizing level as a function of masker duration. Monaural presentation.

conditions for several subjects. The left two groups of bars show the data for monaural presentations and the right group of bars shows the data for binaural presentations. The asterisks mark data where performance under the random level condition was actually better than that under the fixed level condition. For the rest of the bars, the typical case, performance under the fixed level condition was superior. With the WBLD masker (filled bars) the effect of randomizing level is negligible; the average difference is only about .4 dB. If subjects were monitoring the energy in a single critical band and a single integration window under the random level condition, their performance should be much worse than under the fixed level condition. The small differences suggest that the subjects are employing some other strategy, perhaps using information in the spectral and temporal fringe, to avoid the effects of randomizing level. If so, then it should be possible to remove the spectral and temporal fringe, and observe a decrement in performance. Results for the NBSD masker are shown by the open bars. As can be seen, there is a much greater effect of randomizing level when the spectral fringe and temporal fringe are reduced. The average of these open bars is about 4.4 dB, suggesting that subjects are attending to the spectral and temporal fringe of the WBLD masker.

29

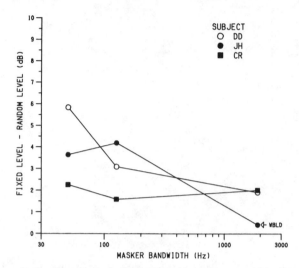

Figure 3. Effect of randomizing level as a function of masker bandwidth. Monaural presentation.

Additional conditions varied masker bandwidth and masker duration separately to determine the individual effects of the spectral fringe and the temporal fringe. Figure 2 shows the difference in threshold attenuation between the fixed level and the random level condition, as a function of the duration of the masker. In all cases the masker is narrow-band, approximately 50 Hz wide. As can be seen, on average there is a reduction in the effect of randomizing level as duration is increased, although for two subjects there is not a great difference between the longest and shortest maskers. For no subject is the information in the temporal fringe of the long duration masker sufficient to reduce the performance difference to that observed with the WBLD masker of Figure 1 (shown here as the arrow in the lower left-hand corner). Figure 3 shows the effect of manipulating the bandwidth of a 56 msec duration masker. Again, there is a reduction in the effect of randomizing level as the bandwidth is increased. For one subject the performance difference is the same as with the WBLD masker, indicating that the increase in bandwidth was sufficient to overcome the effects of randomizing level. For the other two subjects, the effect of randomizing level is greater than with the WBLD masker. Thus, most subjects can use information in either the temporal fringe or the spectral fringe to overcome the effects of

30

randomizing overall level, and there is an added benefit of having both spectral and temporal fringe present.

EXPERIMENT 2 - (from Gilkey et al., 1985; Gilkey and Robinson, 1986)

Experiment 2 provides some indication of the mechanisms that might be underlying the effects observed in Experiment 1. This experiment differs from traditional masking experiments in that reproducible noise samples are used as maskers. The procedures are analogous to those of Ahumada et al. (1975), and others. The detectability of a 100 msec, 500 Hz sinusoid masked by each of 25 reproducible noise samples was investigated. The noise samples were 148 msec long, and had a bandwidth of 100-3000 Hz. A total of 125 different waveforms were employed - 25 noise-alone and 100 signal-plus-noise (25 at each of four signal starting phase angles). The proportion of "yes" responses to each waveform was estimated, based on approximately 100 single-interval yes/no trials per sample. All of the 25 noise samples were presented during each block of 100 trials, but the order of presentation was randomized across blocks. Subjects did not know that the samples were being repeated, and they did not receive trial-by-trial feedback. Thus, they believed they were listening to truly random noise, and did not learn individual samples.

Figure 4 shows the results for each of the 25 noise samples for one subject and a single signal starting phase in ROC space (i.e., P(y) on signal-plus-noise trials as a function of P(y) on noise-alone trials). As can be seen, all samples are not the same, but are distributed fairly broadly throughout this space. These differences across samples can be used to test detection models by presenting these same noise samples to a computer model. The parameters of the model can be adjusted until the model has the same P(y) to the individual samples as do the subjects. Initial results were obtained for the simple model illustrated in Figure 5, which is based on Jeffress (1968). It is composed of a critical band-like filter, followed by a nonlinearity and an integrator with a leak. A sampling strategy is applied to the slowly-varying waveform at the output of the integrator to reduce it to a single number, the model's decision variable, X'. Although it is beyond

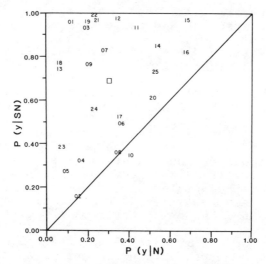

Figure 4.   Hit and false-alarm proportions for individual noise samples shown in ROC space. Data are for
subject SG, with a signal starting phase of Øo.
(From Gilkey et al., 1985, by permission of the
Journal of the Acoustical Society of America.)

the scope of this chapter to provide detailed results of
the fitting process, it is the case that a 5Ø Hz wide
filter, followed by a half-wave rectifier, combined with
integration and sampling strategy stages that
approximate true integration over the signal interval,
predicts the responses of all subjects fairly well.
When the d' of the subjects is about 1.Ø, the model
predicts between 43% and 72% of the variance in the
P(y)s, depending on the subject.

Because the proportion of predictable variance is
large relative to these values, we next combined seven
detectors of this form, each with a 5Ø Hz wide initial

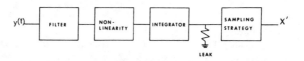

Figure 5.   A block diagram of the electrical analog
model of Jeffress, 1968. (From Gilkey and Robinson,
1986, by permission of the Journal of the
Acoustical Society of America.)

32

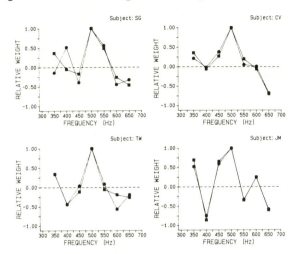

Figure 6. Spectral weighting functions for a multiple-
    detector model. Square and circular symbols are
    for 10 log(E/Nø) of 8.5 and 11.5, respectively.
    (From Gilkey and Robinson, 1986, by permission of
    the Journal of the Acoustical Society of America.)

filter tuned to different frequency regions, at 50 Hz
intervals between 350 and 650 Hz. A new decision
variable was defined as a linear combination of the
seven values of X'. The coefficients, or weights,
applied to each X' in the linear combinations were
manipulated until the combined decision variable again
led to P(y)s for the model that agreed most closely with
the subjects. The curves in Figure 6 show the way the
spectral information was weighted by the model that best
fit the data of each of four subjects. If a single
channel model was adequate, then we would expect to find
positive weights for the channel centered at the signal
frequency, and weights of zero for all of the other
channels (i.e., equivalent to the single channel model
of Figure 5). If, on the other hand, the subject looks
broadly through this frequency region and responds to an
increase in the output of any of the detectors, positive weights would be expected for all of the detectors.
Neither of these patterns was found for any of the
subjects. Instead, a maximum positive weight is assigned to the signal frequency, but negative weights are
assigned to certain other frequencies. The results for
all subjects show negative weights at the highest frequencies, and some show negative weights for a band in

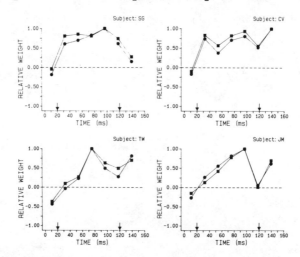

Figure 7. Temporal weighting functions for a multiple-
detector model. Square and circular symbols are
for 1∅ log(E/N∅) of 8.5 and 11.5, respectively.
(From Gilkey and Robinson, 1986, by permission of
the Journal of the Acoustical Society of America.)

the low frequency region. It is as if subjects are
comparing information across frequency regions. That
is, as energy increases in the regions of negative
weight, they are less likely to say yes, unless the
energy also increases in the regions of positive weight.
A similar analysis was performed in the temporal domain.
A linear combination was formed of the average output
over seven 21-ms sub-intervals of the stimulus interval,
and the best-fitting weights were determined, as shown
in Figure 7. Here, the noise begins at ∅ and ends at
148 msec. The small arrows show the onset and offset of
the signal. For all four subjects there is a slight
negative weight given to the interval immediately before
the signal onset. Other regions of the functions show
generally positive weights. The small negative weight
at the beginning is at least suggestive of some sort of
comparison process. But as seen in Experiment 1, the
spectral weighting seems to be more important. The
average increase in the proportion of predicted variance
with the frequency weights is about 8%, and the average
increase with the temporal weights is about 6%.

34

CONCLUSION

The results of both of these experiments suggest that subjects can and do use information in the spectral and temporal fringe of the masker waveform in order to make decisions regarding the presence of a signal. The results of both experiments conflict with simple single filter models of auditory detection. It could be argued that the first experiment, as well as the experiments of Green (1983), does not represent a typical masking situation because the act of randomizing overall level degrades the quality of the information in the critical band centered on the signal frequency. Therefore, subjects are forced to use other information in order to achieve the same level of performance. That is, they do not use the strategy they would in a typical masking task, such as the task investigated by Fletcher. Similar arguments apply to the experiment of Hall et al. (1984). Although the information in the critical band centered on the signal frequency was not degraded, additional information was provided in other critical bands. There is no particular reason to expect the subjects to ignore this additional information. In contrast, the second experiment, from the subject's point of view, was a typical masking situation. There should be no particular advantage for the subjects in attending to information outside the critical band or outside the temporal integration window that contains the signal. Nevertheless, the results of fitting the model suggest that subjects are using this additional information. The results of both of these experiments suggest that even in very simple simultaneous tone-in-noise masking tasks, subjects use listening strategies that are more complicated than would be suggested by a traditional interpretation of the critical band.

ACKNOWLEDGMENTS

Work was supported by NSF (BNS-77-17308, BNS-85-11786), and NIH (NS-03856). Additional support was provided by AFOSR (86-NL-049). The author is indebted to D.E. Robinson, T.E. Hanna, S.F. Cooper, B.D. Simpson, T.A. Meyer, and J.M. Weisenberger.

REFERENCES

Ahumada, A., Marken, R., and Sandusky, A. (1975). "Time and frequency analyses of auditory signal detection," J. Acoust. Soc. Am. 57, 385-390.

Fletcher, H. (1940). "Auditory patterns," Rev. Mod. Phys. 12, 47-65. Reprinted in Psychological Acoustics, edited by E. D. Schubert (Dowden, Hutchinson, and Ross, Stroudsburg, PA, 1979), pp. 221-230.

Gilkey, R.H., Robinson, D.E., and Hanna, T.E. (1985). "Effects of masker waveform and signal-to-masker phase relation on diotic and dichotic masking by reproducible noise," J. Acoust. Soc. Am. 78, 1207-1219.

Gilkey, R.H. and Robinson, D.E. (1986). "Models of auditory masking: A molecular psychophysical approach," J. Acoust. Soc. Am. 79, 1499-1510.

Green, D.M. (1983). "Profile analysis, a different view of auditory intensity discrimination," Am. Psychol. 38, 133-142.

Hall, J.W., Haggard, M.P., and Fernandes, M.A. (1984). "Detection in noise by spectro-temporal pattern analysis," J. Acoust. Soc. Am. 76, 50-56.

Houtgast, T. (1972). "Psychophysical evidence for lateral inhibition in hearing," J. Acoust. Soc. Am. 51, 1885-1894.

Jeffress, L.A. (1968). "Mathematical and electrical models of auditory detection," J. Acoust. Soc. Am. 44, 187-203.

Robinson, D.E. and Trahiotis, C. (1972). "Effects of signal duration and masker duration on detectability under diotic and dichotic listening conditions," Percept. Psychophys. 12, 333-334.

Weber, D.L. (1978). "Suppression and critical bands in band-limiting experiments," J. Acoust. Soc. Am. 64, 141-150.

Simultaneous masking by small numbers of sinusoids under conditions of uncertainty

Donna L. Neff and Brian P. Callaghan
Boys Town National Institute for Communication Disorders
in Children, 555 North 30th St., Omaha, Nebraska 68131

Threshold for a 1000-Hz sinusoidal signal was
measured in the presence of simultaneous maskers composed
of 2 to 200 sinusoidal components. Masker frequencies
were drawn at random for each presentation from a range
of 300-3000 Hz, excluding the signal frequency. To mimic
the properties of components drawn from noise, the amplitude and phase of each component was drawn at random
from Rayleigh or rectangular distributions, respectively.
As in an earlier study, large amounts of masking were
observed for maskers with very few components spread
across a wide frequency range. In the first experiment,
eliminating masker components from a 160-Hz wide critical
band around the signal reduced the amount of masking, but
considerable masking remained even for maskers with 10 or
fewer components. In the second experiment, component
frequencies, amplitudes, or both, were either fixed
or randomized across the two listening intervals of a
forced-choice trial; new frequencies were always presented on each successive trial. Amplitude randomization had
no effect regardless of the number of components in the
masker. Frequency randomization, however, produced large
amounts of masking for maskers with 10 or fewer components. These effects typically show little change with
extensive practice, and appear to be produced primarily
by nonperipheral processes.

INTRODUCTION

Masking is defined operationally as the reduction in
the detectability of one sound, the signal, associated
with the presentation of another sound, the masker.
Masking experiments remain one of the primary tools for
assessing the frequency selectivity of the human auditory
system (e.g., see Patterson and Green, 1978 and Scharf,
1970 for reviews). Out of these many studies has emerged
a generally accepted view of frequency analysis in which
the peripheral auditory system is modeled as a bank of
overlapping bandpass filters and the listener is assumed
to monitor a filter centered on or near the signal fre-

quency where the ratio of signal energy to noise energy
is optimum. Information outside this "critical band" is
presumed to neither help nor hinder detection. Studies
of psychophysical tuning curves, masking patterns, and
auditory filter shape, to name a few, reflect this
single-filter perspective.

In recent years, however, there has been considerable
interest in the ability of the auditory system to make
use of information in regions far removed from the signal
frequency to aid detection. A number of studies have
provided evidence that listeners can indeed use information from filters distant from the signal frequency. A
primary example is the work of Green and colleagues on
profile analysis (e.g., Green, 1983; Spiegel et al.,
1981). Green has shown that threshold for an increment
to a single component of a multicomponent complex can be
improved by as much as 20 dB if additional tones are
added around the tone being incremented. Listeners
appear to use these additional components, even when far
outside the critical band, to build stimulus "profiles"
in long-term memory and use these profiles to improve
signal detection. Similarly, several studies of simultaneous masking report evidence of multichannel processes
that aid signal detection (e.g., Buus, 1985; Hall et al.,
1984). Hall and colleagues have shown that correlating
the temporal envelopes of two stimuli in frequency
regions far outside the critical band around the signal
will reduce the influence of the maskers, an effect they
call "comodulation masking release." Again, in all these
experiments, it is advantageous for the listener to make
use of information in distant frequency regions. Perhaps
it is no great surprise that a sophisticated detection
system can do that when required. The present experiments, however, focus on situations in which the listeners could greatly improve their performance by ignoring
any information falling outside the signal region and
focusing on the output of a single peripheral filter.
Apparently, they are unable to behave as traditional
models would predict, even if it is to their advantage
to do so.

In the initial experiments (Neff and Green, 1986),
our intent was to determine the minimum number of sinusoids necessary to produce the same amount of simultaneous masking as broadband noise. In the process, we
discovered that small numbers of sinusoids could produce
very large amounts of masking if the frequencies of the
sinusoids were changed with each presentation. For

example, as the number of sinusoids in the maskers was increased from 2 to 10, the average amount of masking increased from about 10 to 55 dB. The experiments reported here replicate the basic results of the original study, despite some modifications in the stimuli. (If changed, the original values are given in parentheses in the next section). The goals were to assess the effect of removing masker components from the critical band around the signal frequency, and to compare the effect of randomizing only frequency, only amplitude, or both on the amount of masking produced by the multicomponent maskers.

METHOD

Subjects. Four normal-hearing listeners were tested who received at least 10 hours of practice before data collection began. The stimuli were presented monaurally to the ear with the lower quiet threshold through TDH-39 headphones.

Stimuli. These were simultaneous masking experiments in which the threshold for a 1000-Hz signal was measured in the presence of multicomponent maskers. Note that the signal frequency was never changed and was presented in quiet before each block of trials. Both signal and masker were 200 ms, presented together without ramps. There were two kinds of maskers. One, which served primarily as a reference, was an analog broadband noise, bandpass filtered from 300-3000 Hz (or lowpass-filtered at 5000 Hz), and presented at 60 dB SPL total power. The rest of the maskers were multicomponent complexes in which the number of sinusoidal components was varied from 2 to 200 (or 100) across conditions. With the exception of the broadband noise, the stimuli were computer gener-ated. For the multicomponent maskers, the component frequencies were drawn at random from the same frequency range as the broadband noise. The minimum frequency spacing between components was 5 Hz so that the com-ponents would be orthogonal. The signal frequency could not be drawn as a masker component. Because the original stimuli were intended to sum to make noise, the phase and amplitude of each component were randomly drawn from rectangular and Rayleigh distributions, respectively. The maskers had equal rms values of 60 dB SPL (or an expected value of 60 dB SPL with variation around that value).

39

Procedure. A two-alternative, forced-choice (2AFC), adaptive procedure was used to determine threshold for the signal in quiet and in the presence of a masker, with a decision rule that estimated the 70.7% correct point on the psychometric function (Levitt, 1971). An initial step size of 4 dB was reduced to 2 dB on the fourth reversal. Threshold was defined as the average of the reversal levels recorded during each 100-trial block beginning with the fourth reversal. For each condition, the number of components in the masker was specified and 200 masker waveforms (or 50) with that number of components were generated. In a block of 100 trials, a different masker was drawn at random from this large set for each interval of each trial. At least eight threshold estimates were obtained for each listener and condition. Except for Figure 4, the results presented are averages and standard errors across listeners.

COMPARISON ACROSS GROUPS

Figure 1 compares the average performance of the three listeners in the original experiment and the four listeners in the experiments to be described in the rest of the paper. In this figure (and also Figs. 2 and 3), the amount of masking of the 1000-Hz signal (i.e., masked threshold minus quiet threshold) is plotted as a function of the number of tones in the masker. Error bars are omitted for clarity. The light dashed line shows the

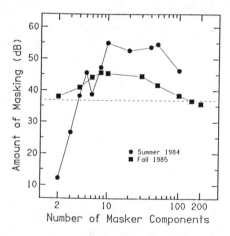

Figure 1. Amount of masking as a function of the number of components in the masker for two groups of listeners. See text for further details.

amount of masking produced by the broadband noise, which happened to be about 37 dB for both groups.

For the 1984 group, the function increased rapidly as the number of components was increased to 10, followed by a plateau or slight decline for maskers with more components. Maskers with 10 components produced up to 55 dB of masking. The masking produced by 100-component maskers was still greater than that produced by the broadband noise. For the 1985 group, the function is flatter. These listeners have much more difficulty with 2-component maskers, which produce almost 40 dB of masking, but about 10 dB less masking is observed for maskers with more than 10 components. The amount of masking equals that produced by broadband noise for maskers with 150 or 200 components. The differences across groups may be due to the use of a narrower frequency range with the later group (2700 vs. 5000 Hz) or perhaps simply to differences across listeners. The frequency range was changed because we were no longer using signals at low and high frequencies, as in the earlier experiments, and because our stimuli would then be similar to those used in related profile analysis experiments (e.g., Spiegel et al., 1981). However, the basic results are the same: large amounts of masking (up to 45 dB) can be measured with very few masker components scattered over a wide frequency range.

The randomization of spectra within a trial appears to be the major factor degrading performance. In the original group, we found that performance improved by as much as 25 dB when the same masker was presented within a trial, but different maskers were presented across trials. This is consistent with a form of profile analysis in which listeners apparently compare spectra across intervals to detect the signal.

CRITICAL BAND COMPONENTS INCLUDED OR EXCLUDED

This experiment tested whether eliminating masker components within a critical band around the signal would affect performance. For maskers with small numbers of components, the absence of critical-band components was not expected to have much effect on threshold, because so few components would fall within that band in the first place. For maskers with large numbers of components, more of an effect would be expected because more components would fall within the critical band. Given the different estimates of the critical band across studies

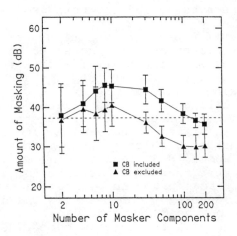

Figure 2. Amount of masking as a function of the number
   of components in the masker, for maskers with
   critical-band components included or excluded. See
   text for further details.

and procedures, a fairly wide bandwidth was chosen
arbitrarily: 160-Hz wide arithmetically centered around
1000 Hz.

   In Figure 2, the upper function is for maskers with
critical-band components included; the lower function is
for critical-band components excluded. The dashed
horizontal line is the masking produced by the broadband
noise, as in Fig. 1. The variability across listeners
is substantial, particularly for maskers with 10 or less
components. For maskers with more than 10 components,
there is clearly less masking when critical-band components are excluded, as expected. For 2- and 4-component
maskers, there is essentially no difference in the
amounts of masking. For maskers with 6, 8, or 10 components, however, significantly less masking is observed
when critical-band components are excluded (p < .05),
although the effect is quite small (about 5 dB). Even
without critical-band components, significant amounts of
masking are produced (e.g., over 40 dB for maskers with
10 components; 37 dB for maskers with 2 components).
Thus, it seems unlikely that this masking can be attributed primarily to peripheral processes based on energy
near the signal frequency.

42

RANDOMIZATION OF AMPLITUDE AND FREQUENCY

In the data presented thus far, both component frequency and component amplitude were varied randomly across intervals within a trial. Certainly, spectral uncertainty is a major variable, but variations in component amplitude might also contribute to the large amounts of masking. Kidd et al. (1986) have shown that profile analysis can be degraded significantly by randomizing the amplitudes of the individual components that form a profile. Therefore, we compared four conditions of randomization within a trial: 1) randomized frequencies and fixed (equal) amplitudes; 2) randomized frequencies and randomized amplitudes; 3) fixed frequencies and fixed (equal) amplitudes; and 4) fixed frequencies and randomized amplitudes. For fixed-frequency conditions, different frequencies were still drawn for each new trial. The results are shown in Figure 3.

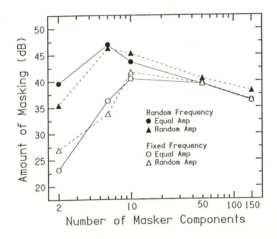

Figure 3. Amount of masking as a function of the number of components in the masker, for combinations of random or fixed component amplitudes and frequencies across the two intervals of a 2AFC trial.

For maskers with 50 or 150 components, there is no effect of manipulating either component frequency or amplitude. However, for maskers with 10 or less components, there is a highly significant effect (p < .001) of randomizing frequency with no significant effect of amplitude (p>.05). For 2-component maskers, for example, randomizing frequency raised the amount of masking by more than 15 dB relative to the fixed-frequency condi-

tion. Even for the fixed frequency/equal amplitude conditions, however, more masking is produced than would be
predicted by classic critical-band models. For example,
6-component maskers produced up to 35 dB of masking,
with very few components falling anywhere near the signal
frequency. Again, nonperipheral processes envoked by
stimulus uncertainty appear to limit performance.

INDIVIDUAL DIFFERENCES AND TRAINING

The effects observed for maskers with small numbers
of components exhibit large individual differences that
are very resistant to training. For conditions with
critical-band components included in which both component
frequency and amplitude were varied, 1800 trials were
presented in blocks of 100 trials. Figure 4 shows
learning curves for two-component maskers. This condition had the largest training effect, although only
one listener (L1-upper left) showed evidence of learning
through sheer repetitive practice in this or any other
condition. When learning occurred, performance stabi-
lized after 500-600 trials. L2, who was the only
musician in the group, typically began with better performance than anyone else, but he did not improve with
time.

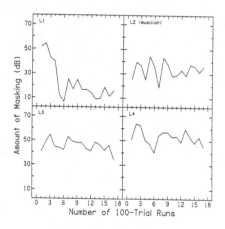

Figure 4. Learning curves for the four listeners for a
    masker with two components.

The observation of large amounts of masking that are
very resistant to training, and the presence of substantial differences in performance both within listeners

44

across repeated conditions and across listeners, is not unexpected for tasks with complex stimuli (Watson, 1980). Large individual differences and learning over a long time course have been shown both for sequential ten-tone patterns, particularly under conditions of high stimulus uncertainty (e.g., Watson et al., 1976), and for profile analysis (Kidd et al., 1986). The general problem of why randomizing masker spectra within a trial produces so much masking remains unsolved.

ACKNOWLEDGMENTS

We wish to thank Walt Jesteadt and John Mott for their comments on earlier drafts of this manuscript. This research was supported by a Biomedical Research Support Grant (#S07RR05999).

REFERENCES

Buus, S. (1985). Release from masking caused by envelope fluctuations, J. Acoust. Soc. Am., 78, 1958-1965.

Green, D.M. (1983). Profile analysis: A different view of auditory intensity discrimination, Am. Psychol., 38, 133-142.

Hall, J.W., Haggard, M.P. and Fernandes, M.A. (1984). Detection in noise by spectro-temporal pattern analysis, J. Acoust. Soc. Am., 76, 50-56.

Kidd, G.Jr., Mason, C.R. and Green, D.M. (1986). Auditory profile analysis of irregular sound spectra, J. Acoust. Soc. Am., 79, 1045-1053.

Levitt, H. (1971). Transformed up-down methods in psycho-acoustics, J. Acoust. Soc. Am., 49, 467-477.

Neff, D.L. and Green, D.M. (1986). Masking produced by spectral uncertainty with multicomponent maskers, Percept. & Psychophys., under review.

Patterson, R.D. and Green, D.M. (1978). Auditory masking, in: Handbook of Perception, Vol. 4: Hearing, E.C. Carterette and M.P. Friedman, eds., Academic Press, New York, 337-361.

Scharf, B. (1970). Critical bands, in: Vol I. Foundations of Modern Auditory Theory, J.V. Tobias, ed., Academic Press, New York, 159-202.

Neff, Callaghan-Masking produced by stimulus uncertainty

Spiegel, M.F., Picardi, M.C. and Green, D.M. (1981).
    Signal and masker uncertainty in intensity discrimi-
    nation, J. Acoust. Soc. Am., 70, 1015-1019.

Watson, C.S. (1980). Time course of auditory perceptual
    learning, Ann. Otol. Rhinol. Laryngol., 89, Suppl.
    74, 96-102.

Watson, C.S., Kelly, W.J. and Wroton, H.W. (1976).
    Factors in the discrimination of tonal patterns. II.
    Selective attention and learning under various levels
    of stimulus uncertainty, J. Acoust. Soc. Am., 60,
    1176-1186.

Discrimination of Frequency Ratios

Neal F. Viemeister and Deborah A. Fantini
Department of Psychology
University of Minnesota
Minneapolis, Minnesota 55455

The ability to extract information about relationships between frequency components in complex sounds may
be of fundamental importance in auditory perception. The
present set of experiments attempts to assess this
ability in a situation for which the observer must
compare the frequencies within a complex in order to
successfully discriminate between different complexes.
Specifically, the observer is required to discriminate
between two-tone complexes which differ, on the average,
only in the ratio of the frequencies of the two simultaneously presented components. The data indicate that
relatively small changes in frequency ratios can be
discriminated: thresholds are similar to those for
simple frequency discrimination measured under conditions of comparable frequency uncertainty. They are also
similar to those shown by trained musicians in discrimination of musical intervals when the two tones
comprising the interval are presented successively.
The data also indicate that as the ratio between
the components in the standard is increased, larger
ratio differences are required to maintain performance.
Discrimination is not unusually acute when the ratio of
the components corresponds to the ratio of small
integers. Generally, these experiments suggest that
observers can discriminate between frequency ratios
remarkably well under a wide range of conditions. It is
not clear how they do this. It does not appear, however,
that discriminations are based upon changes in pitch or
distortion products, or that information about temporal
fine structure is required.

INTRODUCTION

Recent work on "profile analysis" (see Green, 1986)
demonstrates that observers can extract amplitude
relationships between spectral components in complex
sounds. The present work addresses an analogous question
about frequency relationships, namely, how well can
observers extract "higher order" relationships between
the frequencies of components in a complex sound. The

relationship of immediate interest is the ratio.
Frequency ratios may be fundamentally important in
auditory perception-- the identity of musical intervals,
sustained vowels, and other classes of complex sounds is
maintained under the ratio-preserving operation of
transposition.

The experiments to be described assess the
discriminability of two-tone complexes when the stimuli
differ, on the average, only in the ratio of their
frequency components. The general strategy is similar to
that used by Houtsma (1968) and by Burns and Ward (1978)
in experiments on discrimination of musical intervals
with the components of the interval presented
sequentially. The strategy involves randomizing the
frequencies of the components in such a way that the
only reliable information is in the ratio of the
frequencies of the components.

GENERAL METHOD

Fig. 1 shows the idealized spectra on a log
frequency axis for two trials of the 2IFC task used in
the experiments. During each trial two, two-tone complexes are presented, one whose components are at frequencies f and r·f, the other with components at f and
(r+Δr)·f, and the observer is to choose the interval
containing the larger frequency ratio. The base
frequency, f, is random both within and across trials.
Values of f between f-min and f-max are equally likely.

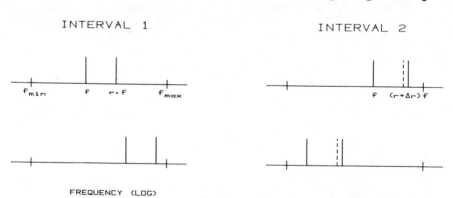

Figure 1. Spectra for two trials of the 2IFC task.
    Interval 2 is the correct interval for both trials.
    Dashed line indicates the frequency of the upper
    component corresponding to the standard ratio (r).

48

The crucial notion is that because of the randomization the observer must, in effect, compare the frequencies within each complex in order to perform well. One natural strategy that does not involve such comparison would be to choose the interval containing the higher frequency of the upper component. This would lead to a correct response for the first trial shown in Fig. 1, but an incorrect response for the second trial. Performance under this strategy will be above chance. For the values of Δr actually used, however, the predicted performance under this strategy is less than 60% correct responses. This is well below that achieved by the subjects.

The stimuli were presented monaurally via a TDH-49 headphone. The duration was 200 ms, including 10-ms rise and decay, and each component in the complex was at 67.5 dB SPL. Both subjects had normal hearing and no musical training. One subject was the second author.

I. PSYCHOMETRIC FUNCTIONS

A comparison of ratio discrimination thresholds across the myriad of conditions possible in these experiments requires a threshold measure such that differences in threshold are at least roughly independent of the level of performance used to define threshold. To determine such a measure, psychometric functions were obtained under three conditions that sampled the extremes of the parameters we planned to investigate. In this experiment, both r and Δr were fixed and f-max/f-min was 1.5. Each point is based upon at least five, 105-trial blocks, of which only the last 100 trials were used for analysis.

The psychometric functions shown in Fig. 2 are plotted with percent correct responses as the ordinate. This P(C) was computed as the average P(C) for those trials on which f for both observation intervals fell within the same frequency "bin", where the bin width was 25% of the randomization range of f. This was done because strong biases were occasionally observed when the two values of f presented on a given trial were near the extremes of the randomization range. When the values of f were within the same bin, there appeared to be no systematic effect of f, i.e., P(C) was roughly independent of the center frequency of the bin.

The abscissa for the psychometric functions, $\log(\Delta r/r)$, was chosen because the functions appear parallel and orderly when plotted using this metric. For the conditions sampled, the slope of the psychometric

49

function around P(C)=75 is about 5% per 0.1 unit in log(Δr/r). Thus, 0.1 unit corresponds, in terms of performance changes, to about 1 dB in simple detection tasks.

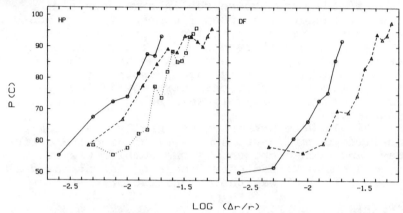

LOG (Δr/r)

Figure 2. Psychometric functions for two subjects for various conditions.

The data shown in Fig. 2 were collected after the subjects had approximately 40 hours of experience in pilot conditions and had reached asymptotic performance in the conditions shown. The ease with which ratio discrimination can be learned can not be readily deter-mined from this because the initial experience with the task involved a wide variety of conditions. Later informal observation with three naive subjects showed that, depending on the subject, from 16 to 80 blocks were required to reach asymptotic performance. It appears that many trials were spent learning to ignore unreliable pitch cues. Learning the task may have been retarded by the randomization necessary to assess ratio discrimination. Thus, no conclusions regarding the "naturalness" of ratio perception can be drawn from the rather protracted course of learning.

II. COMPARISON WITH FREQUENCY DISCRIMINATION

A reasonable basis for evaluating performance in ratio discrimination is to compare such performance with that in simple frequency discrimination. The data of Fig. 2 suggest, not surprisingly, that ratio discrimination is somewhat more difficult than frequency discrimination of a single component: for example, a value [log(Δr/r)] of -2.0, which, as shown in Fig. 2,

yields approximately 71% correct responses for one of
the conditions, corresponds to a 1% change in the
frequency of the upper component. This compares with a
frequency DL, over roughly the same frequency region, of
about 0.2% (Wier et al., 1977). A problem with this
comparison, however, is that, because of the randomization, there is considerably higher stimulus uncertainty
in the ratio discrimination task than in simple frequency discrimination. The higher uncertainty may, in
itself, lead to poorer discrimination (Watson, 1981).

To compare ratio discrimination with frequency
discrimination, thresholds for frequency discrimination
were obtained under conditions of randomization designed
to approximate the uncertainty present in the ratio
task. Thresholds were measured in the 2IFC task
described above, but with a two-down, one-up tracking
procedure (Levitt, 1971). Based upon the psychometric
functions of Fig. 2, steps were in units of $\log(\Delta r/r)$
with a step size of 0.075 units. Each block consisted of
100 trials and all but the first two reversals, of
approximately 30 per block, were used to estimate the
value of $\log(\Delta r/r)$ necessary for 70.7% correct
responses. The reported thresholds are based upon the
average of at least 6 blocks of trials. The standard
deviation of the reversals and of the final threshold
estimate was typically 0.1 unit.

Table I shows the thresholds for the two subjects.
The first two rows show thresholds for simple frequency
discrimination of a 500-Hz tone either in isolation or
in the presence of a fixed 400-Hz tone. In this case,
$\Delta r/r$ is equivalent to $\Delta f/f$ for a 500-Hz tone. A
comparison of these two rows indicates no large effect
of adding a lower frequency component. The third and
fourth rows of Table I are for discrimination in a
situation for which the frequencies were random across
trials, but not within a trial. In this case, the
observer can use the same basic strategy as in simple
frequency discrimination (rows 1 and 2) but there is
considerable uncertainty on any given trial as to where,
in frequency, they should listen. This uncertainty
raises thresholds, particularly for subject HP. It
should be noted that with two components (row 4) ratio
discrimination, rather than simple frequency discrimination is possible. HP's decrease in threshold may
reflect this; the close agreement of DF's thresholds
suggests, however, that she used the same strategy in
both conditions.

The general conclusion from the data of Table I is
that frequency ratio discrimination is quite good and is

comparable to simple frequency discrimination under
conditions of uncertainty similar to those necessitated
by the ratio discrimination experiments. Specifically,
the threshold differences between rows 4 and 5
correspond to differences in P(C) of only about 10% for
both subjects.

Table I. Comparison of thresholds for various conditions
of uncertainty. For the two random conditions and
for ratio discrimination, f-min= 400, f-max=600,
and r=1.25.

CONDITIONS	HP		DF	
	$\Delta r/r$ (%)	LOG($\Delta r/r$)	$\Delta r/r$ (%)	LOG($\Delta r/r$)
ONE COMPONENT NON-RANDOM	0.53	-2.28	0.25	-2.61
TWO COMPONENTS NON-RANDOM	0.46	-2.34	0.38	-2.43
ONE COMPONENT RANDOM ACROSS TRIALS	1.92	-1.72	0.56	-2.25
TWO COMPONENTS RANDOM ACROSS TRIALS	0.98	-2.01	0.58	-2.24
RATIO DISCRIMINATION	1.65	-1.78	0.83	-2.08

III. EFFECTS OF r

The parameter of primary interest for understanding
the basis for ratio discrimination is the standard
frequency ratio, r. The immediate question is whether
discrimination is more acute when r is expressable as
the ratio of small integers. If ratio extraction were
based upon relationships between the temporal fine
structures of the components, such as in correlation or
coincidence detection schemes (Boomsliter and Creel,
1961; Roederer, 1975), then small-integer frequency
ratios would be "special" and one might expect unusually
acute discrimination about these ratios.
Fig. 3 shows the thresholds obtained for various
values of r and for two widely separated frequency
regions. The 2IFC tracking procedure described above
was used but with a fixed number of reversals per block.
Of the 16 total reversals only the last 14 contributed
to the threshold estimate for that block.
The data shown in Fig. 3 for the lower frequency
region (solid lines) are difficult to summarize but do

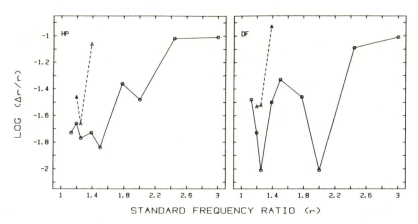

Figure 3. Ratio discrimination thresholds as a function
     of r for f-min= 400 Hz (solid lines) and f-min= 4
     kHz (dashed) with f-max/f-min= 1.5. The integer
     ratios corresponding to r are: 9:8, 239:200, 5:4,
     111:80, 3:2, 711:400, 2:1, 489:200, and 3:1.

suggest an increase in relative thresholds with
increasing r. It is apparent that no simple relationship, such as Weber's law, describes the data. It also
appears that discrimination is not unusual when r is
expressable as the ratio of small integers. To see this,
note that for the solid line, alternate points,
beginning with the leftmost point, correspond to small-
integer ratio values of r. The data for HP shows only
minor local minima at these points; the data for DF do
show pronounced minima at r= 1.25 (5:4) and 2.0, but
also show a local maximum at r=1.5 (3:2). Other data
also support the conclusion that small-integer ratios
are not important in ratio discrimination. Psychometric
functions obtained from HP and DF under conditions
comparable to those for the lower frequency region of
Fig. 3, but with fixed levels and with r= 1.225, show no
unusual behavior when r+∆r= 1.25 (5:4).
     The thresholds for the lower frequency region are
similar to those of the musically trained subjects of
Burns and Ward (1978) in discrimination of musical
intervals with sequential presentation of the two tones
of the interval. In their study the lower frequency
component was randomized over a range of 250-274 Hz and
durations of 500 ms were used (vs 200 ms in the present
study). For r ranging from 1.19 to 1.33 (300 to 500
cents in 50-cent steps), their thresholds, in log(∆r/r),

53

ranged from -1.94 to 1.55 (20 and 48 cents, respectively). As in the present study, thresholds were not unusually small for r in the vicinity of small-integer ratios. The subjects in our study were not musically trained and despite fairly extensive training could not achieve thresholds under sequential presentation similar to those for under simultaneous presentation. Nevertheless, the agreement between our thresholds and those of Burns and Ward indirectly suggests that simultaneous presentation is not necessary to achieve good performance in ratio discrimination.

The data for the high-frequency region, shown in Fig. 3 as dashed lines, indicate that discrimination thresholds can be nearly as good as those at lower frequencies. For the largest tested r there is a substantial increase in threshold. We attribute this increase to detectability limitations and loudness changes of the upper frequency component which, for this r, ranges from 5.6 to 8.3 kHz.

IV. DISCUSSION

These preliminary observations indicate that frequency ratios for two-tone complexes can be discriminated reliably under a fairly wide range of conditions, and with an accuracy that is comparable to simple frequency discrimination under conditions of similar uncertainty. The question is how this discrimination is being performed and, in particular, whether it is being mediated by something other than ratio extraction. We do not see such an alternative basis for ratio discrimination under the conditions of our experiments. One possibility is that the discrimination is based upon changes in the residue pitch of the two-tone complex. Even though the fundamental frequency is random, the often ambiguous residue pitch can, for large Δr, provide a fairly reliable cue. One "golden-eared" observer, of the dozen we have informally tested, showed good performance using what he described as an "obvious pitch clue" (Houtsma, 1986). However, this cue can be shown theoretically, and was shown by this observer, to be unreliable even for values of Δr that were significantly larger than the threshold values shown by our two subjects. Thus, we do not believe that the discrimination is based upon pitch changes. Nor do combination tones appear to be directly involved: adding a broadband noise does not affect threshold until the components themselves are being masked.

It can be readily demonstrated that slightly

54

mistuning the frequencies of a two-tone complex from consonant intervals, most notably the octave and the fifth, produces the sensation of beats. These "beats of mistuned consonances" (Plomp, 1967) may be involved in certain conditions in our experiments. In particular, subject DF reported detecting beats when r= 2.0; this accounts for the unusual minimum shown by her data in Fig. 3. She reported hearing no beats in any other condition and, in informal observation, heard beats only for mistuned octaves and fifths when the component levels were 67.5 dB. [It is not clear why she could not use beats for r= 1.5 (a just fifth) in the discrimination task]. These observations, together with the indication that discrimination is not generally better at "consonant" values of r, suggests that beats of mistuned consonances do not play any general, direct role in our discrimination experiments.

Consideration of the possible role of beats raises the more general question about the role in these experiments of timing information, specifically waveform synchrony. There are several indications that such information is not necessary for ratio discrimination. Assuming that the upper frequency limit for which synchrony is preserved in the auditory nerve is 4-5 kHz, then the indication from Fig. 3 that ratio discrimination can be as good at frequencies above 4 kHz as that at lower frequencies suggests that fine-structure synchrony to the individual components or the resultant, is not necessary. Furthermore, the agreement between our thresholds and those for successive presentation shown by trained musicians in Burns and Ward (1978) suggests, albeit weakly, that temporal interaction, specifically, envelope information, also is not necessary.

One could proceed to model these data by postulating direct computation of ratios. A more realistic implementation would incorporate the quasi-logarithmic mapping of frequency to distance along the basilar membrane. Accordingly, ratio differences become differences in length or extent, and the task becomes superficially, but provocatively, similar to tactile two-point difference thresholds and perhaps visual shape discrimination.

Finally, it should be noted that these data do not, in themselves, indicate direct perception of frequency ratios or that ratios are of fundamental importance in auditory perception. Ratios are important in this task because they are defined to be: the situation is specifically designed such that the stimuli differ, on the average, only in the ratio of their frequency components. We could have chosen other mathematical relationships, such as frequency differences, Bark differences, etc. Comparison of thresholds obtained with other invariant frequency relationships may help to determine whether ratios or other relationships are of special importance in perception.

ACKNOWLEDGMENTS

Our thanks to V.M. Kirby for comments on this paper. Supported by NINCDS NS12125 and NS07889.

REFERENCES

Boomsliter, P. and Creel, W. (1961). The long pattern hypothesis in harmony and hearing. J. Mus. Theory, 5, 2-31.

Burns, E.M. and Ward, W.D. (1978). Categorical perception- phenomenon or epiphenomenon: Evidence from experiments in the perception of melodic musical intervals. J. Acoust. Soc. Am., 63, 456-468.

Green, D.M. (1986). Auditory discrimination of a change in spectral shape. (This volume).

Houtsma, A.J.M. (1968). Discrimination of frequency ratios. J. Acoust. Soc. Am., 44, 383 (Abstract).

Houtsma, A.J.M. (1986). Personal communication and disconcerting demonstration.

Levitt, H. (1971). Transformed up-down methods in psychoacoustics. J. Acoust. Soc. Am., 49, 467-477.

Roederer, J.G. (1975). Introduction to the Physics and Psychophysics of Music, Springer-Verlag, New York.

Plomp, R. (1967). Beats of mistuned consonances. J. Acoust. Soc. Am., 42, 462-474.

Watson, C.S. and Kelly, W.J. (1981). The role of stimulus uncertainty in the discrimination of auditory patterns. In Auditory and Visual Pattern Recognition, D.J. Getty and J.H Howard, eds., L. Earlbaum Associates, Hillsdale.

Wier C.C., Jesteadt, W., and Green, D.M. (1977). Frequency discrimination as a function of frequency and sensation level. J. Acoust. Soc. Am., 61, 178-184.

Experiments on Comodulation Masking Release

Joseph W. Hall III
Department of Communication Sciences and Disorders
Northwestern University

Under some circumstances the auditory system adopts a wideband analysis strategy, even for a task as simple as the detection of a tone in noise. This appears to be the case in modulated noise, where the presence of noise components outside the critical band (CB) centered on the signal provides benefit for detection. This phenomenon is called "comodulation masking release" or "CMR." The present discussion reviews the stimulus variables that affect CMR, the relation between CMR and other psychoacoustical phenomena, and possible explanations of CMR. New data on two variables, the across-frequency level difference of the masker, and the frequency separation between on-signal masking band and comodulated flanking band, are also reported. Data are discussed in terms of the ability of the auditory system to utilize across-frequency difference cues as the frequency difference between comodulated bands increases, and as the level difference between the comodulated bands increases.

INTRODUCTION

Many auditory masking results are consistent with the assumption that the most important factor underlying signal detection is the signal-to-noise ratio at the output of the CB centered on the frequency of the signal (e.g., Fletcher, 1940; Patterson, 1976). Masker energy remote from the signal frequency contributes relatively little to the masking of the signal. Whereas this assumption holds for most cases in random broadband masking noise, the assumption often does not hold in modulated noise, or other noise where there is across-frequency coherence of the temporal envelope. In noise having across-frequency coherence of waveform envelope, noise remote from the frequency of the signal often causes a release from masking, or CMR (Hall, Haggard and Fernandes, 1984a).

Several different paramerters which have been investigated in CMR experiments are summarized below.

1) <u>Rate of modulation</u>. As the rate of modulation increases, the magnitude of CMR decreases in a way that is consistent with the temporal resolving ability of the auditory system (Hall and Haggard, 1983; Buus, 1985).

2) <u>Modulating waveform (sinusoidal, square wave, or random noise)</u>. It does not matter substantially whether the modulation is random or periodic; however CMR is greater for square-wave than for sine wave modulation (Hall and Cokely, 1985).

3) <u>Spectral location of the flanking band with regard to the on-signal band</u>. Masking release is obtained either when the comodulated flanking noise is added below the signal frequency or above the signal frequency (Hall et al., 1984a); the CMR effect occurs for comodulated bands placed nearly an octave below or above the signal frequency (Cohen and Schubert, 1985).

4) <u>The ear to which the comodulated energy is presented (signal ear or non-signal ear)</u>. A masking release occurs when comodulated masking energy is presented to the signal ear, or when the comodualted energy is presented to the non-signal ear (Hall et al., 1984b; Cohen and Schubert, 1985; Harvey et al., 1986).

5) <u>Envelope phase difference between the on-signal masking band and the flanking band</u>. For most subjects CMR is reduced greatly when the flanking band is delayed by more than a few ms (Haggard et al., 1985; McFadden, 1986). However, Haggard et al. report that some subjects continue to show small CMR effects even when the on-signal and flanking band envelopes are 180 degrees out of phase.

6) <u>Relative spectrum levels of the on-signal masking energy versus the comodulated flanking energy</u>. Whereas CMR is greatest when the spectrum level is equal across frequency, CMR also occurs when the level of the flanking band is 20-30 dB greater than the masker level at the signal frequency, or 20-30 dB less than the masker level at the signal frequency (Hall, 1986; Harvey et al., 1986). Somewhat in contrast to this, McFadden (1986) has reported conditions where CMR occurs only when the level difference between the on-signal and flanking bands is about 10 dB or less.

Several possible mechanisims have been proposed to account for CMR. One possibility is that the cue for detection in modulated noise is an across-frequency difference in modulation pattern (Hall et al. 1984a; Hall, 1986). For instance, when the signal is presented, the depth of modulation at the signal frequency will be different from the depth of modulation at flanking frequenies, and the signal may be detected as an across-frequency difference in modulation depth. Another possible explanation is similar to Durlach's (1963) equalization-cancellation theory for the masking-level difference (Buus, 1985; Hall, 1986). Following the extraction of waveform envelope at different CBs, the envelope at the signal CB is subtracted from envelopes at other CBs. A result different from zero indicates the presence of a signal.

Buus (1985) also has proposed an explanation for CMR that does not require detection of an across-frequency difference. According to this view the comodulated flanking energy is used by the auditory system to identify envelope dips. The rule for detection is to "listen in the dips" where the signal-to-noise ratio is best, and to integrate energy over several envelope dips. An explanation based upon suppression has also been proposed (Hall et al., 1984a). This could explain part of the monaural CMR effect, but could not account for the finding that CMR is obtained when comodulated energy is added to the ear contralateral to the signal.

CMR has also been compared to several other psychoacoustical phenomena. For instance, it has been noted that CMR shares attributes with the masking-level difference (Buus, 1985; Cohen and Schubert, 1985; Hall, 1986). CMR also appears to be related to Profile Analysis (e.g., Green et al., 1983; Spiegel et al., 1981), in that in both phenomena detection is based upon across-frequency analysis (see Hall et al., 1984a for further discussion). CMR is also similar to the perceptual cueing effects described by Moore (1981), and to auditory streaming (e.g., Dannenbring and Bregman, 1978; McAdams, 1984). Finally, Cohen and Schubert (1985) note that CMR may be related to the ability of the auditory system to detect temporal coherence of stimulus envelope as processed on different portions of the basilar membrane (e.g., Goldstein, 1967; von Bekesy, 1963).

59

The remainder of this chapter describes two new experiments intended to improve the understanding of the basis of CMR, and the specific stimulus parameters important for the effect.

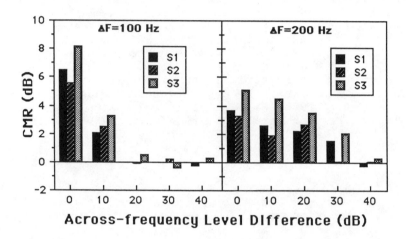

Figure 1.   CMR as a function of level difference between bands for 100 (left) and 200-Hz (right) separation.

EXPERIMENT 1 - CMR, ACROSS-FREQUENCY LEVEL DIFFERENCES, AND FREQUENCY SEPARATION BETWEEN COMODULATED BANDS

The effect of the across-frequency difference of masker level on CMR is somewhat unclear.   Whereas studies by Hall (1986) and Harvey et al. (1986) indicated that CMR can occur for across-frequency masker level differences of from 20 to 30 dB, McFadden (1986) reported a limit of about 10 dB.   The present study attempts to determine the possible reasons for this discrepancy, and to establish better the factors which govern the robustness of CMR to across-frequency level differences.   As noted by McFadden (1986) there are several differences between his method and those of Hall (1986) and Harvey et al. (1986).   Perhaps the most significant difference is that the frequency separation between the on-signal and flanking bands was greater in the experiments of Hall and of Harvey et al. than in the experiment of McFadden.   The present experiment examined both the spectral separation and the difference in level between comodulated bands.

60

METHOD

Comodulated noise was obtained by multiplying a
narrowband noise (30-Hz wide centered on 2500 Hz) by a
two-tone complex. The two-tone complex was either 3000
Hz plus 2900 Hz, or 3000 Hz plus 2800 Hz. This resulted
in comodulated 30-Hz wide bands centered at 400, 500,
5500 and 5400 Hz, or 300, 500, 5500, and 5800 Hz. These
bands were low-pass filtered, leaving comodulated bands
at 400 and 500 Hz (100-Hz separation), or at 300 and 500
Hz (200-Hz separation). The signal was a 500-Hz pure
tone (400-ms duration, 50-ms rise/fall). The spectrum
level of the on-signal masker was always 50 dB/Hz. The
spectrum level of the flanking band was either 50, 40,
30, or 20 dB/Hz. There was also a condition where the
flanking band was not present. Thresholds were determined
using a 3AFC, three-down, one-up strategy (Levitt, 1971).
Four threshold determinations (each being the average of
the final eight of 12 reversals) were averaged to
estimate the threshold for each condition.

RESULTS AND DISCUSSION

Figure 1 shows CMR (threshold for flanker absent
minus threshold for flanker present) as a function of
the level difference between the on-signal band and the
flanking band. The largest CMR occurred when the the
bands had 100-Hz separation and the levels of the two
bands were equal. However, CMR was not robust with
respect to across-frequency level differences at the 100-
Hz separation: Here CMR was reduced to a negligible
amount when the level difference between the comodulated
bands was greater than about 10 dB. When the frequency
separation between the two bands was 200 Hz, CMR was only
about three to five dB even when the two bands were of
equal level. However, CMR was relatively robust to
across-frequency level differences: Here CMR occurred for
across-frequency level differences up to 20 to 30 dB.
Thus CMR is abolished by relatively small differences in
across-frequency level when the comodulated bands are
relatively close in frequency, but is more robust to
level differences when the bands are further apart.

The above results may be explained by considering
the spread of excitation in the auditory periphery. Theoretically, the most favorable condition for CMR would be
where the pure tone signal and the on-signal masking band

are represented only in the CB centered on the signal,
and the flanking band is represented in a "separate" CB.
This would allow for a clear across-frequency difference
cue to occur upon presentation of the signal. However,
because frequency selectivity is not perfect, there will
always be some smearing of spectral components (signal
and masker) across CBs. When the on-signal and flanking
bands are close together, and the signal band is greater
in level than the flanking band, energy in the on-signal
band may significantly affect the response to the flanking band, reducing the across-frequency difference. However, when the bands are separated by a greater frequency
difference, there will be less auditory interaction
between the signal and the flanker, and greater
differences in across-frequency level can be tolerated.
It is possible that the auditory system may use "off-
frequency listening" to aid detection when comodulated
bands are relatively close to one another. This could
help to overcome the problem of the smearing of information across CBs. For instance, if the flanking band is
below the signal frequency (as in the present study), the
auditory system may base detection upon a comparison
between a frequency region above the signal frequency and
below the flanking frequency in order to maximize the
across-frequency difference cue.

EXPERIMENT 2 - CMR AND THE FREQUENCY SEPARATION BETWEEN
ON-SIGNAL AND FLANKING MASKER BANDS

Hall et al. (1984a) showed that CMR occurred whether
a comodulated flanking band was added above or below the
on-signal band. Cohen and Schubert (1985) demonstrated
that when the comodulated bands were separated by an
octave or more, CMR was absent or very small. The present
study examined whether this frequency separation limit is
a general finding, or whether the effect is influenced
significantly by the particular stimuli used. It was
hypothesized that CMR might occur for wider spectral
separations if stimuli were used that were relatively
favorable for CMR in general: a low rate of modulation,
and a comodulated flanking band having a relatively wide
bandwidth (Hall and Haggard, 1983).

METHOD

In a baseline condition a 30-Hz wide band centered on 500 Hz was amplitude modulated (%100) by a 5-Hz or 15-Hz pure tone sinusoid. In the CMR conditions a 300-Hz wide flanking band was added. The 300-Hz wide band was amplitude modulated by the same sine wave used for the 30-Hz wide band, so the bands were comodulated. The parameter was the frequency separation between the 30-Hz wide band centered on 500 Hz and the 300-Hz wide flanker. The spectrum level of the noise was always 50 dB/Hz.

RESULTS AND DISCUSSION

Figure 2 shows CMR as a function of the frequency separation between the on-signal band and the flanking band. The separation was defined as the frequency difference between the upper edge of the flanking band and the lower edge of the on-signal band (flanker below 500 Hz), or the frequency difference between the lower edge of the flanking band and the upper edge of the on-signal band (flanker above 500 Hz). There was also a condition where the masker was a single modulated 300-Hz wide band centered on 500 Hz. As can be seen, at the 5-Hz modulation there is a CMR effect for frequency separations beyond an octave, although the CMR is greater for smaller separations. CMR is smaller in general, and is limited to smaller frequency separations when the sinusoidal modulation rate was 15 Hz.

It is clear that the effect of the separation of the on-signal and flanking bands depends on the stimuli used, and that CMR can occur for bands separated by more than an octave. In general, however, CMR diminishes as the frequency separation between comodulated bands increases. This result may indicate that the auditory system has difficulty in coding the comodulation of noise bands having relatively large frequency separations. One reason for this may be a decorrelation of envelopes as processed on different regions of the basilar membrane, due in part to the delay time of the travelling wave (e.g., Bekesy, 1963; Cohen and Schubert, 1985). It is of interest to note that in a pilot experiment where a double-balanced multiplication was used (rather than 100% amplitude modulation) CMR effects were extremely small or absent for frequency separations an octave or greater. The modulation frequency was 2.5 Hz, which resulted in a

63

5-Hz modulation, but a cusp-shaped envelope similar in shape to a rectified sine wave. Such an envelope is characterized by relatively short dips and relatively long peaks. It is reasonable to conclude that CMR occurs for wide frequency separations only when the modulation frequency is low and envelope dips are long in duration.

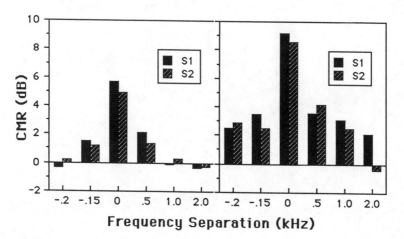

Figure 2. CMR as a function of frequency separation between bands for 15-Hz (right) and 5-Hz (left) modulation.

If indeed comodulated stimuli resolved on different regions of the basilar membrane suffer decorrelation, decorrelation in the region of envelope dips should be less for low-frequency, sinusoidal modulation than for high-frequency, cusp-shaped modulation.

CONCLUDING REMARKS

The two experiments reported here demonstrate two contrasting effects concerning the frequency separation between comodulated bands. Whereas experiment 2 indicated that CMR generally decreases as the frequency separation between the comodulated bands increases, experiment 1 showed that CMR can sometimes benefit from an increase in the frequency separation between bands (when there are across-frequency differences in masker level). Eventhough these results might appear to be in conflict at first glance, they can be reconciled, and are

helpful in identifying different factors which contribute
to CMR. The results from both experiments are consistent
with the hypothesis that CMR is based upon the ability of
the auditory system to code the comodulation of noise
bands, and the ability to code the across-frequency
difference which results upon signal presentation. When
the comodulated bands are very close in frequency and/or
the bands differ greatly in level, CMR may be diminished
because the limited frequency selectivity of the ear
fails to preserve across-frequency difference cues. On
the other hand, when the comodulated bands are far apart,
CMR may be diminished because the auditory system is
unable to code precisely the comodulation of the bands.

REFERENCES

Buus, S. (1985). Release from masking caused by envelope
fluctuations, J. Acoust. Soc. Am., 78, 1958-1965.

Cohen, M.F. and Schubert, E.D. (1985). Place synchrony
and the masking-level difference, J. Acoust. Soc. Am. 77,
S49.

Dannenbring, G.L. and Bregman, A.S. (1978). Streaming vs.
fusion of sinusoidal components of complex sounds,
Percept. Psychophys., 24, 369-376.

Fletcher, H. (1940). Auditory Patterns, Rev. Mod. Phys.
12, 47-61.

Goldstein, J.L. (1967). Auditory spectral filtering and
monaural phase perception. J. Acoust. Soc. Am., 41, 458-
479.

Green, D.M., Kid, G., and Picardi, M.C. (1983). Successive versus simultaneous comparison in auditory intensity
discrimination, J. Acoust. Soc. Am., 73, 639-643.

Haggard, M.P., Harvey, A.D.G. and Carlyon, R.P. (1985).
Peripheral and central components of comodulation masking
release, J. Acoust. Soc. Am., 78, S63.

Hall, J. W. (1986). The effect of across-frequency
differences in masking level on spectro-temporal pattern
analysis, J. Acoust. Soc. Am., 79, 781-787.

Hall, J.W. and Cokely, J.A. (1986). Signal detection for combined monaural and binaural masking release, (manuscript in preparation).

Hall, J. W. and Haggard, M. P. (1983). Co-modulation - a principle for auditory pattern analysis in speech, Proc. 11th I.C.A., 4, 69-71.

Hall, J. W., Haggard, M. P., and Fernandes, M. A. (1984a). Detection in noise by spectro-temporal pattern analysis, J. Acoust. Soc. Am., 76, 50-56.

Hall, J. W., Haggard, M. P., and Harvey, M. A. (1984b). Release from masking through ipsilateral and contralateral comodulation of a flanking band, J. Acoust. Soc. Am., 76, S76.

Harvey, A.D.G., Haggard, M.P., and Hall, J.W. CMR for monotic, dichotic, and pseudo-dichotic flanking bands, (manuscript submitted for publication).

Levitt, H. (1971). Transformed up-down methods in psychoacoustics, J. Acoust. Soc. Am. 49, 467-477.

McAdams, S. (1984). Spectral fusion, spectral parsing, and the formation of auditory images, Ph.D. thesis, Stanford Univ., Stanford Dept. Mus. Rep. STAN-M22 (unpublished).

McFadden, D.M. (1986). Comodulation masking release: Effects of varying the level, duration, and time delay of the cue band, J. Acoust. Soc. Am. (to be published).

Moore, B.C.J. (1981). Interaction of masker bandwidth with signal duration and delay in forward masking, J. Acoust. Soc. Am., 70, 62-68.

Patterson, R. D. (1976). Auditory filter shapes derived with noise stimuli, J. Acoust. Soc. Am., 59, 640-654.

Spiegel, M.F., Picardi, M.C. and Green, D.M. (1981). Signal and masker uncertainty in intensity discrimination, J. Acoust. Soc. Am., 70, 1015-1019.

von Bekesy, G. (1963). Three experiments concerned with pitch perception, J. Acoust. Soc. Am., 35, 602-606.

CENTRAL AND PERIPHERAL FACTORS AIDING SIGNAL DETECTION WITH COMPLEX STIMULI

ROBERT P. CARLYON
MRC Institute of Hearing Research, University Park,
Nottingham NG7 2RD, England

This paper reports a set of conditions under which a continuous random noise with a spectral notch causes a release from masking. Subjects are required to detect a brief tone in a burst of bandpass noise, and the addition of the continuous random noise, with a notch centered on the signal frequency, reduces thresholds by up to 11 dB. This masking release builds up within 320 ms of notched noise onset, persists for about 160 ms after its offset, and is greatest when thresholds in the absence of notched noise are high. A smaller (7 dB) masking release is obtained with a continuous bandpass noise. The effect is similar in many ways to the "overshoot" effect reported by Zwicker (1965a,b), and it is argued that both these effects may be attributed to peripheral short-term adaptation. It is likely that additional, possibly more central, mechanisms are responsible for part of the effect.

INTRODUCTION

In a classical signal detection experiment a sinusoid is masked by a single burst of random noise. In such an experiment components of the noise falling within one critical band around the signal contribute to its masking, and more remote components have no effect (Zwicker et al, 1957). In this volume, both Green and Hall report experiments involving more complex stimuli which show that energy at frequencies remote from that of the signal can produce a release from masking. These "profile analysis" and "comodulation" phenomena are largely attributed to central mechanisms. This chapter describes a masking release which, it is argued, is mediated at least in part by more peripheral mechanisms. In the experiments to be described subjects are required to detect a brief signal in a burst of random noise. The addition of a continuous independent random noise, with a notch centered on the signal frequency, produces a reduction in signal threshold of up to 11 dB. Before describing this masking release in more detail, I shall review two findings that have already been reported in the literature related to it.

Zwicker (1965a,b) has shown that the threshold for a brief sinusoidal signal presented against a longer-duration noise masker decreases as the delay between masker and signal onset is increased. He termed this finding the "overshoot" effect. In one experimental condition he found that adding a continuous white noise to a pulsed tone-in-noise detectioon task produced a release from masking, and attributed this finding to the overshoot effect. More recently, a number of researchers have proposed that the overshoot effect (and therefore, presumably, the masking release caused by the continuous noise) is attributable to peripheral short-term adaptation (Green, 1969; Smith and Zwislocki, 1975; Carlyon, 1984; Bacon and Viemeister, 1985; Carlyon and Moore, 1986a). This is consistent with physiological evidence (Smith, 1979), which shows auditory-nerve adaptation to be additive: exposure to a prior adapting stimulus reduces the responses to the masker alone and to the masker+signal equally, thereby increasing the proportional increment in firing rate caused by the signal. (For example, if the unadapted response of a fiber were 100 spikes/sec to a masker alone, and 110 with the signal added, adaptation might reduce these amounts to 60 and 50 respectively, raising the increase caused by the signal from 10% to 20%). If this is true, then it might also explain the masking release caused by continuous notched noise, as this noise should also produce some adaptation in the signal frequency region via "spread of excitation." One should also be able to obtain at least as big an effect by using as an adaptor a continuous bandpass noise centered on the signal frequency.

A second relevant finding has been reported by Viemeister (1980). He measured thresholds for a 1-kHz tone in a pulsed harmonic complex which had the 1-kHz component filtered out. He found that presenting 2.4 seconds of an identical complex before the masker and signal were turned on could produce a 13 dB release from masking, but did not speculate as to the precise mechanism which underlay this finding. In marked contrast to the overshoot effect, no masking release occurred when the adaptor contained energy in the frequency region of the signal.

The experiments reported here were designed to investigate the release from masking by continuous notched noise in detail, and to attempt to determine

68

the mechanisms which underly it with reference to the two findings reported above.

EFFECTS OF FREQUENCY AND OF NOTCHED NOISE LEVEL

Stimuli and Procedure

Experiment 1 investigated how the effect varies with masker and signal frequency, and with the level of continuous notched noise used.

Signals were 10-ms sinusoids of frequencies 1000, 3000 and 6500 Hz, gated on and off with 2-ms ramps. Maskers were 10-ms bursts of bandpass noise centered on the signal frequency (fs) and of bandwidth 0.4fs, gated on and off in each of two possible signal intervals. The level of the masker passing through a hypothetical auditory filter centered on the signal frequency was 60 dB SPL (Moore and Glasberg, 1983). This level was 21, 27 and 30 dB above the spectrum level of the maskers centered on 1000, 3000 and 6500 Hz respectively. Independent, random continuous notched noise consisted of two bands of noise 0.3fs wide, separated by a notch 0.2fs wide centered on the signal frequency. For each signal frequency tested spectrum levels of this noise of −20, −10, −5, 0, +5, +10 or +20 dB relative to that of the signal were used, as well as a condition in which it was absent. More detailed information on all stimuli is reported by Carlyon (1986).

RESULTS

Results are represented by the solid lines in Figure 1. The unconnected points on the left are thresholds in the absence of notched noise. There were some inter-subject differences, but all three subjects show the same general trend, so mean data are presented.

Thresholds are expressed as 10 log ($\Delta I/I$), where ΔI is the signal level and I is the level of the masker (60 dB in these experiments) passing through a hypothetical auditory filter centered on the signal frequency. For all frequencies thresholds decrease as notched noise level is increased to a certain level. This "optimum level" is +5 dB for the 3000-Hz and 6500-

69

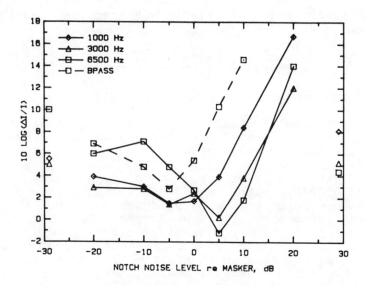

Figure 1. Thresholds for signals of three different
frequencies masked by bursts of noise, as a
function of the spectrum level of a continuous
noise relative to that of the masker.

Hz conditions, and 0 dB for the 1000-Hz condition. It
is likely that the threshold increase observed as
notched noise is raised beyond its optimum level is due
to ·it becoming so intense as to actually mask the
signal.

Thresholds in the absence of any continuous noise
are highest at 6500 Hz, in agreement with the results
of Carlyon and Moore(1986b) for a 60-dB masker level.
As thresholds at the optimum level of notched noise are
broadly similar across frequency, this means that the
greatest masking release occurs at 6500 Hz. This is
consistent with the data obtained on the overshoot
effect (Zwicker, 1965a). It is not consistent with
Viemeister's (1980) results.

EFFECT OF A CONTINUOUS BANDPASS NOISE

If the present effect is related to the overshoot
effect reported by Zwicker (1965a,b), then a similar

masking release should also be obtainable with a
continuous bandpass noise adaptor. If it is related to
Viemeister's (1980) effect, then no masking release
should be seen with a bandpass noise.

Experiment 2 repeated the 6500-Hz condition of
Experiment 1, except that the continuous notched noise
was replaced by a bandpass noise of bandwidth 0.4fs.
Continuous bandpass noise levels of -20, -10, -5, 0, +5
and +10 dB were used.

The results of this experiment are shown by the
dashed lines of Figure 1. The bandpass noise does
produce a masking release, but the lowest threshold
observed is 4 dB higher than that seen with the notched
noise at the same frequency, and occurs at a continuous
noise level of -5 dB. This suggests that notched noise
masking release may be partly, but not totally,
mediated by the same mechanisms that are responsible
for the overshoot effect.

BUILD UP OF MASKING RELEASE

Experiment 3 was designed to determine the time
course of the build up of the effect. A +5 dB level of
notched noise from the 6500-Hz condition of Experiment
1 was gated on and off at different times relative to
the masker and signal.

Briefly, the results of this experiment showed
that when the masker and signal were presented 320 ms
after the onset of a 430-ms notched noise, thresholds
were within 1 dB of those obtained when the notched
noise was continuous. It was concluded that the build
up of the effect was complete within 320 ms. This time
course is similar to that of both the overshoot effect
and of Viemeister's (1980) results.

DECLINE OF MASKING RELEASE

Experiment 4 was designed to determine whether a
release from masking would occur when the notched noise
was turned off before masker onset, and, if so, how
thresholds would vary with delay time. Testing was
carried out at 6500 Hz with a 320-ms burst of notched
noise that ended 2.5, 5, 10, 20, 40, 80, 160, 320 or

640 ms before masker and signal onset. Notched levels
of -5, +5, +15 and +25 dB were used.

Mean data are presented in Figure 2. For the -5
dB notched noise level, thresholds do not vary
systematically as a function of delay time. For the
higher noise levels thresholds change only slightly
with increases in delay time beyond 160 ms. For the +5
and +15 dB levels, thresholds increase monotonically as
delay time is increased from 2.5 to 160ms, at rates of
3.9 and 5.2 dB/decade respectively. For the +25 dB
level, threshold decreases as delay time increases from
2.5 to 10ms. This may be due to the notched noise
being so intense as to completely forward mask the
signal, by rendering the responses to it less than that
at absolute threshold. As delay time is further
increased to 160 ms, threshold increases at a rate of
5.1 dB/decade. For all four noise levels thresholds
are always lower than in the absence of any continuous
noise, even at a 640-ms delay. Thus, some very slow

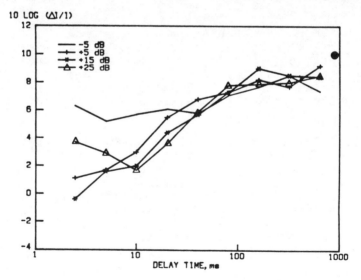

Figure 2. Thresholds (expressed as 10 log(ΔI/I) for
    10-ms 6500-Hz signals masked by bursts of bandpass
    noise as a function of the delay after the offset
    of a 320-ms notched noise. Data for four
    different notched noise levels are shown. The
    filled circle on the right of the graph is the
    threshold in the absence of any continuous noise.

72

decline of the effect may be taking place at delay
times longer than this.

No comparable data are available for the overshoot
effect. However, as the overshoot effect has been
attributed to peripheral short-term adaptation, and as
a similar explanation is often used to explain forward
masking (Harris and Dallos, 1979), it is interesting to
compare the present data with those for the recovery
from forward masking. Such a comparison reveals two
similarities. One is the delay time of 160 ms beyond
which thresholds do not change markedly. This is
similar to the value of 178 ms for forward masking of
4-kHz signals predicted by Jesteadt et al's (1982) fit
to their data. The second is the finding that this
delay time is independent of the adaptor level used,
for both the data presented here and for forward
masking.

Viemeister's (1980) functions relating threshold
to delay time show a different time course. His
functions are well fitted by straight lines on log
delay/dB threshold co-ordinate for delays up to 6400
ms. However, it is possible that this difference is
due to the much longer (2.4 s) adaptor used in his
study.

DISCUSSION

Two findings reported in this chapter are
consistent with the overshoot effect, but not with
Viemeister's (1980) results. The first of these is
that a continuous bandpass noise can produce a
substantial masking release. The second is that the
size of the effect is greatest at high frequencies
(Zwicker, 1965a) where "unreleased" thresholds are
highest. However, the greater effectiveness of
notched- than of bandpass-noise (see Figure 1) suggests
that additional mechanisms are involved, and these may
be similar to those responsible for Viemeister's
results. Any such mechanism would have to affect the
representation of masker and signal in such a way as to
render the signal more detectable. Elsewhere (Carlyon,
1986) I propose two mechanisms which fulfill these
criteria.

The results presented here add to the list of

73

findings which show that off-frequency components can produce a release from masking. Whereas both Hall and Green in this volume demonstrate that these components can produce a release by providing information about the masker (on the fluctuations in this envelope in Hall's comodulation experiments, and on its overall level in Green's profile analysis paradigm), the notched noise described in this chapter provides no such information. This leads to the conclusion that in complex situations a number of mechanisms operate to render the signal more detectable, and I have argued that these can operate at peripheral as well as central sites.

REFERENCES

Bacon, S.P. and Viemeister, N.F. (1985). The temporal course of simultaneous tone-on-tone masking, J. Acoust. Soc. Am. 78, 1231-1235.

Carlyon, R.P. (1984). Intensity discrimmination in hearing. Ph.D. thesis, University of Cambridge.

Carlyon, R.P. (1986). A release from masking by continuous random notched noise. J. Acoust. Soc. Am. In Press.

Carlyon, R.P. and Moore, B.C.J. (1986a). Continuous versus gated maskers and the "severe departure" from Weber's Law. J. Acoust. Soc. Am. 79, 453-460.

Carlyon. R.P. and Moore, B.C.J. (1986b). Detection of tones in noise and the "severe departure" from Weber's Law. J. Acoust. Soc. Am. 79, 461-464.

Green, D.M. (1969). Masking with continuous and pulsed sinusoids. J. Acoust. Soc. Am. 46, 939-946.

Harris, D.M. and Dallos, P. (1979). Forward masking of auditory-nerve fiber responses. J. Neurophysiol. 42, 1083-1107.

Jesteadt, W., Bacon, S.P. and Lehman, J.R. (1982). Forward masking as a function of frequency, masker level, and signal delay. J. Acoust. Soc. Am. 71, 950-962.

Moore, B.C.J. and Glasberg, B.R. (1983). Suggested formulae for calculating auditory-filter bandwidths and excitation patterns. J. Acoust. Soc. Am. 74, 750-753.

Smith, R.L. (1979). Adaptation, saturation, and physiological masking in single auditory-nerve fibers. J. Acoust. Soc. Am. 65, 166-178.

Smith, R.L. and Zwislocki, J.J. (1975). Short-term
     adaptation and incremental response of single
     auditory-nerve fibers. Biol. Cybernetics, 17,
     169-182.
Viemeister, N.F. (1980). Adaptation of masking, in:
     Psychophysical, physiological and behavioural
     studies in hearing, eds: G. van den Brink and
     F.A. Bilsen, Delft University Press, Delft.
Wilson, J.P. (1970). An auditory afterimage, in:
     Frequency analysis and psychophysics of hearing,
     eds: R. Plomp and G.F. Smoorenburg, Sijthoff,
     Leiden, Netherlands.
Zwicker, E. (1965a). Temporal effects in simultaneous
     masking by white-noise bursts. J. Acoust. Soc.
     Am. 37, 653-663.
Zwicker, E. (1965b). Temporal effects in simultaneous
     masking and loudness. J. Acoust. Soc. Am. 38,
     132-141.
Zwicker, E., Flottorp, G. and Stephens, S.S. (1957).
     Critical bandwidths in loudness summation. J.
     Acoust. Soc. Am. 29, 548-557.

ADDITIONAL REFERENCES

Elliot, L.L. (1965). Changes in the simultaneous
     masked threshold of brief tones. J. Acoust. Soc.
     Am. 38, 738-746.
Lummis, R.C., Guttman, N. and Bock, D.E. (1966).
     Auditory afterimages in gated noise. J. Acoust.
     Soc. Am. 40, 1240.
Smith, R.L. (1977). Short-term adaptation in single
     auditory nerve fibers: some poststimulatory
     effects. J. Neurophysiol. 40, 1098-1112.
Summerfield, A.Q., Haggard, M.P., Foster, J. and Gray,
     S. (1984). Perceiving vowels from uniform
     spectra: phonetic exploration of an auditory
     aftereffect. Percept. Psychophys. 35, 203-213.
Summerfield, A.Q., Sidwell, A.S. and Nelson, A.
     (1986). Auditory enhancement of increments in
     spectral amplitude. J. Acoust. Soc. Am.
     Submitted.
Viemeister, N.F. and Bacon, S.P. (1982). Forward
     masking by enhanced components in harmonic
     complexes. J. Acoust. Soc. Am. 79, 1502-1507.
Wilson, J.P. (1970). An auditory afterimage, in:
     Frequency Analysis and Psychophysics of Hearing,
     eds: R. Plomp and G. F. Smoorenburg, Sijthoff,
     Leiden, Netherlands.

DEMODULATION PROCESSES IN AUDITORY PERCEPTION

Lawrence L. Feth and Lisa J. Stover
Department of Speech-Language-Hearing
University of Kansas, Lawrence, KS   66045

Complex sounds exhibit fluctuations of amplitude and
frequency. This paper reviews a model of auditory
processing of simultaneous amplitude and frequency
modulations derived from studies of Voelcker's elementary modulated signals. A digital computer simulation of the model using the discrete Hilbert
transform indicates its usefulness in understanding
the perception of more complex sounds. Applying the
model to the complex sounds used in "auditory profile
analysis" studies predicts a consistent pitch difference between sounds thought to be discriminable
only because of small spectral-envelope differences.

INTRODUCTION

Temporal modulations of the amplitude and (phase)
angle of continuous signals are known to carry the information in most naturally occurring sounds (e.g., Lauter
and Hirsh, 1985). Some of the earliest work in modern
psychoacoustics reflected the time-varying nature of
speech, music and other environmentally important sounds
(e.g., Riesz, 1928; Shower and Biddulph, 1931; Tiffin,
1931), but we are still far from understanding the
process(es) by which the auditory system extracts information from temporally complex sounds. A popular approach has been to eliminate much of the complexity of
"real" sounds so that auditory processing of simple signals could be understood. One problem with that approach
lies in the choice of basis (i.e., simple) signals.
Harmuth (1970) indicates that a number of sets of orthogonal functions could be used as the basis signals in
communications; however, the set of harmonically related
sinusoids (Fourier series) has been most widely used.
Such sinusoids are basis signals only for true periodic
signals processed by linear, time-invariant systems.
Real sounds are rarely periodic, and recent evidence
indicates that the auditory system is not best represented as linear.

76

Voelcker (1966a,b) suggested a set of basic functions for modulated signals that would unify the representation of various modulation processes. Feth and his colleagues (1974, 1977, 1982) have investigated the auditory processing of the simplest of Voelcker's signals, two-component signals that are simultaneously modulated in amplitude and frequency. Schematic representations of these signals are given in Figure 1. For each signal, the figure shows a line spectrum, envelope function, and instantaneous frequency function. In the upper half of

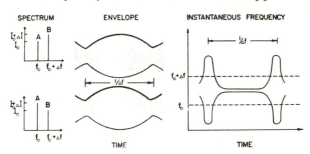

Figure 1. Line spectra, envelope functions and frequency fluctuations for a complementary pair of Voelcker signals. Component tones differ in frequency by Δf and in amplitude by ΔI. (Feth and O'Malley, 1977; reprinted by permission.)

the figure, the higher frequency component is also greater in amplitude; in the lower half, the lower frequency component is larger. The frequency separation is indicated by Δf; the amplitude difference by ΔI. Each resulting complex tone is periodic with period 1/Δf. The envelope fluctuations for each complex tone are identical, if Δf and ΔI are the same for both. However, the frequency fluctuations are symmetric about a horizontal line. That is, while the modulations in the upper trace move upward in frequency periodically, those in the lower trace move downward. These excursions in frequency occur as the envelope is moving toward its minimum value. Near envelope maxima, the frequency remains nearly constant at a value just above, or just below, the average of the two component frequencies.

THE EWAIF MODEL

Our previous work has indicated that the discriminability of complementary pairs of Voelcker signals can be predicted from the envelope-weighted average of instantaneous frequency (EWAIF) fluctuations. A typical compound psychometric function for the discriminability of a

77

pair of Voelcker signals in shown in Figure 2. Here, at
1000 Hz, the discriminability of a pair of two-component
complex tones is seen to improve from about 75% to nearly
100% as Δf is increased from 5 to 50 Hz. From 50 to
about 300 Hz, performance remains near 100%, then as Δf

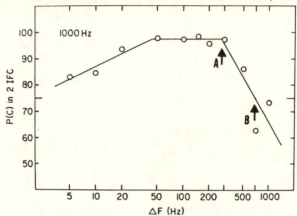

Figure 2. A typical compound psychometric function for the discrimination of complementary
Voelcker signals. Here, ΔI is 1 dB; Δf, as shown
on the abscissa, was always centered on 1000 Hz.
A is a "breakpoint" estimate; B is based on the
difference limen. (Feth and O'Malley, 1977; reprinted by permission.)

is increased further, performance drops toward chance.
For this example, ΔI remained at 1 dB. That is, the
ratio of the two amplitudes was equal to 1 dB. Feth and
O'Malley (1977) used such compound psychometric functions to indicate the frequency-resolving power of normal
hearing human listeners. To do so, they had to determine
an indicator of the frequency separation at which the two
components were resolved by the peripheral auditory system. When so resolved, the frequency fluctuations
inherent in the two-component complex sound could not be
perceived by the listener. Without the frequency fluctuations, the two complementary complex tones become
indiscriminable. Figure 2 shows two possible ways to
define this resolution bandwidth. The arrow marked A
indicates a "break point" definition of resolution as
typically used in indicators of the critical bandwidth
(e.g., Scharf, 1970). The arrow marked B indicates the
frequency for which listener performance drops back to
75% in a two-interval forced-choice task. For simple
psychometric functions the 75% point is used to define
the difference limen (DL) or just-noticeable-difference
(jnd). By analogy, we suggested that the downward cross-

78

ing of the 75% level should be used to delimit the
resolving power of the listener's ear. Figure 3 shows
the bandwidth estimates so obtained from our crew of
listeners for center frequencies from 250 to 4000 Hz.

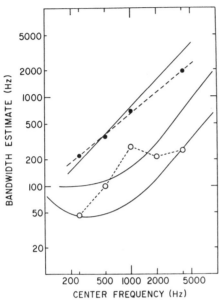

The break-point
estimates are
shown as open cir-
cles; the jnd
estimates as
filled circles.
The two curves
shown are the
empirical and
critical ratio
estimates of the
critical band-
width. While
there is little
order to our
break-point esti-
mates, the jnd
estimates fall on
a straight line.
(The solid line
shown is taken
from Green's
(1965) estimate of
the 3 dB points on
Bekesy's traveling
wave envelopes.)
The reader is di-
rected to the orig-
inal paper for de-
tails of this work.

Figure 3. Resolution bandwidth as a function of
center frequency. Open circles denote breakpoint
estimates; filled circles are jnd estimates. The
curves are the familiar "empirical" and critical
ratio estimates of the critical bandwidth (Scharf,
1970). The solid straight line reflects Green's
(1965) estimate of the 3 dB bandwidths from
Bekesy's traveling wave envelopes. (Feth and
O'Malley, 1977; reprinted by permission.)

The pitch perceived in each of the Voelcker signals
appears to be related to the envelope-weighted average of
instantaneous frequency. Feth et al. (1982) demonstrated
this relationship by asking well-trained listeners to
match the pitch they heard in each two-component Voelcker
tone. In general, the more discriminable complex tone
pairs exhibited larger differences in the pitch matches.
Further, they found that the pitch of a particular Voelcker
tone was predicted by calculating the envelope-weighted
average of its instantaneous frequency fluctuations.
When predictions and listener performance differed, the
model always predicted better performance than was
evident in the data. That is, the model predicted better
discrimination performance and larger pitch differences

79

than our listeners were able to produce. Again, the reader is directed to the original paper for details of this work.

COMPUTER IMPLEMENTATION OF THE MODEL

Previous work on the EWAIF model has been limited to two- or three-component signals because predictions required the analytical calculation of envelope and instantaneous frequency functions for each of the test signals. In general, (McGillem, 1979)

$$f(t) = E(t) \cos\{p(t)\}$$

where $E(t)$ is the instantaneous envelope, and $p(t)$ is the instantaneous phase (angle). Using the analytic signal $g(t) = f(t) + jH(t)$, where $j=(-1)^{\frac{1}{2}}$ and $H(t)= -f(t)*(1/\pi t)$, is the Hilbert transform of $f(t)$,

$$E(t) = [f^2(t) + H^2(t)]^{\frac{1}{2}}$$
$$p(t) = \tan^{-1}\{-H(t)/f(t)\}$$

and the instantaneous frequency, $\omega(t) = dp(t)/dt$, or

$$\omega(t) = \{H(t) \times f'(t) - f(t) \times H'(t)\}/ \{f^2(t) + H^2(t)\}.$$

The * denotes convolution and ' denotes the first time derivative.

Recently, we have implemented a computer simulation of the model using the discrete Hilbert transform. Using the computer implementation of the model, the instantaneous envelope and frequency functions can be calculated for any sampled signal. Figure 4 shows the output of the computer implementation for the two-component Voelcker signals discussed above. The upper panel shows the sampled signal, envelope function, and the instantaneous frequency function for a signal in which the higher frequency component is the more intense. The lower panel shows the same functions for the complementary signal.

Predictions from the computer simulation agree with the analytical form of the model and with data from discrimination and pitch-matching experiments. Also, the discrete form of the model is able to predict the pitch heard in simple amplitude modulated (AM) and frequency modulated (FM) tones. Further, the pitch shifts associated with phase differences between simultaneous AM and

80

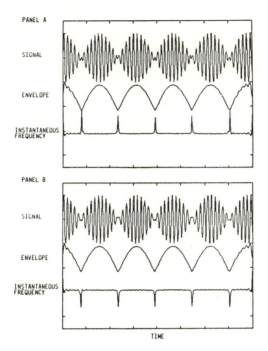

PANEL A

SIGNAL

ENVELOPE

INSTANTANEOUS FREQUENCY

PANEL B

SIGNAL

ENVELOPE

INSTANTANEOUS FREQUENCY

TIME

FIGURE 4. Sampled signal, envelope functions, and instantaneous frequency fluctuations for the computer simulation of the EWAIF model. The signals are a typical complementary pair of Voelcker tones.

FM modulators (Iwamiya et al., 1984) are well described by the model.

PROFILE ANALYSIS SIGNALS
    Recently, we have applied the EWAIF model to the multi-component complex tones used in the series of studies on profile analysis (Mason et al., 1984; Green, 1983; Green et al., 1984, 1983). Green and his co-workers (personal communication, 1985) were concerned that profile complexes with a small number of components (e.g., three) might have a frequency-fluctuation cue associated with the increment to the center component. Figure 5, reproduced from Green et al. (1984), illustrates a curious result in profile analysis. Open symbols indicate the level of an increment to the center component of a three-component profile array that is just detectable in a two-interval forced-choice adaptive tracking task. For each three-component profile array,

81

the Fmax and Fmin values represent the frequencies of the "edge" components. Listener performance is slightly poorer at the narrowest bandwidth, but overall it is fairly constant as the three components are spread wider in frequency. The filled symbols in the figure represent

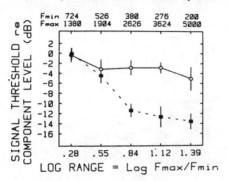

the just-detectable increment for those same listeners, in the same paradigm, when more components are added to the profile array. Starting at the narrowest band-width, there are three, five, seven, nine, and eleven components, respectively, in the profile com-plex. As components are added to the array, the just de-tectable increment becomes progressively smaller.

Figure 5. Profile analysis results reproduced from Green et al. (1984). Open symbols represent three-component arrays; filled symbols represent three, five, seven, nine and eleven components in equal logarithmic spacing over the corresponding frequency range. (Reprinted by permission.)

Using the just-detectable increment for each datum in Figure 5 and passing each equal-amplitude and incre-mented array pair through the EWAIF model produces some surprising results. If the just detectable increments were discriminable by pitch, one would expect the pre-dicted pitch differences to be similar. Table I shows the predicted differences in pitch between the equal-amplitude profile signals and their incremented coun-terparts. The predictions for the three component com-

Log Range	Predicted Difference	
	Three-component	Multi-component
.28	21.1	21.1
.55	82.7	29.5
.84	204.2	21.8
1.12	381.0	23.7
1.39	222.5	33.6

Table I. EWAIF predictions of pitch differences between equal-amplitude profile signals and their incremented counterparts (with threshold incre-ments).

82

plexes appear, at first, to be unusable. However, we have seen above that if the components of the signal are resolved, the frequency modulations can no longer be used for discrimination. The narrowest bandwidth signal may not be resolved but the components of the others surely would. In this case, we would not expect the EWAIF to predict listener's performance.

The EWAIF predictions for the multi-component complexes, however, show a remarkable similarity. The pitch differences are of the same order of magnitude ranging from about 20 Hz to just under 40 Hz. These differences are certainly larger than would be expected based on pure tone frequency DL studies; however, given the built-in uncertainties of the experimental paradigm, they seem reasonable. Since these results represent equal discrimination (detection) performance, it may be more reasonable to assume that the listeners are responding to pitch differences between equal-amplitude and incremented profile arrays rather than detecting an ever smaller "bump" on the line-spectrum representation of these complex sounds. Thus, the model can explain both the different performance between the three- and multi-component signal discrimination and the ability of the listeners to detect very small increments in the multi-component signals.

It should be noted that each entry in Table I is an average of three complementary pairs of signals. For each pair, the initial phase of every component in the flat spectrum signal is the same as its incremented counterpart. The model is phase sensitive in that a different phase randomization for a given signal may change the predicted pitch. To explore this aspect further we generated an additional set of five randomizations of phase for the five- and eleven-component profile signals. The results of these phase differences are summarized in Table II. Phase has very little effect on the five-component signals and would be expected to add only

	Eleven-component			Five-component		
	Flat	Increment	Diff.	Flat	Increment	Diff.
Mean	1593.5	1560.2	33.3	1114.6	1086.5	28.1
St. Dev.	57.4	55.9	10.9	3.3	3.2	2.5
Range	1484-1674	1452-1632	12-46	1110-1120	1083-1094	25-32

Table II. Means, standard deviations and ranges of EWAIF predictions for eight different phase randomizations.

83

some variability to the data. For the eleven-component signals, on the other hand, a different randomization of the initial phase may change the pitch of the flat spectrum signal by as much as 200 Hz. Adding the increment, however, produces a consistent pitch shift which is only slightly affected by phase. Green and Mason (1985) reported that changing relative phase did not affect the listener's performance. Examination of their data reveals a slight variability in increment threshold on the order of about 3 dB for different phase randomizations. A change of 3 dB when passed through the EWAIF model produces a change in predicted pitch of 10 - 15 Hz for a five-component complex and 5 - 7 Hz for an eleven-component signal. Thus phase effects would not be expected to change the overall performance but would seem to add some variability to the data.

CONCLUSIONS

The amplitude and frequency modulations inherent in many complex sounds may strongly influence the detection and discrimination of subtle manipulations of the signal parameters. Work with simple two-component complex sounds, the Voelcker signals, indicated the influence of small amplitude and frequency differences in the perceived pitch. From that work, we formulated a signal-processing model of listener performance that does a reasonably good job of predicting listener performance in frequency discrimination and pitch matching tasks for simple signals. The model also predicts the pitch-shifts associated with manipulation of the phase relationship between simultaneous amplitude and frequency modulators. Perhaps most surprising is the prediction of constant pitch differences between equal-amplitude and incremented multi-component complex tones used in the profile analysis experiments.

**We would like to thank Dave Green and his co-workers for their comments on a preliminary version of this manuscript.

REFERENCES

Feth, L. L. (1974) "Frequency discrimination of complex periodic tones," Percept. Psychophys., 15, 375-379.
Feth, L. L. and O'Malley, H. (1977) "Two-tone auditory spectral resolution," J. Acoust. Soc. Amer., 62, 940-497.

Feth, L. L., O'Malley, H. and Ramsey, J. (1982) "Pitch of unresolved, two-component complex tones," J. Acoust. Soc. Amer., 72, 1403-1412.

Green, D. M. (1983) "Profile analysis: A different view of auditory intensity discrimination," American Psychologist, 39, 133-142.

Green, D. M. (1965) "Masking with two tones," J. Acoust. Soc. Amer., 37, 803-813.

Green, D. M. and Mason, C. R. (1985) "Auditory profile analysis: Frequency, phase, and Weber's Law," J. Acoust. Soc. Amer., 77, 1155-1161.

Green, D. M., Mason, C. R. and Kidd, G. (1984) "Profile analysis: Critical bands and duration," J. Acoust. Soc. Amer., 75, 1163-1167.

Green, D. M. and Kidd, G. (1983) "Further studies of auditory profile analysis," J. Acoust. Soc. Amer., 73, 1260-1265.

Green, D. M.,Kidd, G. and Picardi, M. C. (1983) "Successive versus simultaneous comparison in auditory intensity discrimination," J. Acoust. Soc. Amer., 73, 639-643.

Harmuth, H. F. (1970) Transmission of Information by Orthogonal Functions, Springer-Verlag, Berlin.

Iwamiya, S., Nishikawa, S. and Kitamura, O. (1984) "Perceived principal pitch of FM-AM tones when the phase difference between frequency modulation and amplitude modulation is in-phase and anti-phase," J. Acoust. Soc. Jap., 5, 59-69.

Lauter, J. L. and Hirsh, I. J. (1985) "Speech as temporal pattern: A psychophysical profile," Speech Communication, 4, 41-54.

Mason, C. R., Kidd, G., Hanna, T. E. and Green, D. M. (1984) "Profile analysis and level variation," Hearing Research, 13, 169-175.

McGillem, C. D. (1979) Hilbert Thansforms and Analytic Signals, Unpublished notes on signal processing. Purdue Univeristy.

Riesz, R. R. (1928) "Differential intensity sensitivity of the ear for pure tones," Physics Review, 31, 867-875.

Scharf, B. (1970) "Critical Bands," in: Foundations of Modern Auditory Theory Vol. I, J. V. Tobias, ed., Academic Press, New York.

Shower, E. G. and Biddulph, G. R. (1931) "Differential pitch sensitivity of the ear," J. Acoust. Soc. Amer., 3, 275-287.

Tiffin, J. (1931) "Some aspects of the psychophysics of the vibrato," Psych, Rev. Monogr., 41, 153-200.

Voelcker, H. (1966a) "Toward a unified theory of
modulation - Part I: Phase-envelope relationships,"
Proc. IEEE, 54, 340-353.
Voelcker, H. (1966b) "Toward a unified theory of
modulation - Part II: Zero manipulation," Proc.IEEE,
54, 735,755.

The Perception of Repetitive Auditory Temporal Patterns

Donald A. Robin
Department of Speech Pathology and Audiology
The University of Iowa, Iowa City, IA 52242

Fred L. Royer
Case Western Reserve University, Cleveland, OH 44106

Paul J. Abbas
The University of Iowa, Iowa City, IA 52242

    The temporal patterning of sound provides the organism with
important information about objects and events in the world about
it. Temporal patterns emerge when listening to cyclic sets of
temporally dispersed soundbursts, but only when the rate of
presentation lies within a limited range. At extremely slow
rates, no pattern is heard; at some faster rate, pattern
organization of discrete events occurs; at still faster rates, the
perception of pattern in discrete events passes to perception of a
repeating unit; at still faster rates, the perception of
unitization passes to perception of texture or timbre. We review
temporal pattern perception, the phenomenon of unitization, and a
model suggested by the phenomenon. Finally, we discuss possible
neurophysiological processes underlying or contributing to
auditory temporal pattern perception.

INTRODUCTION
    A taxonomy of complex sounds would necessarily include the
class of amplitude modulated signals. We are especially
interested in a subclass of these signals that are characterized
by steady state conditions because listening to them evokes a
unique perceptual process. This process is one in which the
cyclic repetition of a series of discrete soundbursts distributed
in time evokes the perception of rhythmic organization.
Incredibly, a psychological organization emerges in which a
particular burst in some temporal relation to others gains a
salience that gives it temporal position such that the listener
can describe it as beginning a pattern. This is remarkable
because there is no event in a cyclic pattern that logically marks
a beginning or end. That is to say that a physicist examining the
signal on an oscilloscope could not discern anything about the
various bursts that are elements of the cyclic pattern. For
example, let X represent one tone and 0 represent another. The
cyclic sequence ...0XX0XX... can be organized logically in three
ways, XX0, X0X, and 0XX. However, the perception of X0X as an
organization would be highly unlikely. Royer and Garner (1966)
found that almost all listeners will report the sequence
...XXXXX000..., repeated endlessly, as beginning with the first of
the run of X's or the first of the run of 0's, which the listeners

perceive as stressed despite the absence of any physical difference in the stimulus.

That the listener can differentiate the elements of the pattern poses special questions for both perception and psychoacoustics. Can the psychological organization emerge only from some yet-to-be-defined "higher" level processes? Can the organization be a by-product of the levels of the nervous system? The review of temporal pattern perception that follows suggests that currently the best bet for understanding such percepts lies in a signal processing model.

AUDITORY PATTERN PERCEPTION

Royer and Garner (1966) presented listeners with all 256 different possible 8-element sequences of two sounds (binary patterns). Their results established that listeners perceived only a few of the logically possible organizations and that the number of organizations reported for a particular temporal sequence of two sounds was related to the difficulty of manually tracking the pattern and the delay before tracking began. They established that a run of sounds of the same type formed a unit and that perceived pattern organization began with runs. For example, the sequence ...XXXOOXOO.. might be organized as XXXOOXOO, OOXOOXXX, or OOXXXOOX, but not as XXOOXOOX or OXOOXXXO because these would entail a break in the run of elements of the same type in the cycle.

This work was followed by studies that attempted to define the principles governing the perceived organization of sequences. Royer and Garner (1970) showed that principles of temporal balance and temporal progression or run lengths governed perception of 9-element binary patterns. This study established that perception of auditory sequences could not be other than a wholistic or Gestalt one; the structure of all element of a sequence determined organization, not its serial statistics. The cognitive approach to sequential events as seen in the work of Restle (1970) was inadequate to account for the results. The evidence for wholistic principles was striking from the finding that if a pattern had a particular organization preferred by a large number of subjects and there existed another pattern for which a mirror-reversal organization of the first was possible, it was predictable that the reversal would be the preferred second pattern's organization.

Preusser et al (1970) observed that Royer-Garner binary patterns could be dissected into two interdigitated temporal patterns which were called "half-patterns" and we will call "unary" patterns because of their fundamental character. Two primary principles emerged, the run and gap. The run principle states that the first element of the longest run is perceived as the beginning of a pattern; while the gap principle states that the first element following the longest gap (silent interval) is the perceived beginning of a pattern. The organization of Royer-Garner patterns could be explained comprehensively by the interaction of the strength of run and gap principles within and between component unary patterns. When the principles applying to the component unary patterns are in conflict or are incompatible, pattern organization is difficult and labile. When they are compatible organization is easy and stable.

Later experiments explored the effects of various stimulus parameters and compared the results with temporal pattern perception in other modalities. Garner and Gottwald (1968) found that the ease of description measured by delay and accuracy was related to the rate of element presentation. They showed that the listening time for binary patterns was a U-shaped function of presentation rate with the minimum at 2.67 events/sec. Preusser (1972) found that pattern descriptions tended to be governed by the run principle at a slow presentation rate (1 Hz) and by the gap principle at the fastest rate (4 Hz); he also found that the slope of the function was steeper for verbal than for manual tapping modes of description.

Garner and Gottwald (1968) found a similar U-shaped function for visual patterns of two lights, but observation time was longer than for auditory sequences. Handel and Buffardi (1968, 1969) showed that pattern organization is essentially the same for auditory, tactile, and visual temporal patterns, but that ease of description as a function of rate depended on whether the patterns were in one modality, were switched between modalities alternately, or were interleaved between modalities so that one pattern element was auditory and the other was visual or tactile for example.

The principles of organization have been the same whether the binary sequences were generated with buzzers (Preusser et al, 1970; Royer & Garner, 1966), complex tones (Preusser, 1972; Royer & Garner, 1970), or pure tones (Handel, 1974). Effects of frequency of pattern elements are not clear; there was no effect in Royer and Garner (1966), a bias toward the higher tone in Royer and Garner (1970), an interaction with rate in Preusser (1972), and an interaction with run and gap structure in Handel (1974).

Handel (1973) began a series of experiments varying other stimulus dimensions. First pauses were placed between pattern elements at different locations in the sequence. Segmented patterns were identified well if increased interburst interval occurred at locations that Royer and Garner (1966, 1970) found were strong organization points (compatibly segmented); however, incompatibly segmented patterns could be identified only by learning them element by element. Handel (1974) then explored the effects of frequency, intensity, duration, interval, and the interaction of frequency with duration and interval. The description of a patterns as X's and O's above may represent two

89

different frequencies, different intensities, or different durations. Also, it may represent two intervals separating the same recurrent soundburst, so that XXOXOOXO would become X.X.X-X.X-X-X.X- where a dot (.) represents a short interval, a dash (-) a long interval, and X a sound of fixed duration, intensity and frequency. Frequency induced a preference for which of the two sounds was foreground or background depending on run and gap structure. Intensity induced a preference for the more intense element as figure and the gap principle dominated. A short duration element was preferred as the beginning element and run organization dominated. Interval introduced a very different perception (the cycle time is much longer and the pattern is basically unary); results were complex. The results of frequency and interval or duration interactions were also complex, leading Handel (1974) to the pessimistic conclusion that although the organization of different types of temporal patterns may be analyzed empirically, "it is possible that no complete set of principles can ever be found." We will show shortly that this pessimism is unwarranted.

Handel and Yoder (1975) examined intensity and interval effects in both auditory and visual patterns. These results, like those of Handel (1974), were complex and differences were found between auditory and visual pattern identification.

An interesting alternative interpretation of pattern organizing principles was provided by Sturges and Martin (1974), who applied Martin's (1972) general theory of hierarchical rhythmic structure to the Royer-Garner patterns. They showed that the "goodness" of a pattern and the ability of listeners to discriminate a change in the pattern was determined by the extent to which the pattern was hierarchically constructed. If implied accents fell on even subdivisions of the pattern (1st, 5th, 3rd, and/or 7th elements), the pattern was good and listeners made few errors; if implied accents fell elsewhere, the pattern was poor and listeners made more errors. Such patterns were described as metrical or ametrical (syncopated), respectively. As we have pointed out elsewhere (Royer & Robin, 1986) Martin's theory is incomplete because it can not account for differences in pattern perception arising from rate changes. However, hierarchical structure can be incorporated into a more powerful explanatory system.

UNITIZATION AND A FILTER MODEL OF TEMPORAL PATTERN PROCESSING

A simple apparatus that maintains a constant duty cycle for soundburst duration and interburst interval while presentation rate is being increased or decreased will yield rate effects that are purely perceptual and independent of problems of performance (encoding of perception into manual or verbal responses). At extremely slow rates, one hears only discrete, temporally unorganized sounds. At a sufficiently fast rate, one hears an organized temporal pattern. At a very fast rate, one hears a buzzy texture or a tone with some characteristic rough timbre. Importantly, just between these latter perceptions one hears a particular phenomenon; the perception of discrete organized bursts gives way to the perception of a repeating packet of bursts having the duration of the pattern cycle. Royer and Robin (1986) described this as "unitization."

What is the significance of this rate-dependent phenomenon or, for that matter, the significance of all of these rate-dependent perceptions? Royer and Robin (1986) noted that the cyclic stimuli fall in the class of amplitude modulated signals, with the temporal pattern being the modulator and the soundburst being the carrier. In the case of a pure tone carrier, the Fourier spectrum of the modulator is centered about the carrier frequency; under the steady state listening conditions, however, one does not hear an harmonically complex sound but a pure tone. At rates exceeding unitization, however, one does hear the harmonic complexity. During unitization and at rates below that, the auditory system seems to separate the signals by some demodulation process. What does it do with the extracted modulation signal, which is now in an "infra-low pitch" range and is perceptually pitchless? Royer and Robin (1986) hypothesized that the modulation signal is processed by a filter that has at least a low-pass component which, in the time domain, smooths the envelope of the signal. The existence of the phenomenon of unitization is strong evidence for such a filter mechanism. At rates yielding pattern organization, smoothing is partial, but at rates yielding unitization, smoothing produces a single envelope encompassing one full cycle of the pattern. At rates beyond this, output is flat; the system can no longer demodulate.

Royer and Robin (1986) had subjects listen to eight unary cyclic patterns with a period of eight events (below X is a soundburst of some duration followed by a silent interval 1, ' is a silent interval 2 equal in duration to burst duration plus interval 1); two patterns had three elements (X'X'X''', and X''X'X''), three patterns had four elements (XXX'X''', XXX''X'', and XX'X''X'), two patterns had five elements (XXX'X'XX' and XX'X'XX'), the remaining pattern had six elements (XXXX'XX'). At least one of the 3, 4, and 5 elements patterns is strongly organized in one way; the others are perceptually ambiguous, with respect to organization and having a lability that sometimes results in shifts like a Necker-cube illusion in vision. According to Martin (1972), stable and labile patterns would be metrical and ametrical, respectively.

In the experiment, subjects were tested in two procedures. In one the interburst interval was fixed at 10, 20, 30, 40, or 50 msec and the duration of the burst was adjusted by the method of limits to yield the unitization (the shortening of the duration decreases cycle time, hence increases rate and vice versa). In the other procedure, duration was fixed at the same levels and interval was adjusted.

Results depicting critical durations and intervals are shown in Figure 1. There is an obvious inverse linear relationship between duration and interval, demonstrating a highly reliable phenomenon. Note that critical duration and interval vary systematically with the number of elements in the pattern such that the total pattern cycle length at unitization is shorter for three element than four element, shorter for four element than five element, etc. These results are consistent with expectations of the time domain output of a smoothing filter.

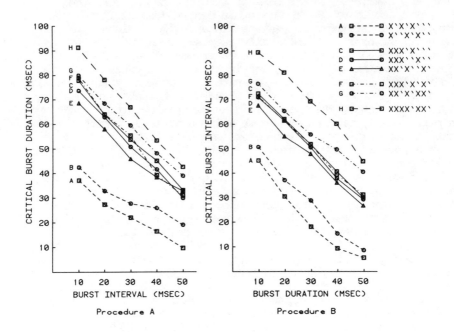

Figure 1.   Left panel, critical tone-burst duration as a function of interburst interval.   Right panel, critical interburst interval as a function of tone-burst duration for eight patterns.   Reprinted by permission of Psychonomics Society, Inc.

From this theoretical stance unitization is a consequence of filtering, hence is a consequence of the spectrum of the modulators.   Fourier analyses of the modulation waveforms, with durations and intervals being those at unitization, showed that the harmonics of different patterns having the greatest energy were aligned in a way consistent with filter inputs that would produce equivalent smoothing of outputs.

The Fourier analysis suggested there may be theoretical explanatory power in the more general model proposed by Royer and Robin (1986). They hypothesized a temporal frequency analytic system operating in parallel with the pitch analytic system and associated with the filter system. Their stable, unambiguously organized patterns had major amounts of energy in harmonics that are in an octave relationship to the fundamental, while their labile, ambiguously organized patterns had energy distributed in harmonics that are not in an octave relationship. The proposed temporal frequency system may function like the parallel pitch frequency system; thus octave relationships of temporal frequency will be perceptually like the octave relationships of pitch frequency. Rate chroma would parallel tone chroma. Such a system would account for the observations of Martin (1972); pattern organization would appear hierarchically biased because the presence of elements at "accent points" increases the power in octave relation harmonics.

The proposed model deals only with unary patterns. Its extension to binary patterns will entail problems closely related to those of stream segregation studied by Bregman (1978). Such patterns are multiplexed amplitude modulated signals and the separation of carrier signals in the demodulation process is a special matter. It is worth noting in passing that however the demodulation is accomplished, the filter model would predict that there should be evidence of the temporal reversal principle discovered by Royer and Garner (1970). If two patterns differ in that one is a temporal reversal of the other, they have identical power spectra, but phase spectra differing by 180 degrees. Also worth noting is that the pattern having the greatest delay in reproduction and the largest number of errors in Royer and Garner (1966) is unique in its structure. The pattern is XXOXOOXO. It is composed of two unary patterns that are simply time shifted versions of one another (XX'X''X' and ''O'OO'O). They have identical power spectra, but different phase spectra. Filtering of each unary pattern would yield identical output. Finally, we emphasize that the manipulations of stimulus dimensions by Handel (1973, 1974; Handel & Yoder, 1975) which yielded complex results will all produce markedly different magnitude and phase spectra. Thus, Handel's pessimism may have to yield to our optimistic view that temporal pattern perception obeys the expectancies of a signal processing model.

PHYSIOLOGICAL PROCESSES RELATED TO TEMPORAL PATTERN PERCEPTION
The history of acoustics shows that advances in auditory physiology and acoustics move in concert. Neural processes paralleling psychophysical observations should be expected with a model that assumes neural filtering. Royer (1979) observed evoked potentials from vertex leads in humans during listening to several unary and binary patterns. Positive potentials with median latencies between 50 and 70 msec and negative potentials with median latencies between 130 and 140, as well as the difference potential, were greatest for the first element of the longest run in pattern XXX'X'X and for the first element after the longest gap in pattern X'X'X'''. Potentials were nearly equal for the first elements in both runs of length two in pattern XX'XX'X' and for the elements after the gaps of equal length two in pattern ''X''X'X. No effects could be observed with binary patterns formed by interdigitating the appropriate patterns above.

Completely independently of the above, two of us (Robin and Abbas) undertook the measurement of evoked brain stem responses in the cat to the unambiguous, stable pattern XXX'X''' and the labile, ambiguous pattern XX'X'XX'. Preferred pattern beginnings are indicated by underlining. Much of the basis for complex pattern perception may be central. However, responses observed at the auditory periphery, both in single unit responses (Smith, 1977) and in far field potentials (Eggermont and Spoon, 1973), show properties of adaptation that may be relevant to perception. As a preliminary step for providing information on the relationship of complex auditory patterns to neurophysiological responses we performed an experiment measuring auditory evoked brainstem potentials in a cat. These data are preliminary and are meant to illustrate the approach we are taking. Our apriori hypothesis was that pattern organization based on run and gap principles could in part be explained by adaptation and recovery of the neuronal response at a relatively peripheral level of the nervous system.

Responses were collected at slow presentation rates comparable to rhythmic pattern organization and at fast presentation rates comparable to perceived unitization. Data were collected synchronized for onset of each element within the patterns. The amplitude of response was measured from the negative peak to the following positive. Averages for 1024 sweeps were collected for each pattern element.

The amplitude of the P3 and P4 wave of the brain stem evoked potential are shown in Figure 2. Figure 2a represents the unambiguous pattern. At slow rates, response amplitude was greatest at element 1 of the pattern. Response amplitude decreased over the next two elements of the pattern. Finally, one observes recovery of amplitude in element 4 of the pattern. At fast rates, a similar pattern was observed. Fast presentation

94

rates result in greater differences between amplitudes for each element.

Figure 2b represents the responses for the ambiguous pattern. At slow rates relative amplitude was greatest at elements 1, 3, and 4, those elements that define starting points. Similar results were observed for fast rates, except, again, amplitude differences in the fast condition were greater. Comparing these results with the unambiguous pattern in Figure 2a one sees less differentiation between amplitude peaks in the ambiguous pattern. Thus, pattern ambiguity may be related to the relative difference between peaks.

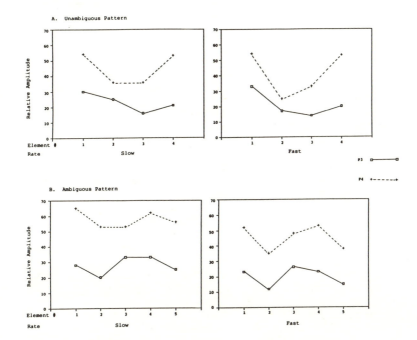

Figure 2. Relative amplitude of evoked potential responses, waves P3 and P4. A. Unambiguous pattern (XXX'X'''). B. Ambiguous pattern (XX'X'XX'). Left side of figure, slow presentation rate (X = tone duration of 70 msec followed by silent interval of 70 msec, ' = interval of 140 msec), right side, fast presentation rate (X = tone duration of 25 msec followed by an interval of 25 msec, ' = interval of 50 msec). In the figure, each X is represented by an element numbered successively from left to right.

SUMMARY

The perception of repetitive auditory patterns is related to the presentation rate. At fast rates, within a very limited range, unitization is heard. At rates above unitization within a larger range, organization is perceived. We interpret the findings on pattern unitization and organization as evidence for a temporal frequency analyzer in the auditory system that has a filter with a low-pass component. Evoked potential responses provide evidence that the organization of auditory patterns is related to the adaptation and recovery of the neuronal response at central and peripheral levels. It is likely that the periphery of the auditory nervous system sets the limits or constraints that the perceptual system must work within.

REFERENCES

Bregman, A.S. (1978). The formation of auditory streams. In J. Reguim (Ed.), Attenuation and Performance VII. Hillsdale, NJ: Erlbaum Associates.

Eggemont, J.J., & Spoon, A. (1973). Cochlear adaptation in guinea pigs. Audiology, 12, 193-220.

Garner, W.R., & Gottwald, R.L. (1968). The perception and learning of temporal patterns. Quarterly Journal of Experimental Psychology, 20, 97-109.

Handel, S. (1973). Temporal segmentation of repeating auditory patterns. Journal of Experimental Psychology, 101, 46-54.

Handel, S. (1974). Perceiving melodic and rhythmic auditory patterns. Journal of Experimental Psychology, 103, 922-933.

Handel, S., & Buffardi, L. (1968). Pattern perception: Integrating information presented in two modalities. Science, 162, 1026-1028.

Handel, S., & Buffardi, L. (1969). Using several modalities to perceive one temporal pattern. Quarterly Journal of Experimental Psychology, 21, 256-266.

Handel, S., & Yoder, D. (1975). The effects of intensity and interval rhythms on the perception of auditory and visual temporal patterns. Quarterly Journal of Experimental Psychology, 27, 111-122.

Martin, J.G. (1972). Rhythmic (hierarchical) versus serial structure in speech and other behavior. Psychological Review, 79, 487-509.

Preusser, D. (1972). The effect of structure and rate on the recognition and description of auditory temporal patterns. Perception & Psychophysics, 11, 233-240.

Preusser, D., Garner, W.R., & Gottwald, R.L. (1970). Perceptual organization of two-element temporal patterns as a function of their component one-element patterns. American Journal of Psychology, 83, 151-170.

Restle, F. (1970). Theory of serial pattern learning: Structural trees. Psychological Review, 77, 481-495.

Royer, F.L. (1979). Cortical coding of auditory temporal patterns. Bulletin of Psychonomics Society, 14, 242.

Royer, F.L., & Garner, W.R. (1966). Response uncertainty and perceptual difficulty of auditory temporal patterns. Perception & Psychophysics, 1, 41-47.

Royer, F.L., & Garner, W.R. (1970). Perceptual organization of nine-element auditory temporal patterns. Perception & Psychophysics, 7, 115-120.

Royer, F.L., & Robin, D.A. (1986). On the perceived unitization of repeating auditory sequences. Perception & Psychophysics, 39(1), 9-18.

Smith, R.L. (1977). Short-term adaptation in single auditory-nerve fibers: Some poststimulatory effects. Journal of Neurology, 40, 1098-1112.

Sturges, P.S., & Martin, J.G. (1974). Rhythmic structure in auditory temporal pattern perception and immediate memory. Journal of Experimental Psychology, 102, 377-383.

ADDITIONAL REFERENCES

Abbas, P.J. (1979). Effects of stimulus frequency on adaptation in auditory-nerve fibers. Journal of the Acoustical Society of America, 65, 162-165.

Abbas, P.J., & Gorga, M.P. (1981). AP responses in forward-masking paradigms and their relationship to responses of auditory-nerve fibers. Journal of the Acoustical Society of America, 69, 492-498.

Aitkin, L.M., & Dunlop, C.W. (1968). Interplay of excitation and inhibition in the cat medial geniculate body. Journal of Neurophysiology, 31, 44.

Beauvillain, C. (1983). Auditory perception of dissonant polyrhythms. Perception & Psychophysics, 34, 585-592.

Bregman, A.S. (1978). Auditory streaming: Competition among alternative organizations. Perception & Psychophysics, 23, 391-398.

Bregman, A.S. (1978). Auditory streaming is cumulative. Journal of Experimental Psychology: Human Perception and Performance, 4, 380-387.

Bregman, A.S. (1981). Asking the "What for" question in auditory perception. In M. Kubovy & J.R. Pomerantz (Eds.), Perceptual Organization. Hillsdale, NJ: Earlbaum Associates.

Bregman, A.S., Abramson, J., Doehring, P., & Darwin, C. (1985). Spectral integration based on common amplitude modulation. Perception & Psychophysics, 37, 483-493.

Bregman, A.S., & Campbell, J. (1971). Primary auditory stream segregation and perception of order in rapid sequences of tones. Journal of Experimental Psychology, 89, 244-249.

Bregman, A.S., & Dannebring, G. (1976). Effect of silence between tones on auditory stream segregation. Journal of the Acoustical Society of America, 59, 987-989.

Bregman, A.S., & Dannebring, G.L. (1977). Auditory continuity and amplitude edges. Canadian Journal of Psychology, 31, 151-159.

Bregman, A.S., & Pinker, S. (1978). Auditory streaming and the building of timbre. Canadian Journal of Psychology, 32, 19-31.

Broadbent, D.E., & Ladefoged, P. (1957). On the fusion of sounds reaching different sense organs. Journal of the Acoustical Society of America, 29, 708-710.

Broadbent, D.E., & Ladefoged, P. (1959). Auditory perception of temporal order. Journal of the Acoustical Society of America, 31, 1539.

Chiang, C. (1976). A theory of ambiguous pattern perception. Bulletin of Mathematical Biology, 38, 497-504.

Cooper, L.A., & Shepard, R.N. (1984). Turning something over in the mind. Scientific American, 251, 106.

Creelman, C.D. (1967). Human discrimination of auditory duration. Journal of the Acoustical Society of America, 34, 582-593.

Dannebring, G.L., & Bregman, A.S. (1976). Effect of silence between tones on auditory stream segregation. Journal of the Acoustical Society of America, 59, 987-989.

Dannebring, G.L., & Bregman, A.S. (1976). Stream segregation and the illusion of overlap. Journal of Experimental Psychology: Human Perception and Performance, 2, 544-555.

Dannebring, G.L., & Bregman, A.S. (1978). Streaming vs. fusion of sinusoidal components of complex tones. Perception & Psychophysics, 24, 369-376.

Darwin, C.J. (1981). Perceptual grouping of speech components differing in fundamental frequency and onset-time. Quarterly Journal of Experimental Psychology, 33A, 185-207.

David, E., Keidel, W.D., Kallert, S., Bechtereva, N.P., & Bundzen, P.V. (1977). Decoding processes in the auditory system and human speech analysis. In E.F. Evans and J.P. Wilson, (Eds.), Psychophysics and physiology of hearing. London: Academic Press.

Delgutte, B. (1980). Representation of speechlike sounds in the discharge patterns of auditory-nerve fibers. Journal of Acoustical Society of America, 68, 843.

Deutsch, D. (1975). Musical illusions. Scientific American, 233, 92-104.

Deutsch, D. (1980). The processing of structured and unstructured tonal sequences. Perception & Psychophysics, 28, 381-389.

Deutsch, D. (1981). The octave illusion and auditory perceptual integration. Hearing Research and Theory, 1, 99-142.

de Ribaupierre, F., Goldstein, M.H., & Yeni-Komshian, G. (1972). Cortical coding of repetitive acoustic pulses. Brain Research, 48, 205.

Divenyi, P.L., & Danner, W.F. (1977). Discrimination of time intervals marked by brief acoustic pulses of various intensities and spectra. Perception & Psychophysics, 21, 125-142.

Divenyi, P.L., & Hirsh, I.J. (1978). Some figural properties of auditory patterns. Journal of the Acoustical Society of America, 64, 1369-1385.

Divenyi, P.L., & Sachs, R.M. (1978). Discrimination of time intervals bounded by tone bursts. Perception & Psychophysics, 24, 429-436.

Elliott, L.L. (1971). Backward and forward masking. Audiology, 10, 65-76.

Essens, P.J., & Povel, D.J. (1985). Metrical and nonmetrical representations of temporal patterns. Perception & Psychophysics, 37, 1-7.

Evans, E.F. (1974). Neural processes for the detection of acoustic patterns and from sound localization. In F.O. Schmitt (Ed.), Neurosciences: A third study program. Boston: MIT Press.

Evans, E.V. (1968). Cortical representation. In A.V.S. de Resick and J. Knight (Eds.), Hearing mechanisms in vertebrates. London: J & A Churchill.

Fitzgibbons, P.J. (1984). Tracking a temporal gap in band-limited noise: Frequency and level effects. Perception & Psychophysics, 35, 446-450.

Fitzgibbons, P.J., Pollatsek, A., & Thomas, I.B. (1974). Detection of temporal gaps within and between perceptual tonal groups. Perception and Psychophysics, 16, 522-528.

Fraisse, P. (1982). Rhythm and tempo. In D. Deutch (Ed.), The Psychology of Music. NY: Academic Press.

Frisshkopf, L.S., Capranica, R.R., & Goldstein, M.H.Jr. (1968). Neural coding in the bullfrog's auditory system - A teleological approach. Proceedings of the IEEE, 56(6), 969-980.

Fruhstrofer, H. (1971). Habituation and dishabituation of the human vertex response. Electroencephalography and Clinical Neurophysiology, 30, 306-312.

Garner, W.R. (1974). The processing of information and structure. Hillsdale, NJ: Erlbaum Associates.

Glass, I., & Wollberg, Z. (1983). Responses of cells in the auditory cortex of awake squirrel monkeys to normal and reversed species-specific vocalizations. Hearing Research, 9, 27.

Goldstein, R., Rodman, L.B., & Karlovich, R.S. (1972). Effects of stimulus rate and number on the early components of the averaged electroencephalic response. Journal of Speech and Hearing Research, 15, 559-566.

Gorga, M.P., McGee, J., Walsh, E.J., Jarvel, E., & Farley, G.R. (1983). ABR measurements in the cat using a forward-masking paradigm. Journal of the Acoustical Society of America, 73, 256-261.

Halpern, A.R., & Darwin, C.J. (1982). Duration discrimination in a series of rhythmic events. Perception & Psychophysics, 31, 86-89.

Handel, S., & Lewis, W.E. (1970). Effect of practice on the perception of temporal patterns. Quarterly Journal of Experimental Psychology, 22, 97-108.

Handel, S., & Oshinsky, J.S. (1981). The meter of syncopated auditory polyrhythms. Perception & Psychophysics, 30, 1-9.

Handel, S., Weaver, M.S., & Lawson, G. (1983). Effects of rhythmic grouping on stream segregation. Journal of Experimental Psychology: Human Perception and Performance, 9, 637-651.

Harris, D.M., & Dallos, P. (1979). Forward masking of auditory nerve fiber responses. Journal of Neurophysiology, 42, 1083.

Hawkins, J.E., & Kniazuk, M. (1950). The recovery of auditory nerve action potentials after masking. Science, 11, 567-568.

Heise, G.A., & Miller, G.A. (1951). An experimental study of auditory patterns. American Journal of Psychology, 64, 68-77.

Hibi, S. (1982). A study of rhythm perception in repetitive sounds sequence. Annual Bulletin of RILP, 16, 103-124.

Jones, M.R. (1976). Time, our lost dimension: Toward a new theory of perception, attention, and memory. Psychological Review, 82, 323-355.

Jones, M.R. (1978). Auditory patterns: Studies in the perception of structure. In E.L. Carterette & M.P. Friedman (Eds.), Handbook of perception: Vol. VIII, perceptual coding. NY: Academic Press.

Jones, M.R. (1981). A tutorial on some issues and methods in serial patterns research. Perception & Psychophysics, 30, 492-504.

Keidel, W.D. (1974). Information processing in the higher parts of the auditory pathway. In E. Zwicker and E. Terhardt, (Eds.), Facts and models in hearing. New York: Springer-Verlag.

Kubovy, M. (1981). Concurrent-pitch segregation and the theory of indispensable attributes. In M. Kubovy & J.R. Pomerantz, Perceptual Organization. Hillsdale, NJ: Earlbaum Associates.

Ladefoged, P., & Broadbent, D.E. (1960). Perception of sequence in auditory events. Quarterly Journal of Experimental Psychology, 12, 162-170.

Leek, M.R., & Watson, C.S. (1984). Learning to detect auditory pattern components. Journal of the Acoustical Society of America, 76, 1037-1044.

McAdams, S. (1982). Spectral fusion and the creation of auditory images. In M. Clynes (Ed.), Music, mind, and brain: The neuropsychology of music. New York: Plenum Press.

McNally, K.A., & Handel, S. (1977). Effect of element composition on streaming and the ordering of repeating sequences. Journal of Experimental Psychology: Human Perception & Performance, 3, 451-460.

Miller, G.A., & Heise, G.A. (1950). The trill threshold. Journal of the Acoustical Society of America, 22, 637-638.

Moller, A.R. (1976). Dynamic properties of the responses of single neurons in the cochlear nucleus. Journal of Physiology, 259, 63.

Nakajima, Y., Shimojo, S., & Sugita, Y. (1980). On the perception of two successive sound bursts. Psychological Research, 41, 335-344.

Natale, M. (1977). Perception of nonlinguistic auditory rhythms by the speech hemisphere. Brain and Language, 4, 32-44.

Neff, D.L., Jesteadt, W., & Brown, E.L. (1982). The relation between gap discrimination and auditory stream segregation. Perception & Psychophysics, 31, 493-501.

Newman, J.D., & Wollberg, Z. (1973). Multiple coding of species-specific vocalizations in the auditory cortex of squirrel monkeys. Brain Research, 54, 287.

Oshinsky, J.S., & Handel, S. (1978). Syncopated auditory polyrhythms: Discontinuous reversals in meter interpretation. Journal of the Acoustical Society of America, 63(3), 936-939.

Parsons, T.W. (1976). Separation of speech from interfering speech by means of harmonic selection. Journal of the Acoustical Society of America, 60, 911-918.

Picton, T.W., Hillgard, S.A., & Galambos, R. (1976). Habituation and attention in the auditory system. In W.D. Kendal and W.D. Neff (Eds.), Handbook of sensory physiology, Vol. V, Auditory systems, Part 3. Heidelberg: Springer-Verlag.

Povel, D.J. (1981). Internal representation of simple temporal patterns. Journal of Experimental Psychology: Human Perception and Performance, 7, 3-18.

Robin, D.A. (1984). Auditory temporal processing: Two-tone flutter-fusion and a negative exponential decay model. Unpublished dissertation. Cleveland: Case Western Reserve University.

Robin, D.A., Royer, F.L., & Gruhn, J.J. (1985). Age related changes in auditory temporal processing. Journal of the Acoustical Society of America, 77, Suppl. 1, S37.

Rosenblith, W.A. (1950). Auditory masking and fatigue. Journal of the Acoustical Society of America, 22, 792-800.

Rousseau, R., Poirier, J., & Lenyre, L. (1983). Duration discrimination of empty time intervals by intermodal pulses. Perception & Psychophysics, 34, 541-548.

Smith, J., Jausfeld, S., Power, R.P., & Gorta, A. (1982). Ambiguous musical figures and auditory streaming. Perception & Psychophysics, 32, 454-464.

Sorkin, R.D., Boggs, G.J., & Brady, S.L. (1982). Discrimination of temporal jitter in patterned sequences of tones. Journal of Experimental Psychology: Human Perception and Performance, 8, 46-57.

Sovijarvi, A.R.A. (1975). Detection of natural complex sounds in the primary auditory cortex of the cat. Acta Physiologica Scandinavia, 93, 318-335.

Steiger, H., & Bregman, A.S. (1982). Competition among auditory streaming, dichotic fusion, and diotic fusion. Perception and Psychophysics, 32, 153-162.

ten Hoopen, G., van Meurs, G., & Akerboom, S. (1982). The perceived tempi of coherent and streaming tone sequences. Perception & Psychophysics, 31, 256-260.

Thurlow, W.R., & Elfuer, L.F. (1959). Continuity effects with alternately sounding tones. Journal of the Acoustical Society of America, 31, 1337-1339.

Townsend, R.E., House, J.F., & Johnson, L.L. (1976). Auditory evoked potential in stage 2 and REM sleep during a 30-day exposure to tone pulses. Psychophysiology, 13, 54-57.

Viemeister, N.F. (1979). Temporal modulation transfer functions based upon modulation thresholds. Journal of the Acoustical Society of America, 66, 1364-1380.

Vos, J. (1984). Spectral effects in the perception of pure and temporal intervals: Discrimination and beats. Perception and Psychophysics, 35, 173-185.

Warren, R.M. (1984). Perceptual restoration of obliterated sounds. Psychological Bulletin, 96, 371-383.

Warren, R.M., Obusek, C.J., Farmer, R.M., & Warren, R.P. (1969). Auditory sequences: Confusions of patterns other than speech or music. Science, 164, 586-587.

Watson, C.S. (1980). Time course of auditory perceptual learning. Annuals of Otology, Rhinology and Laryngology, Suppl. 74, 96-102.

Watson, C.S., & Foyle, D.C. (1985). Central factors in the discrimination and identification of complex sounds. Journal of the Acoustical Society of America, 78, 375-380.

Whitfield, I.C., & Evans, E.F. (1965). Responses of auditory cortical neurons to stimuli of changing frequency. Journal of Neurophysiology, 28, 655.

Computational Models of Tonal Sequence Discrimination

Robert D. Sorkin
Department of Psychological Sciences
Purdue University, W. Lafayette, IN 47907

Human subjects were asked to compare the frequency patterns defined by two sequences of tones. When each tonal sequence had a unique timing pattern, variability in the tone onset times or tone durations had a deleterious effect on discrimination performance. Two sequence comparison algorithms were evaluated on the same stimulus sequences heard by the human subjects. The overall pattern of performance for the two computational algorithms was similar to that of the human subjects. However, the subject responses did not correlate highly with the algorithm measures over experimental trials. This study demonstrates that sequence comparison algorithms may be useful in modelling how humans process sequential stimuli.

INTRODUCTION

A "simple" sound, such as a brief pure tone, can be made into a "complex" sound by concatenating the "simple" sounds into sequences. Our goal is to understand how such tonal sequences are processed by the human auditory system. Previously, our laboratory (Sorkin, 1984) reported qualitative support for a discrimination model developed by Durlach and Braida (1969) applied to the sequence discrimination task. In the present paper, we summarize some results of an alternative approach to modelling sequence discrimination. First, we apply two sequence comparison algorithms to the pattern discrimination task. We then examine the differences between the performance of the algorithms and the human subjects, and suggest some ways in which models of human pattern discrimination might be developed.

When a subject must judge the similarity of the frequency patterns defined by each of two sequences of tones, variation in the timing of the tones can have a deleterious effect on performance. This effect is most evident when each of the tonal sequences has a unique timing pattern. Under such conditions, it may be difficult for the subject to tell whether or not the frequency patterns are the same or different. A major aim of this investigation is to specify how performance depends on the magnitude of this temporal variation.

Watson and his colleagues have reported that varying the parameters of a tonal sequence can have a large effect on a listener's performance in a discrimination or detection task (e.g. Watson, Kelly & Wroton, 1976; Watson & Kelly, 1981; Spiegel, & Watson, 1981; and Leek & Watson, 1984). We have reported similar effects in an experiment on the discrimination of temporal jitter in tonal sequences (Sorkin, Boggs & Brady, 1982). In that study, subjects were to report which of two tonal sequences had temporal jitter added to the time gap between each tone. The tones were chosen from a set of two frequencies. We were interested in specifying how performance depended on the binary pattern of tone frequency. When the frequency pattern was regular, a satisfactory fit of the data to an independent filter-band model was obtained. However, when the frequency pattern for each pair of sequences was randomly varied, performance was much poorer than it was in the regular pattern conditions. No quantitative model of performance in the random conditions was proposed.

The deleterious effects of varying the frequency pattern are analogous to those found in experiments in which the subject must discriminate the frequency pattern, while the temporal pattern is varied (Sorkin, 1984). In these experiments subjects are presented with a pair of tonal sequences and must determine whether the frequency pattern in the two sequences is the same or different. Subjects are supposed to ignore variations in the temporal structure of the sequences, such as jitter in the tone onsets, durations, or inter-tone gaps.

When the temporal variations in the sequences are uncorrelated within a trial, e.g. when each sequence has a unique timing pattern, performance decreases as the magnitude of the jitter variance is increased. When the temporal variation is across trials, rather than within trials, there is no drop in performance with increases in jitter magnitude. We would like to specify the sequence comparison process employed by the

observer in this task. Toward that goal, we consider
two sequence comparison algorithms as preliminary
models of performance in the task. An important aspect
of this approach is that assumptions about observer
processing strategy are not required; a fixed
comparison mechanism is postulated and then tested in
all the experimental conditions.

METHODS

Some examples of the tonal sequences present on
experiment trials in our experiment are illustrated in
Figure 1. Three types of temporal matching conditions
were studied. In condition, C, the correlated
condition, the pattern of tone onsets, durations, and
inter-tone gaps is identical in the two sequences.

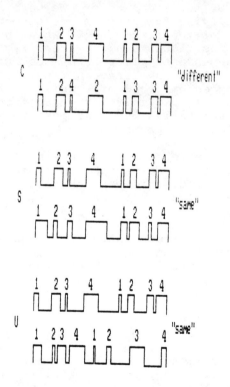

Figure 1. Examples of the pairs of sequences present on
the three types of expermental trials (see text).

106

Note that for this particular pair of sequences the frequency pattern is different in the two sequences, so that the correct response is "different" on this trial. The second pair of sequences illustrates condition S, the synchronized case. In this condition the tone onsets are identical in the two sequences, but the durations and gaps vary. In this particular pair of sequences the frequency pattern is identical, so the correct response is "same". The last pair of sequences illustrates condition U, the uncorrelated condition. Here the tone onsets, durations, and gaps are uncorrelated between the two sequences. The frequency pattern is identical on the trial shown, hence the correct response is "same". The tones in each of these cases were drawn from a set of eight tones at frequencies of 500, 909, 1667, and 2857 Hz. On "same" trials, the identical frequency pattern was present in both sequences; on "different trials" a subset of the tones was randomly changed in frequency.

Subjects were three undergraduate students paid an hourly rate plus a fractional incentive bonus for correct responses. All had normal hearing and extensive experience with psychoacoustic tasks. Subjects were seated in a double-walled Industrial Acoustics chamber. Stimuli were presented to the subject's right ear over TDH-39 headphones. All timing, signal synthesis, and data recording were controlled by an IBM-PC computer. Stimuli were generated via a Data Translation DT2801-A 12 bit digital-to-analog converter, sampling at 20 KHz. The converter output was low pass filtered at 5 KHz. All tone bursts were sinusoidal segments with 2 ms. linear onset and offset envelopes. The time interval between sequences was 500 ms. On each trial, subjects answered via a set of four pushbuttons corresponding to the responses: "I'm sure the sequences were different", "I think the sequences were different", "I think the sequences were the same", and "I'm sure the sequences were the same". Feedback about the correct response on each trial was provided.

The tonal sequences were composed of eight tones; each tone was selected from a set of four frequencies: 500, 909, 1667, and 2857 Hz. Tones were presented at sound pressure levels of 71 dB(A). The frequency pattern of the first sequence of each trial was randomly determined but subject to the constraint that

107

each frequency appeared twice. The frequency pattern in the second sequence was either the same as the first (a "same" trial), or was different than the first (a "different" trial). On "different" trials, three of the tone positions of the sequence were randomly selected to be changed. The first and last tone position were excluded from this selection. The selected positions were than randomly changed from their original frequency to one of the three remaining frequencies.

Manipulation of the temporal characteristics of the two sequences was accomplished in the following manner: The gap durations were randomly selected from a set of possible gaps to approximate a Gaussian distribution (bounded by a gap of 0 ms. and 2.5 times the gap standard deviation). The mean of the gap distribution was 50 ms. The standard deviation of the gap distribution was either 5, 10, 20, 30, or 40 ms. The duration of the tones was controlled by a different procedure. The tone durations were randomly selected from a distribution of five durations (20, 30, 40, 50, and 60 ms) having a mean duration of 40 ms and a standard deviation of 12.25 ms.

Subjects were trained on each of the three types of temporal matching conditions until consistent performance was obtained. Daily testing sessions were 1-1/2 to 2 hours in duration and consisted of from 5 to 7 blocks of 100 trials. The experimental conditions were constant within each block; only one temporal matching condition (C, S, or U) was run in a given session. The gap standard deviation was randomly changed from block to block within each session.

SEQUENCE COMPARISON ALGORITHMS

Consider the general problem of sequence comparison: A sequence, a, is a series of elements, $a_1, a_2, ..., a_n$ where the elements a_i are drawn from some defined alphabet. One wishes to compute a measure of the difference or similarity between sequence a and b. Traditional methods for comparing sequences include Euclidean distance metrics, the Hamming distance measure, and others.

These traditional measures sum the results of all comparisons between element pairs, a_i and b_i. In the case of tone burst sequences, this measure would be a function of the frequency difference between the tones. For the Euclidean distance measure the difference, d^{ab}, between sequence a and b is given by:

$$d^{ab} = [\sum_{i=1}^{n} (a_i - b_i)^2]^{1/2}$$

For the Hamming distance measure,

$$d^{ab} = \sum_{i=1}^{n} d_i \quad \text{where } d_i = 0 \text{ if } a_i = b_i$$
$$d_i = 1 \text{ if } a_i \neq b_i$$

Both these measures sum the results of comparisons made on corresponding elements in each sequence. When the sequences are composed of different numbers of elements, or when there is no correspondence between the elements of each sequence, more sophisticated measures are needed. The requirement for comparing sequences in which there are non-corresponding elements is a problem common to many sequence comparison situations. For example, a deleted or added element may upset the normal correspondence between a_i and b_i at position i in the sequence. Distortions in the time periods between the sequence elements or in the duration of the elements also may occur. These are the sort of sequence transformations to be expected in natural stimuli such as speech. We would expect that the human pattern processing mechanism would be able to handle these types of distortions and transformations without undue difficulty. Many applications of sequence comparison algorithms (including speech) are described in a recent book edited by Sankoff and Kruskal (1983).

An example of a more complex distance measure is one derived from the weighted average of comparisons made between all pairs of elements, a_i, b_j, in each sequence. Element pairs that are offset by a large difference in their respective position receive a smaller weight in the comparison measure. The weighted average measure which we employed is based on one used by Bradley and Bradley (1983) in a study of sequence comparison techniques applied to the study of bird songs. Bradley and Bradley compared two different types of sequence comparison algorithms: a weighted average algorithm and an optimal matching algorithm. We used modified versions of those algorithms as candidate comparator mechanisms for our tonal sequence task with human subjects.

The weighted average algorithm employed by Bradley and Bradley uses the average of all inter-element distances for all pairs, i,j, of elements from the two sequences. Measures on the distance between each pair of elements are weighted by the function, W_{ij}, which is a linear function of the distance between positions i and j. Their algorithm is defined as follows:

$$M^{ab} = max\ [\ (\sum_{i=1}^{m} \sum_{j=1}^{n} W_{ij}^{mn} D_{ij}^{ab}\ ) -$$

$$- \frac{1}{2}\ \{\ (\sum_{i=1}^{m} \sum_{j=1}^{n} W_{ij}^{mm} D_{ij}^{aa}\ ) + (\sum_{i=1}^{m} \sum_{j=1}^{n} W_{ij}^{nn} D_{ij}^{bb}\ )\ \}, \emptyset\ ]$$

where:

M^{ab} is the distance from a to b

D_{ij}^{ab} is the distance function on element i,j

m,n are the number of elements in a and b

W_{ij}^{mn} is the weighting for element pair at position i,j

and

$$W_{ij}^{mn} = k(1 - |\frac{i-1}{m-1} - \frac{j-1}{n-1}|)$$

with k chosen so $\sum_{i=1}^{m} \sum_{j=1}^{n} W_{ij}^{mn} = 1.$

The weighted average algorithm we employed was the same as the Bradley and Bradley procedure except that we allowed the computation of negative distances between sequences, and we employed a modified weighting

110

function. If the span between element position i and j
exceeded a constant (about 20% of the sequence
duration), the weight was set equal to zero. If the
span was less than or equal to that constant, a unit
weight was applied. The distance between elements,
D_{ij}, was defined as a function of the tone frequency.
The lowest tone frequency was assigned the value 1, the
next 2, etc. D_{ij} was then defined as two times the
absolute difference between those values. If either,
but not both, of the elements was a silent period, D_{ij}
was set equal to unity.

The second algorithm employed by Bradley and
Bradley was an optimal matching procedure based on the
concept of the Levenshtein distance metric (Kruskal,
1983). These metrics allow comparisons of sequences
which have suffered insertion/deletion or time
compression/expansion transformations. These metrics
evaluate the summed total cost of the basic operations
needed to transform one sequence into another. For
example, the substitution of very dissimilar tones
would add more cost than would the substitution of
similar tones. The minimum possible cost for the
entire set of operations then defines the distance
between the sequences. Following Bradley and Bradley
(1983), the algorithm for the specific optimal matching
metric we used is recursively defined as follows:

$$S^{ab} = S^{ab}_{mn} / \max(m,n)$$

where

$$S^{ab}_{ij} = \min \left[S^{ab}_{i-1,j-1} + D^{ab}_{ij} , \quad S^{ab}_{i-1,j} + C^{a}_{i} , \quad S^{ab}_{i,j-1} + C^{b}_{j} \right]$$

$$S^{ab}_{00} = 0, \quad S^{ab}_{i0} = \sum_{k=1}^{i} C^{a}_{k} , \quad S^{ab}_{0j} = \sum_{k=1}^{j} C^{b}_{k}$$

$$S^{ab} \quad \text{is the distance from } a \text{ to } b$$

$$D^{ab}_{ij} \quad \text{is the element substitution cost}$$

111

$$C_k^a \quad \text{is the insertion and deletion cost for}$$
element k of sequence **a**

and m,n are the lengths of sequence a and b.

A constant value of 1.9 was used for the insertion/deletion cost of a silent element, and a constant value of 3.6 was used for the cost of inserting or deleting any tone element. The cost of substituting an element of tone frequency i for an element of tone frequency j was set equal to 2.3 times the absolute difference between the tone numbers (lowest frequency equals tone number 1, next frequency equals 2, etc., as described for the weighted average algorithm). (A Pascal routine is available from the author which implements the optimal matching procedure using a dynamic-programming technique, rather than explicit recursion.)

Each algorithm was tested on transformed versions of the stimulus sequences used in the human experiments. The computer representation of each stimulus sequence was sliced into a sequence of segments 10 ms in duration. These segments then became the elements of the sequences subjected to the comparison algorithms. Both of the algorithms incorporate parameters which will affect the resulting discrimination performance. No attempt was made to evaluate a large volume of the parameter performance space. Values of the parameters were tried until a reasonable range of performance was obtained for the stimulus sequences employed in the experiment. The goal was to determine whether some of the general features of the observed human behavior would be matched by the algorithm, rather than to compute a fit of the algorithm to the human data.

RESULTS AND DISCUSSION

The effects of gap variability on the discriminability of the stimulus sequences in the conditions run are illustrated in Figure 2. The plotted points are data averaged from the three human subjects. Data from individual subjects was similar to that of the average data. These points are based on at least 200 trials per subject; standard errors for data from individual subjects were less than 0.2 d' units.

Performance in the Correlated condition is essentially independent of the gap variability. Performance in the Synchronized condition improves slightly at high gap variabilities. Performance in the Uncorrelated condition drops quickly and then levels off. (The rise in d' for the 40 ms uncorrelated condition is the consequence of data from one observer.) These results are consistent with data we have obtained in similar tasks involving longer and shorter sequences, binary sequence patterns, and different rules describing the frequency-difference manipulation.

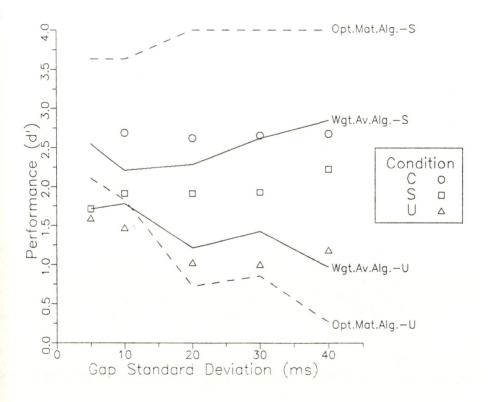

Figure 2. Average performance as a function of the gap standard deviation and condition (C,S,U) for the human subjects (plotted symbols) and for the two comparison algorithms (solid and dashed lines).

The performance of the two algorithms tested is
shown as the solid and dashed lines in Figure 2; the
weighted average algorithm is the solid line and the
optimal matching algorithm is the dashed line. The
standard deviation of the algorithm's responses was
different on same and different trials, preventing use
of a direct d' measure. The performance of the
algorithms was evaluated by determining the area under
the Receiver Operating Characteristic (ROC) curves
(based on the algorithm's trial by trial responses) and
then converting to equivalent yes/no d' values. The
performance of both algorithms was perfect in the
correlated condition, and is not shown. In the
uncorrelated condition, the performance of both
algorithms decreased as a function of gap variability.

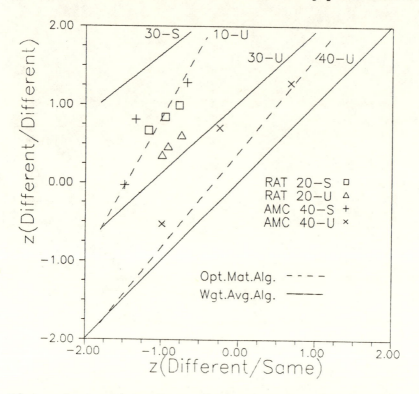

Figure 3. Receiver Operating Characteristic (ROC)
    curves for human observers RAT and AMC (plotted
    points) and best linear fits to the algorithms
    (solid and dashed lines).

114

Figure 3 shows representative ROC curves (plotted on normal probability axes) obtained for both algorithms and for two of the subjects. The slope of the normal probability ROC functions depended somewhat on the algorithm employed; slopes generally were less than 1.0 for the weighted average algorithm and exceeded 1.0 for the warp algorithm. Slopes for the human ROC curves were consistently near 1.0.

The correlation between human and algorithm performance was computed on the trial by trial responses of the human subjects (ratings) and the algorithms (computed responses). Because the magnitude of such correlations depends on the level of performance, the most revealing correlations are on the conditions having the poorest performance. At the uncorrelated 30 ms or 40 ms conditions, the correlations obtained between individual subjects and either of the algorithms was generally less than 0.4. Neither algorithm correlated consistently higher than the other. Correlations between the algorithms or between pairs of subjects also were generally less than 0.4. Apparently, the subjects and the algorithms (for the particular parameter values chosen) order the similarity of sequence pairs in idiosyncratic ways.

Both of the algorithms tested produced performance which was similar to the profile of human performance over the different experimental conditions studied. However, note that these comparison algorithms are not models of human tone pattern discrimination. To construct such a model, we would need to postulate internal noise in order to obtain less than perfect model performance in the correlated condition. A reasonable assumption would be that this internal noise would take the form of uncorrelated temporal jitter added to the tone onsets. To estimate the magnitude of this internal jitter, we could observe the performance of the algorithm in low levels of uncorrelated jitter. When the performance of the algorithm in the uncorrelated jitter matched that of the human in the correlated jitter, an estimate of the internal jitter could be obtained.

This application of sequence comparison procedures was not intended to serve as a test of whether these specific algorithms will be good models of tonal sequence discrimination. Rather, our analysis

115

demonstrates that such algorithms may be a useful starting point in modelling how humans process serially defined stimuli. A number of other computational procedures and variations of these algorithms could have been tested. For example, optimal matching procedures can incorporate the costs of changes in the durations of the tones or in the gaps between the tones. Algorithms of this type have been developed for the machine processing of speech. Such algorithms could be evaluated in tone pattern discrimination or in other tasks involving stimulus sequences. Other investigators have reported the effects of specific types of sequence context manipulations on the salience and discriminability of subsequences (see Leek, 1987, this volume). It would be interesting to see whether the performance of specific comparison algorithms would resemble the human observer's sensitivity (or lack of sensitivity) to such contextual manipulations.

ACKNOWLEDGMENT

Research sponsored by the Air Force Office of Scientific Research, Air Force Systems Command, USAF, under grant or cooperative agreement number, AFOSR-84-0302. The US government is authorized to reproduce and distribute reprints for Governmental purposes notwithstanding any copyright notation thereon.

REFERENCES

Bradley, D. W., and Bradley, R. A. (1983). Application of Sequence Comparison to the Study of Bird Songs, in: Time Warps, String Edits, and Macromolecules: The Theory and Practice of Sequence Comparison, D. Sankoff and J. B. Kruskal, eds., Addison-Wesley, Reading.

Durlach, N. I., and Braida, L. D. (1969). Intensity perception I. Preliminary theory of intensity resolution, J. Acoust. Soc. of Am., 46, 372-383.

Kruskal, J. B. (1983). An Overview of Sequence Comparison, in: Time Warps, String Edits, and Macromolecules: The Theory and Practice of Sequence Comparison, D., Sankoff and J. B. Kruskal, eds., Addison-Wesley, Reading.

Leek, M. R. (1987). The role of attention in complex sound resolution, in: Complex Sound Perception, W. A. Yost and C. S. Watson, eds., Erlbaum, Hillsdale.

Leek, M. R. and Watson, C. S. (1984). Learning to
    detect auditory pattern components, J. Acoust.
    Soc. of Am., 76, 1037-1044.
Sankoff, D., and Kruskal, J. B. (1983). Time Warps,
    String Edits, and Macromolecules: The Theory and
    Practice of Sequence Comparison, Addison-Wesley,
    Reading.
Sorkin, R. D., Boggs, G. J., and Brady, S. L. (1982).
    Discrimination of temporal jitter in patterned
    sequences of tones. J. Exper. Psych.: Human
    Performance and Perception, 8, 46-57.
Sorkin, R. D. (1984). Discrimination of binary tone
    sequences, J. Acoust. Soc. of Am., S75, 21.
Spiegel M. F.,and Watson, C. S. (1981). Factors in the
    discrimination of tonal patterns. III. Selective
    attention and the level of target tones, J.
    Acoust. Soc. of Am., 69, 223-230.
Watson, C. S., and Kelly, W. J. (1981). The role of
    stimulus uncertainty in the discrimination of
    auditory patterns, in: Auditory and Visual Pattern
    Recognition, D. J. Getty and J. H. Howard, eds.,
    Erlbaum, Hillsdale.
Watson, C. S., Kelly, W. J., and Wroton, H. W. (1976).
    Factors in the discrimination of tonal patterns.
    II. Selective attention and learning under various
    levels of stimulus uncertainty, J. Acoust. Soc. of
    Am., 60, 1176-1186.

On the significance of spectral synchrony for signal detection

T. Houtgast
TNO Institute for Perception
P.O. Box 23, 3769 DE Soesterberg, The Netherlands

A compound stimulus consists of a combination of nine individual Gaussian-shaped tone pulses, each tone pulse covering a well defined and restricted area in the frequency-time domain. All nine individual tone pulses have the same masked threshold (in pink noise). The masked threshold of the compound stimulus is measured as a function of the configuration of the nine tone pulses in the frequency-time domain. Each configuration fits within a restricted frequency-time window of 500-3170 Hz along the frequency scale and 100 ms along the time scale, and the nine individual tone pulses are always well separated in frequency and/or time. Various of such configurations are considered, including the case of perfect spectral synchrony: nine tone pulses with different carrier frequencies and coinciding peaks of the Gaussian envelopes. Of all configurations considered, the latter appears to lead to optimal detectability. The effect of spectral synchrony on signal detection amounts to about 5 dB, and appears to be restricted to very brief signals only.

INTRODUCTION

Many sounds (pulses, bursts, also plosives) have a brief and broad-band character, showing a high degree of temporal synchronization along the frequency scale. For instance, after 1/3-octave band filtering, the resulting envelopes will peak at approximately the same instance. Thus, in general, such sounds will lead to a synchronized stimulation in many critical bands. This paper is concerned with the significance of this stimulus parameter - the degree of spectral synchrony - for signal detection. For that purpose a compound stimulus is considered consisting of nine elementary signals, with a distribution in frequency and time which can be varied systematically.

STIMULI

The elementary signal, a Gaussian-shaped tone pulse, is described in fig. 1. Parameters are the nominal frequency and temporal

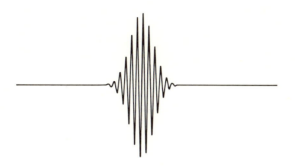

Figure 1. Description of the elementary signal, covering a restricted area in the frequency-time domain. A compound stimulus consists of nine such signals, with various combinations of (f_o, t_o).

$$f(t) = const. \; f_o^{1/2} \sin\left[2\pi f_o(t-t_o)\right] . \exp\left[-\pi(a f_o(t-t_o))^2\right]$$

$a = 0.2$

eff. bandwidth $\Delta f = 0.2 f_o$
eff. duration $\Delta t = 5/f_o$ (approx. -6 dB points)

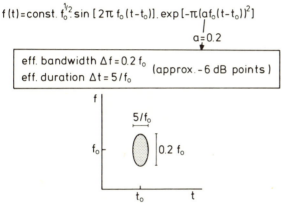

values f_o and t_o. The multiplication factor $f_o^{1/2}$ is to make the energy of a tone pulse independent of f_o.

The value of a in the argument of the exponent determines the effective duration and bandwidth. For a=0.2 the compromise in limiting both duration and bandwidth leads to the values for Δt and Δf as indicated. Note that $\Delta f=0.2 f_o$ implies that the effective band-width is a constant proportion of the nominal frequency (thus, the bandwidth is slightly smaller than 1/3 octave). Note also, that $\Delta t=5/f_o$ implies that the effective duration is five periods of the nominal (carrier) frequency, which amounts to 10 ms at 500 Hz and shortens with increasing f_o. The lower part of fig. 1 indicates how the elementary signal can be characterized in the frequency-time domain.

Fig. 2 displays several configurations for a compound stimulus. The grid in the frequency-time domain is defined by nine positions along the frequency scale (at 1/3-octave intervals) and nine positions

119

along the time scale (at 10-ms intervals). Note that by the definition of the elementary signal, the grid ensures that the elementary
signals are well separated in frequency and/or time.

The configuration indicated in the upper-right panel in fig. 2 is
the one of special interest, i.e. the case of spectral synchrony.
Besides the ones illustrated in fig. 2, several other stimulus
configurations were considered as well. A complete listing is given
in Table I. All stimuli were calculated and stored digitally (40-µs
samples, 12-bit D-A conversion).

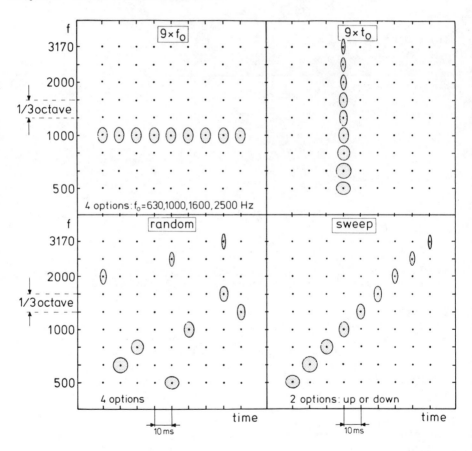

Figure 2. Four examples of compound stimuli. The nine elementary
      signals are distributed on a 9x9 grid such that they are well
      separated in frequency and/or time.

120

Table I. Listing of the six types of stimuli involved. Since most stimulus types include several options the total number of stimuli amounts to 16.

===
Stimulus		Symbol in fig. 3
Single	one elementary signal	o
	options: f_o = 630, 1000, 1600 or 2500 H_z	
$9xf_o$	nine equal-f_o signals at 10 ms intervals	F
	options: f_o = 630, 1000, 1600 or 2500 H_z	
$9xt_o$	nine equal-t_o signals at 1/3-oct. intervals	S
RANDOM	nine random combinations of (f_o, t_o)	R
	options: four frozen configurations	
SWEEP	nine sweep-like combinations of (f_o, t_o)	U , D
	options: sweep up or down	
9x9	all 81 possible combinations of (f_o, t_o)	●
===

METHOD

Subjects listened by headphone (Beyer DT-48). The masker was continuous pink noise (spectral level - 3 dB/octave) at a Sensation Level of about 50 dB. In a pilot experiment it was verified that for the pink-noise masker, each elementary signal with f_o in the range of 500-3170 Hz did lead to the same masked threshold (recall that the energy of the elementary signals were the same).

Detection thresholds were determined by a four-interval forced-choice procedure, with feedback. The four intervals in a trial were indicated by signal lights. During a run, four of the 16 possible stimuli (Table I) were considered, and at each individual trial a random selector determined which of those four stimuli was to be presented. The presentation levels of each of the four possible stimuli were kept within the relevant range by an adaptive procedure (stimulus level -/+ 2 dB after correct/incorrect responses). A run consisted typically of 400 trials, 100 for each stimulus. Each of the 16 possible stimuli were included in at least four runs. Responses were pooled for each stimulus and each stimulus level, and are plotted as psychometric functions.

The procedure of combining several possible stimuli within a run prevents the subject from tuning in on one particular stimulus; the subject has to keep an "open mind" in both frequency and time.

121

Especially in case of a random configuration, it may well be that threshold decreases after prolonged training on one particular frozen sample. The present procedure leads to what might be called the "spontaneous" masked threshold.

RESULTS

The results of two subjects are presented in fig. 3. All levels are presented relative to the masked threshold (62.5% score) for the single elementary signals. Of the compound stimuli consisting of

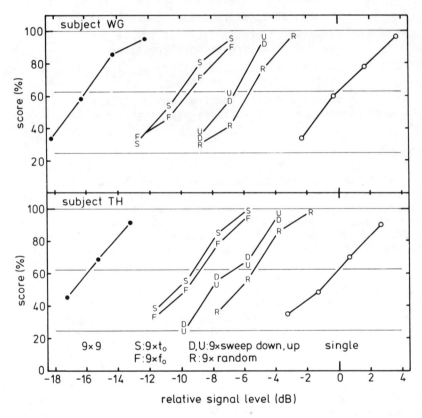

Figure 3. Scores obtained for two subjects in a four-alternative forced choice procedure for various signal levels for the six types of stimuli involved (specified in Table I). Levels are expressed relative to the masked threshold level of the single elementary signals (defined by a score of 62,5%).

nine elementary signals, the one labeled S (synchrony) yields the lowest masked threshold.

In terms of total energy, the summation of nine elementary signals leads to an increase of 9.5 dB, and 81 corresponds to 19.1 dB. When this is taken into account, the masked threshold depends on the stimulus configuration as presented in fig. 4. (These data represent the mean of nine subjects, and were obtained with a method somewhat different from the one described before.)

DISCUSSION

Fig. 4 leads to the following observation. Given a continuous pink-noise masker and given a frequency-time window of 500-3170 Hz along the frequency scale and 100 ms along the time scale, the distribution of stimulus energy within that window influences detection threshold. <u>Concentrating</u> the energy in frequency and/or time (single, $9xf_o$, $9xt_o$) leads to better detectability than distributing the energy over both frequency and time (9x RANDOM, 9x9).

equal-energy thresholds

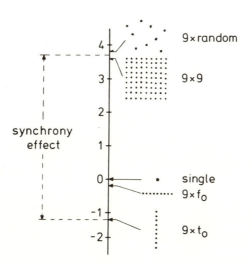

Figure 4. Relation among the masked threshold levels of five types of stimuli after compensation for the energy increment when adding nine (+ 9.5 dB) or 81 (+ 19.1 dB) elementary signals. Mean data of nine subjects.

123

The close relation between "single" and "9xf$_o$" is a traditional result: both stimuli are restricted in bandwidth to 1/3-octave and thus the total energy essentially determines masked threshold (at least for a duration up to 100 ms). The equally important effect of concentrating stimulus energy in the time domain (9xt$_o$) illustrates the significance of spectral synchrony. As indicated in fig. 4, the effect amounts to about 5 dB: for a broad-band stimulus with energy distributed from 500 to 3170 Hz a brief synchronized presentation yields a 5 dB lower threshold than a non-synchronized presentation within a 100 ms interval.

EFFECT OF SIGNAL DURATION

Fig. 5 indicates that the duration of the tone pulses is a critical parameter for the synchrony effect. Tone pulse duration is

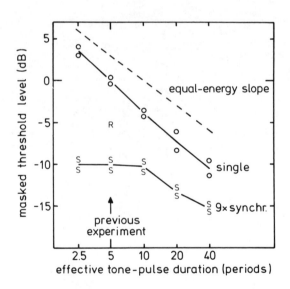

Figure 5. The relative masked threshold for two stimulus conditions (single and 9xt$_o$, see Table I), are given as a function of tone-pulse duration. For the duration of 5 periods the data relate to the previous experiments.

varied from 2.5 up to 40 periods, including the condition of 5 periods considered in the previous experiments. (The effective duration is manipulated by varying the value of $\underline{a}$ in fig. 1 from 0.4 down to 0.025.) For each duration, two stimulus conditions are considered, single and $9xt_o$ (see Table I), thus concentrating on the effect of synchrony on signal detection. Mean data of two subjects are given, again with 0 dB defined as the masked threshold for the single tone pulses at an effective duration of 5 periods. For larger durations, the gain of adding nine elementary signals can be seen to reduce rapidly to about 5 dB, a value which was found to apply also to a random, non-synchronized combination of nine elementary signals. Apparently, the benefit of synchrony for signal detection is lost for longer durations. Towards extreme short durations, the difference between single and $9xt_o$ increases, suggesting that the benefit of synchrony when adding nine signals becomes larger for very brief signals. However, the interpretation may be more complicated since, for the shortest duration considered, there is some degree of spectral overlap of the elementary signals, thus violating the basic concept of this study, namely that the elementary signals in a compound stimulus are essentially separated in frequency and/or time.

CONCLUSION

The masked threshold of brief broad-band stimuli benefits from spectral synchrony, i.e. when the temporal envelopes for different frequency regions peak at the same instance. This finding of synchrony-facilitated broad-band detection has interesting theoretical implications. Traditional detection theories are strongly critical-band oriented, and spectral synchrony is not acknowledged as a relevant parameter. In case of broad-band detection (i.e., the threshold being approached in a number of individual critical bands), some process of across-frequency integration must be involved. Apparently, the efficiency of that process benefits from spectral synchrony, especially for very brief stimuli.

REFERENCES
(added by Editors)

The interested reader should consult the literature on frequency uncertainty and detection, e.g., Green, D. M. (1961) "Detection of auditory sinusoids of uncertain frequency," J. Acoust. Soc. Am. 33, 897-903, or the literature on temporal uncertainty and detection, e.g., Green, D. M. (1980) "Detection of temporally uncertain signals," J. Acoust. Soc. Am. 67, 1304-1311. In addition the chapters in this book by C. S. Watson and M. Leek, and some of their cited references are relevant to the topic of T. Houtgast's chapter.

TEMPORAL FLUCTUATIONS AND THE DISCRIMINATION OF SPECTRALLY DENSE SIGNALS BY HUMAN LISTENERS.

W.M. Hartmann
Physics Department, Michigan State University,
E. Lansing, MI 48824

This report begins with a discussion of the statistical nature of noise, giving particular attention to the difference between thermal noise and fixed-amplitude random-phase noise. Then two measures of noise power fluctuations are introduced, the fourth moment of the waveform and the fourth moment of the envelope. It is argued that the latter measure provides the more pertinent description for psychoacoustical purposes. Experiments are described suggesting that noise power fluctuations can contribute about 5 dB of masking to the familiar signal in noise detection experiment and that these fluctuations are the basis for the discrimination of spectral density for small noise bandwidths.

INTRODUCTION

A thermal noise waveform of duration T can be described as a sum of sine components separated in frequency by the reciprocal of T, i.e.

$$x(t) = \sum_{n=n_1}^{n_1+N-1} a_n \cos(2\pi\, nt/T) + b_n \sin(2\pi\, nt/T). \quad (1)$$

The coefficients $\{a_n, b_n\}$ form a set of 2N independent random variables, normally distributed with zero mean and variance σ^2 (Rice, 1952). The mean and variance in this instance refer to an ensemble average, which we will indicate by the symbol $\langle...\rangle$, e.g. $\langle a_n^2 \rangle = \langle b_n^2 \rangle = \sigma^2$. The ensemble average is an average over all possible waveforms which are consistent with the rules defining the parameters, in this case, independent normal distributions for a_n and b_n.

Because of the orthogonality of the trigonometric functions on interval T the long-run time-average power (denoted with a bar) is:

$$\bar{P} = \frac{1}{2} \sum_n (a_n^2 + b_n^2). \quad (2)$$

The ensemble-average $\langle a_n b_n \rangle$ is zero. Therefore the ensemble-averaged power is $\langle P(t) \rangle = N \sigma^2$. In the limit that the number of components N becomes large we expect that $\bar{P} = \langle P(t) \rangle$. This is actually true if the noise is ergodic.

An alternative description of the noise waveform in Eq. (1) is the amplitude and phase form,

$$x(t) = \sum_n X_n \cos (2\pi nt/T + \phi_n), \qquad (3)$$

where

$$X_n^2 = a_n^2 + b_n^2 \qquad \text{and} \qquad \tan(\phi_n) = b_n/a_n. \quad (4)$$

With a_n and b_n independent and normally distributed, the distribution of the amplitude X_n is chi-square with two degrees of freedom. This distribution is called the Rayleigh distribution, and it has the density

$$f_R(X) = \frac{X}{\sigma^2} e^{-X^2/2\sigma^2}. \qquad (5)$$

The phase angles ϕ_n are distributed rectangularly from 0 to 2π.

NUMERICAL GENERATION OF NOISE

The elements of the human auditory system are tuned according to frequency. Therefore, the representation of noise in Eq. (3), where the power spectrum $X^2(f)$ is explicit, is a convenient starting point for the generation of noise for psychoacoustical experiments. Historically bands of noise have been produced by passing the output of a broad-band thermal noise generator through a filter to obtain the desired power spectrum. Increasingly nowadays noise is generated numerically by starting with the spectral representation $\{X_n, \phi_n\}$ and then computing the inverse Fourier transform (usually a Fast Fourier Transform) to create the noise waveform.

It is not difficult to generate thermal noise in this way, starting with an algorithm which generates random numbers q with a rectangular distribution, $0 < q < 1$. The indefinite integral of the Rayleigh distribution is given by

$$y(X) = \int_0^X dX' f_R(X') = 1 - e^{-X^2/2\sigma^2}, \qquad (6)$$

127

and this can be inverted. Therefore, starting with a rectangular distribution of random numbers y, the quantity X, given by

$$X = \sigma\sqrt{-2 \ln(1-y)} \tag{7}$$

will have a Rayleigh distribution.

What is used at least as often in psychoacoustical work is "fixed-amplitude random-phase" noise, where the amplitudes X_n are set equal to the desired spectrum and ϕ_n assumes random values between 0 and 2π. This kind of noise would seem to be an attractive alternative because any particular noise waveform then has a power spectrum equal to the ensemble-averaged power spectrum for thermal noise. And because the autocorrelation function is the Fourier transform of the power spectrum, the autocorrelation function, or any function depending linearly upon autocorrelation, for the fixed-amplitude noise is also the same as the ensemble-averaged function for thermal noise.

In studies which use frozen noise the listener hears the same noise waveform throughout the experiment. One is naturally concerned that any particular sample of thermal noise might be special in some way, casting doubt on the generality of the experimental results. Such a concern is minimized if one chooses fixed-amplitude noise as a stimulus. Frequent use is made of the special case of "equal-amplitude random-phase" noise, where $X_n = 1$ for all n, so that the power spectrum is rectangular.

A second look at the fixed-amplitude random-phase noise, however, makes it appear less attractive. The case of equal-amplitude noise demonstrates the problem: If $a_n^2 + b_n^2$ is constrained to equal unity then, by Eqs.(4) we must have $b_n = \sin(\phi_n)$. Because ϕ_n is uniformly distributed, the distribution for b_n (or for a_n) is

$$
\begin{aligned}
f_F(b_n) &= \pi^{-1}(1-b_n^2)^{-1/2} & 0 < |b_n| < 1 \\
&= 0 & |b_n| > 1.
\end{aligned}
\tag{8}
$$

The density f_F is minimum for $b_n = 0$ and maximum for extreme values of b_n. This is quite different from the correct density for thermal noise which is Gaussian. Further, although coefficients a_n and b_n are both distributed according to f_F, they are not independent. Once a value has been chosen for b_n, for example, there are only two possibilities for a_n, namely $\pm (1-b_n^2)^{1/2}$.

The anomalous density for fixed-amplitude noise suggests that this noise might be quite different from thermal noise. One way to compare the two kinds of noise is to make a numerical study of the distribution of the noise waveform in each case. Our study is an example of an ensemble-average calculation, of which there are several in this report. The calculation begins with a particular set of randomly-selected parameters $\{X_n, \phi_n\}$, consistent with the statistical rules for the noise. The corresponding waveform is sampled at 2000 points and the values are put into a histogram. Then the calculation is repeated 99 more times, starting each time with a different random set of parameters. All the sampled-waveform values are put into the same histogram.

Figure 1 shows such a histogram for thermal noise (Rayleigh distributed X_n) and for equal-amplitude noise when there are only three components ($N = 3$). As might be expected, the two distributions differ considerably. Careful comparison with a Gaussian waveform having the same variance shows that the thermal noise differs from normal only by sampling errors, whereas the equal-amplitude noise is not even close to normal.

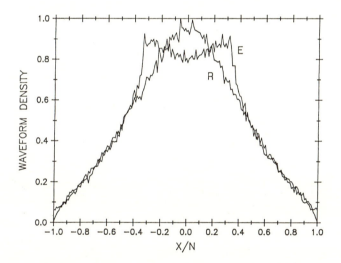

Figure 1. Distribution of sampled values of noise having only three spectral components, (R) Rayleigh distributed amplitudes and (E) equal amplitudes.

As the number of spectral components increases, however, the distribution of sampled noise values for equal-amplitude noise rapidly approaches a normal distribution. For N as small as 6 one cannot tell by eye that the equal-amplitude noise is less normal than the Rayleigh thermal noise; one must make a numerical comparison with a Gaussian to learn that. For N equal to 12, our calculation with only 200,000 points is barely able to distinguish between the two. Thus, the "law of large numbers" comes to the rescue of the equal-amplitude noise, despite an inauspicious beginning, even when the numbers aren't really very large. Of course, the above argument is incomplete. Fixed amplitude noise might yet differ from true thermal noise in some systematic way, a way which is not apparent in either the ensemble-averaged distribution or the autocorrelation function.

FLUCTUATIONS

There are numerous possible ways to describe the fluctuations in the average power of noise. Here we examine two of them, the fourth moment of the waveform and the fourth moment of the envelope.

The fourth moment of the waveform, normalized by the square of the average power, is the quantity W, given by

$$W = \int_0^T x^4(t)dt / [\int_0^T x^2(t)dt]^2. \qquad (9)$$

The standard deviation of the power about its time-averaged value P is given by

$$S = \sqrt{W-1} \ \overline{P}. \qquad (10)$$

The ensemble-averaged value of W is $\langle W \rangle = 3 - 3/(2N)$, where N is the number of spectral components.

To compute the distribution of W we performed an ensemble-average computation as described earlier. There were 2048 sampled values in each waveform, from which a single value of W was computed, and there were 2000 different waveforms. The ensemble distributions for waveforms having 51 and 151 spectral components of equal amplitude are shown in Figure 2. As would be expected from the distribution of x(t) itself, it does not matter whether the amplitudes are all equal or whether the amplitudes are Rayleigh distributed with a rectangular ensemble-averaged power spectrum. The distribution for W is the same in either case.

130

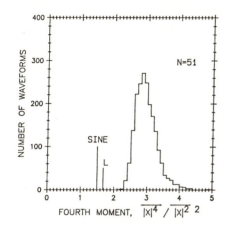 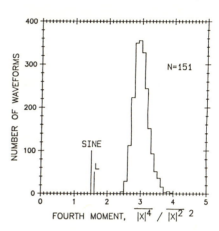

Figure 2. The vertical axis value is the number of waveforms, out of 2000, for which the normalized fourth moment falls in a histogram bin corresponding to the horizontal axis value.

Although the fourth moment of the waveform provides a correct physical description of the power fluctuations, there is something not quite right about it from a perceptual point of view. One obvious difficulty is that even a single sine waveform has power fluctuations ($S^2 = 1/2$), and yet these fluctuations are never perceived as such. These fluctuations actually correspond to oscillations in power at twice the sine frequency, and these are too rapid to be perceived. The contribution of rapidly oscillating terms to the power fluctuation is actually the root of the problem in general. To see this one can write an expression for the instantaneous power by squaring Eq. (3). A band of N components of unit amplitude will serve as an example.

$$x(t) = \sum_n \frac{1}{2} + \sum_n \sum_{n'<n} \cos(Z_n - Z_{n'}) + \sum_n \sum_{n'<n} \cos(Z_n + Z_{n'})$$
$$+ \frac{1}{2} \sum_n \cos(2Z_n), \tag{11}$$

where $Z_n = 2\pi nt/T + \phi_n$.

The fluctuation about the average power, $N/2$, includes both sum and difference terms. The sum terms, as well as the terms in $2Z_n$, oscillate at frequencies higher than the component frequencies of

131

the noise, and most, if not all, of these will not contribute to the perceived fluctuations. Therefore, the fourth moment of the waveform overestimates the relevant fluctuations.

An alternative measure of fluctuations is the envelope fourth moment. The envelope is the absolute value of the analytic signal, given by

$$E(t) = \left| \sum_n X_n \, e^{i(2\pi nt/N + \phi_n)} \right| . \qquad (12)$$

This can easily be calculated from an inverse FFT by removing the negative frequency components from the spectrum. The expression for E is the same as the right hand side of Eq. (11), except that only the frequency difference terms are present. The ensemble-averaged value $\langle E^4 \rangle / \langle E^2 \rangle$ is equal to $2 - 1/N$. Figure 3 shows the distribution of the fourth moment of E for noise with 51 or 151 spectral components in the band. As the number of components increases the distribution becomes remarkably narrow.

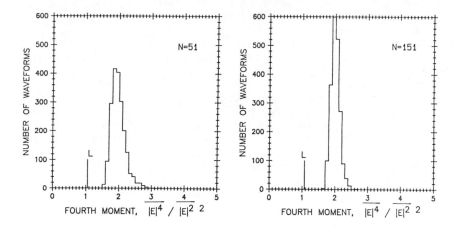

Figure 3. Distributions of the normalized envelope fourth moment for 51 and 151 spectral components.

FLUCTUATIONS AND MASKING

The theory of signal detection in noise asserts that the signal creates an increment in the total stimulus power, which the listener considers significant or not depending upon the size of the increment compared to the fluctuations. These fluctuations are of two kinds, those due to the stimulus noise and those due to the listener's internal noise (de Boer, 1966, Green and Swets, 1966). Much of the recent history of psychoacoustics can be viewed as an attempt to fit an enormous volume of data by using a consistent set of assumptions concerning these two kinds of fluctuations. To manipulate the internal noise experimenters have compared thresholds resulting from different psychophysical procedures. To a lesser extent there have been attempts to control the stimulus fluctuations, by using frozen noise, for example (Raab and Goldberg, 1975, Hanna and Robinson, 1985).

Recently it has become possible to control the stimulus fluctuations in a straight-forward way. The low-noise noise algorithm of Pumplin (1985) provides a way to minimize the fluctuation S^2 in Eq. (10). The input to the algorithm is an amplitude spectrum $\{X_n\}$, the output is a set of phase angles $\{\phi_n'\}$ which correspond to a local minimum of S^2 in the N-dimensional space of phase angles. The algorithm therefore produces fixed-amplitude noise; it can make a noise with small power fluctuations for any desired amplitude spectrum. The local minima discovered by the algorithm turn out to be good minima. Symbols "L" in figures 2 and 3 show the values of the fourth moment achieved for 51 and 151 components. They are well below the average distributions; they are close to the values for sine waveforms.

To study the role of fluctuations in masking we (Hartmann and Pumplin, 1986) found masked thresholds for 1000 Hz sine tones in noise bands centered on 1000 Hz. One set of noise bands, with 51 components, was 100 Hz wide; the other set, with 151 components, was 300 Hz wide. For each bandwidth we used both random-phase noise and low-noise noise, having the same power spectra.

Experimental details were these: The experiment was a two-interval forced-choice task with noise at 64 dB SPL on two 490 ms intervals, separated by a 250 ms gap. Noises were turned on and off with 10ms raised cosine envelopes. The signal was turned on and off with the noise, but with a 30ms envelope entirely enclosed by the noise envelope. Detection thresholds were found by the standard two-and-one staircase technique, with a 2 dB step size on the signal level. Values of $[\overline{E^4}/\overline{E^2}^2 - 1]$ for random-phase noise were 1.0 or 1.1; for low-noise noise they were 0.05 and 0.07. For each kind of noise, signal detection thresholds were found for six different starting phases of the signal, 60, 120,...360 degrees. The six thresholds were averaged to find a final threshold. There were six subjects.

The data showed that average thresholds for the 100 Hz bandwidth were 5 dB less for the low-noise noise than for the random-phase noise, leading us to conclude that in a typical detection task, the noise fluctuations contribute about 5 dB of masking. For the 300 Hz bandwidth, masked thresholds did not depend upon the form of the noise. Our interpretation of this result is that filtering by the auditory system, perhaps by a critical band filter 160 Hz wide, reintroduced power fluctuations into the 300 Hz low-noise noise.

FLUCTUATIONS AND DISCRIMINATION OF SPECTRAL DENSITY

Hartmann et al. (1986) measured the ability of listeners to discriminate between noises with different spectral densities. A band, having width W and centered on frequency f, either contained a large number of spectral components or a smaller number N. The listener's task was to distinguish between these two when their average power was the same.

Experimental details were these: The noises were generated by a digital synthesizer in such a way that component frequencies and phases on a given trial were different from those on any other trial. Components were placed randomly and uniformly in frequency bins, of width W/N. The large number of components was N = 60 and the small number was N = 3,5,7...25. A trial included two 500 ms intervals, with noise at 75 dbA, separated by a 500 ms gap. One interval included a 60-component noise, the other had a N-component noise. From 30 trials at each N we constructed a psychometric function and used the 75% correct point to find, the just-discriminable value for N.

The data included a number of surprises. First, for small bandwidths only a few components were required to simulate a dense spectrum. For example, for W = 50 Hz, a noise with only four spectral components was barely distinguishable from a noise with 60 components. Second, for small bandwidths, W = 50 or 100 Hz, the performance did not depend upon the center frequency f (f = 500, 1000, 2000 Hz), and for W = 200 Hz performance depended only weakly upon f. We concluded that the discrimination in these cases was not based upon spectral resolution but upon the perception of fluctuations in the envelope power, which depend upon bandwidth but

134

are independent of band center frequency. The model which successfully fitted the data for narrow bands was based upon the fluctuation in envelope power, essentially the quantity $\langle E^4 \rangle / \langle E^2 \rangle^2 - 1$, as passed through a low-pass filter with a time constant of 3 ms. The application of the model included the ad hoc assumption that the jnd in average fluctuation is about 5 to 10 percent. This value is not known from experiment, but at this time work on the perceptual aspects of noise power fluctuations is just beginning.

The two experimental studies described above are examples of an increasing appreciation of the role which noise fluctuations play in the study of human hearing. Other chapters of this book, notably those by J.W. Hall and R.H. Gilkey, provide other examples.

REFERENCES

de Boer, E. (1966) "Intensity discrimination of fluctuating signals," J. Acoust. Soc. Am. 40, 552-560.

Green, D.M. and Swets, J.A. (1966) Signal Detection and Psychophysics, Wiley, New York.

Hanna, T.E. and Robinson, D.E. "Phase effects for a sine wave masked by reproducible noise," J. Acoust. Soc. Am. 77, 1129-1140.

Hartmann, W.M., McAdams, S., Gerzso, A., and Boulez, P. (1986) "Discrimination of spectral density," J. Acoust. Soc. Am. 79, 1915-1925.

Hartmann, W.M. and Pumplin J. (1986) "Noise power fluctuations and the masking of sine signals," J. Acoust. Soc. Am. (submitted)

Pumplin, J. (1985) "Low-noise noise," J. Acoust. Soc. Am. 78, 100-104.

Raab, D.H. and Goldberg, I.A. "Auditory intensity discrimination with bursts of reproducible noise," J. Acoust. Soc. Am. 57, 437-447.

Rice, S.O. (1954) "Mathematical analysis of random noise," in Selected Papers on Noise and Stochastic Processes, ed. N. Wax, Dover, New York.

Perception of the Temporal Envelope of Amplitude-
Modulated Noise by Hearing-Imparied Listeners

C. Formby
Departments of Communicative Disorders and Neurology,
University of Florida, Gainesville, FL   32610, USA

The temporal envelope plays an important role in
communication for many hearing-impaired listeners and
may, in profound impairments, be one of the few auditory cues that remains available. This paper reviews
some recent studies of hearing-impaired listeners'
abilities to detect and to discriminate the special
class of complex stimuli represented by sinusoidally
amplitude-modulated noise.

INTRODUCTION

Since the early experiments of Miller and Taylor
(1948) with chopped noise, theorists have attempted to
understand the stimulus properties and mechanisms that
are important for detection and discrimination of the
temporal envelope of amplitude-modulated noise. Experiments with normal human listeners have ranged from
parametric investigations of the stimulus and its role
in modulation detection (Rodenburg, 1977; Viemeister,
1977,1979; van Zanten, 1980) to studies of the melodic
information conveyed by modulated noise (e.g., Burns
and Viemeister, 1976). From these experiments, models
have been proposed to account for normal modulation
detection (Rodenburg, 1977; Viemeister, 1977, 1979).
Detection and rate discrimination of amplitude-modulated noise also have been studied in an assortment of
non-human species ranging from parakeet to goldfish
(Dooling and Searcy, 1979; Fay, 1982; Long and Clark,
1984). With increasing knowledge about the normal perception of modulated noise, investigators (Formby,
1982; Lamore et al., 1983, 1984; Formby, 1984; Bacon
and Viemeister, 1985) have begun to explore clinical
populations of hearing-impaired listeners and their
abilities to make use of the temporal envelope of
modulated noise.

TEMPORAL ENVELOPE DETECTION

First, consider the measurement of detection
threshold for sinusoidally amplitude-modulated noise.
The general pattern of modulation detection is

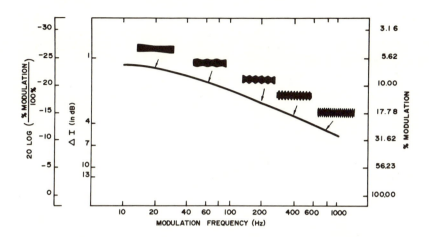

Fig. 1. Idealized MTF for a normal listener.
Smoothed modulation waveforms at detection threshold are superimposed for selected frequencies.

illustrated for an idealized normal listener in Fig. 1.
A modulation-threshold function (MTF) is plotted such
that the depth of modulation at threshold is mapped
inversely on the ordinate and the frequency of modulation is displayed on the abscissa. Also shown are
waveforms depicting the smoothed modulation envelopes
measured at threshold for several modulation frequencies. The pattern of the normal MTF crudely
resembles the shape of a lowpass filter transfer function. By rough analogy to the latter, the MTF may be
characterized as having a cutoff frequency, f_c, which
varies with the psychophysical method of measurement
between 35-60 Hz. The rate of attenuation of MTF above
f_c has generally been reported to be about 3 to 4
dB/octave.

To date, MTFs have been measured for patients suffering (1) chronic Meniere's disease (Formby, 1982),
(2) high-frequency sensorineural hearing loss (Bacon
and Viemeister, 1983, 1985), (3) acoustic neuroma
(Formby, 1986b), and (4) severe hearing loss from
multiple etiologies (Lamore et al., 1984).

Consider first Meniere's disease and the chronic
Meniere impairment (Formby, 1982). The disorder arises

137

from altered function of cochlear mechanics due to en-
dolymphatic hydrops. Audiometry typically reveals a
unilateral and relatively flat or gently sloping
hearing-loss configuration and positive cochlear symp-
toms. Frequency selectivity is characteristically
poor.

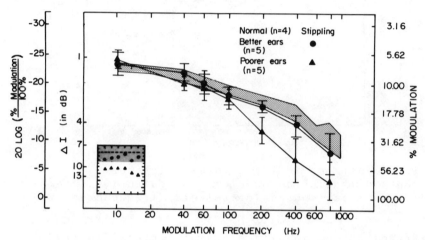

Fig. 2. Forced-choice MTFs for normal listeners and
for better and poorer ears of chronic Meniere
patients. A composite audiogram is inset for the
patients.

Average modulation thresholds for five Meniere
patients, along with their composite audiogram, which
is inset, are shown in Fig. 2. Also shown by stippling
are mean modulation thresholds, $\pm$ 1 standard deviation,
for four normally hearing listeners. All of these data
were measured using an adaptive forced-choice procedure. No attempt was made to compensate for the
dc-component of the modulated noise sample in the
mesurements. The modulation thresholds for the
normally hearing listeners were obtained with a carrier
spectrum level of 38 dB SPL. The better-ear modulation
thresholds of the Meniere patients (filled circles)
were obtained with a carrier spectrum level of 30 dB
SPL. As expected, these two sets of data were very
similar. By way of comparison, the normal values were
typically within 1 dB of modulation thresholds
previously reported by Viemeister (1977), who used a
generally similar method. The mean MTF for the

138

impaired ears is shown here as filled triangles.
Presentation levels for the impaired ears were matched
for equal loudness to that presented to the good ear of
each patient. These data were similar to the better-
ear MTF below 100 Hz, above which sensitivity declined
at an abnormally rapid rate of about 6 dB/octave.
These findings indicate that chronic Meniere patients,
when listening with their impaired ears, detected
amplitude modulation in a near-normal manner at low
modulation frequencies. The patients had considerable
difficulty however detecting amplitude modulation at
the higher modulation frequencies.

A rather different pattern of modulation thresholds has emerged in the other studies with hearing-
impaired listeners (Bacon and Viemeister, 1983, 1985;
Lamore et al., 1984; Formby, 1986b). Common among
these studies is a general elevation in modulation
threshold across modulation frequency. Also common to
these studies is the high-frequency pattern of hearing
loss among most of these patients. The modulation data
are typified in Fig. 3 by average modulation thresholds for six acoustic neuroma patients. Better-ear
thresholds for the neuroma patients are shown by filled
circles and the neuroma-ear thresholds by open
circles. The normative range is shown by stippling.

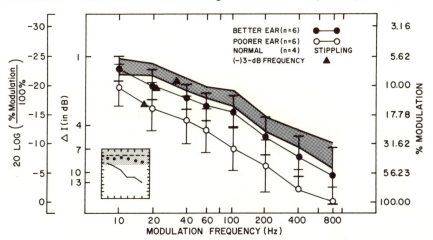

Fig. 3. Method-of-adjustment MTFs for normal listeners
and for better and poorer ears of acoustic neuroma
patients. A composite audiogram is inset for the
patients (from Formby, 1986b).

All of these modulation thresholds were measured by a method-of-adjustment (MOA) procedure. Presentation level for the normally hearing listeners was at 30 dB SL and at 40-50 dB SL for each ear of the patients. Filled triangles attached to each function denote a 3-dB increase in modulation threshold relative to the minimum threshold value measured at 10 Hz. A composite audiogram for the six patients is inset.

The better-ear modulation thresholds coincided with the border of the mean range of the normally hearing listeners. Both functions increased at a rate of 2 to 3 dB/octave. Note, however, that the better-ear thresholds were increased by 3 dB near 20 Hz, whereas for the normally hearing listeners the 3-dB increase in threshold was near 35 Hz. Since the normally hearing listeners were all well practiced for MOA prior to collecting data, the differences in the f_c shown here for MOA and the 60-Hz value measured earlier for the forced-choice method presumably reflect differences in the two psychophysical procedures. The lower f_c for the better ears of the neuroma patients is due to the inclusion of a pair of bilaterally affected patients. Although each exhibited normal hearing sensitivity in the better ear, one had a small neurofibroma in the better ear and the second had a large space-filling tumor that affected auditory brainstem recordings for the off-side better ear. The neuroma-ear thresholds reveal that, on the average, the patients required from 5 to 8 dB more modulation than the average normal listener at any frequency to achieve threshold in the affected ear. Moreover, the average neuroma threshold was increased by 3 dB at a frequency approximately half the normal value. However, the attenuation rate of the neuroma MTF remained between 2 to 3 dB/octave above the f_c. This pattern of the neuroma data is in contrast to the Meniere thresholds which were near normal at low modulation frequencies, but above the f_c were attenuated at twice the normal rate.

The neuroma data are similar qualitatively to findings for patients with high-frequency sensorineural hearing losses (Bacon and Viemiester, 1983, 1985) and also to findings for noise-exposed chinchillas suffering temporary high-frequency hearing losses (Henderson et al., 1984). In fact, the pattern of modulation data measured for patients suffering high-frequency sensorineural hearing losses may be simulated

140

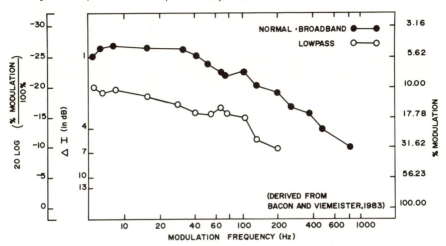

Fig. 4. Bacon and Viemeister's (1983) MTFs for a
broad-band noise carrier and for a filtered-noise
carrier simulating high-frequency hearing loss
(from Formby, 1986b).

reasonably well with normally hearing listeners. As
may be seen by the lower curve in Fig. 4, Bacon and
Viemeister (1983) were able to simulate elevated
modulation thresholds and a lower f_c by restricting the
presentation of the noise carrier to lower spectral
frequencies. The upper curve reflects the expected
normal performance with a broad-band noise carrier. It
remains unclear at this time whether the elevated
modulation thresholds measured for patients with high-
frequency audiometric impairments reflect their reduced
listening bandwidths (Bacon and Viemeister, 1985) or
their inabilities to hear the higher audiometric
frequencies, which arguably are the most critical for
normal modulation detection (Patterson, 1977; van
Zanten, 1980).

The differences in the Meniere and neuroma
patients' modulation thresholds may reflect differences
in their audiometric configurations or the presentation
levels used. Differences probably arise also because
of changes in the auditory filter mechanism in
Meniere's disease (Formby, 1984). We do not know
whether eighth-nerve tumor affects peripheral
filtering.

141

TEMPORAL ENVELOPE DISCRIMINATION

We have seen that the hearing-impaired listener can detect modulation, although this ability may be more or less impaired. However, we know almost nothing about hearing-impaired listeners' abilities to make use of the temporal envelope after detection. Rate-discrimination data are shown in Fig. 5 for the Meniere patients presented earlier. The circles code the better-ear data and the triangles the poorer-ear values. Stippling reflects the normal range of values. The Meniere patients could discriminate normally between different rates of 100% sinusoidally amplitude-modulated noise at the lower modulation frequencies, but they had difficulty discriminating modulation rates at modulation frequencies above 100 Hz. That is, deficits were measurable only at modulation frequencies where modulation thresholds also were elevated. This pattern is in agreement with reports for normally hearing listeners which indicate that rate discrimination is limited largely by the listener's ability to detect modulation (Burns and Viemeister, 1976; Patterson et al., 1978; Formby, 1985).

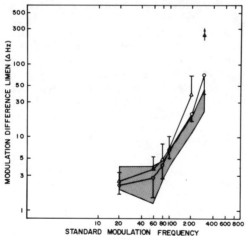

Fig. 5. Geometric-mean modulation-rate DLs (±1 s.d.) for normal listeners (stippling) and for better (circles) and poorer (triangles) ears of chronic Meniere patients (from Formby, 1986a).

142

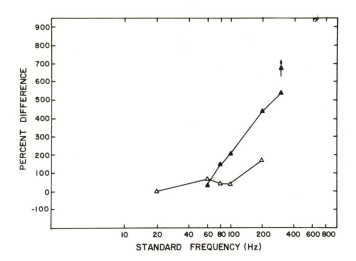

Fig. 6. Index of relative impairment for pure-tone
frequency (filled triangles) and modulation-rate
(open triangles) DLs of chronic Meniere patients
(from Formby, 1986a).

    The Meniere patients' rate discrimination data
suggest that the temporal envelope cue is relatively
resistant to the Meniere disorder, at least when compared to their deficits for simple pure-tone frequency
discrimination (Formby, 1986a). This is demonstrated
in Fig. 6 by a relative index of impairment for pure-
tone frequency discrimination and modulation-rate
discrimination. The index plots percent-difference
values versus standard frequency. These values were
calculated by taking the difference between the average
Meniere frequency DL or rate DL and the corresponding
DLs measured for a group of normal listeners at each
standard frequency. Each difference value then was
multiplied by 100% to obtain a percent difference value
at each standard frequency. Except at 60 Hz, the
Meniere disorder was relatively more detrimental to
frequency discrimination than to rate discrimination at
all standard frequencies where both tasks could be
measured. Moreover, as standard frequency was
increased, the relative deficit increased much more
rapidly for pure-tone frequency discrimination than for
modulation-rate discrimination.
    Based on the limited experimental data available,
it seems that despite deficits in temporal envelope

143

perception, the temporal envelope remains a relatively robust cue for the hearing impaired. As a practical matter, the syllable is the unit of speech probably most directly related to temporal envelope rate (Calvert and Silverman, 1975). Fortunately, syllable rates important for speech are typically less than 8 per second. So this information would appear available to most hearing-impaired listeners. Other information also may be available in the temporal envelope such as cues for voicing and voice pitch (F_0), voice rhythm (prosody), and consonant/vowel boundaries (see Erber, 1972; Goldstein and Proctor, 1985).

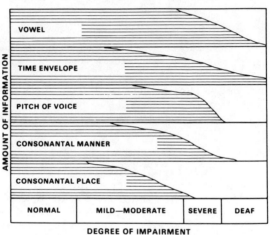

Fig. 7. J.D. Miller's estimates of the relative impairment to information carriers in the speech signal as a function of severity of hearing loss (from Calvert and Silverman, 1975).

It remains to be established how great the severity of hearing loss must be to render temporal envelope cues useless. J.D. Miller (Calvert and Silverman, 1975) has estimated roughly the relative impairment to the temporal envelope cue and to other types of information contained in the speech signal. These estimates of relative impairment are presented in Fig. 7 as a function of the severity of hearing loss. Future studies will be needed to verify Miller's estimates and to extend our understanding of deficits in temporal envelope perception.

ACKNOWLEDGMENTS

American Speech and Hearing Association, S. Karger, and the A.G. Bell Association granted permission to use Figs. 3 and 4, Figs. 5 and 6, and Fig. 7, respectively. Laura Ellsworth kindly provided editorial assistance.

REFERENCES

Bacon, S.P. and Viemeister, N.F. (1983). Detection of amplitude modulation by normal-hearing and hearing-impaired subjects. J. Acoust. Soc. Am., 73, Suppl. 1, S93.

Bacon, S.P. and Viemeister, N.F. (1985). Temporal modulation transfer functions in normal-hearing and hearing-impaired listeners. Audiology, 24, 117-134.

Burns, E.M. and Viemeister, N.F. (1976). Nonspectral pitch. J. Acoust. Soc. Am., 60, 863-868.

Calvert, D.R. and Silverman, S.R. (1975). Speech and Deafness. Alexander Graham Bell Assoc. for the Deaf, Washington, D.C.

Dooling, R. and Searcy, M. (1979). Amplitude modulation thresholds for the parakeet (Melopsittacus and latus). J. Acoust. Soc. Am., 66, Suppl 1., S34.

Erber, N.P. (1972). Speech-envelope cues as an acoustic aid to lipreading for profoundly deaf children. J. Acoust. Soc. Am., 51, 1224-1227.

Fay, R.R. (1982). Neural mechanisms of an auditory temporal discrimination by the goldfish. J. Comp. Physiol., 147, 201-216.

Formby, C. (1982). Differential sensitivity to tonal frequency and to the rate of modulation of broadband noise by hearing-impaired listeners. Unpublished doctoral dissertation, Washington University, St. Louis, MO.

Formby, C. (1984). Modulation thresholds for Meniere's and neuroma patients. J. Acoust. Soc. Am., 76, Suppl. 1, S61.

Formby, C. (1985). Differential sensitivity to tonal frequency and to the rate of modulation of broadband noise by normally hearing listeners. J. Acoust. Soc. Am. 78, 70-77.

Formby, C. (1986a). Frequency and rate discrimination by Meniere patients. Audiology, 25: 10-18.

Formby, C. (1986b). Modulation detection by patients

with eighth-nerve tumors. J. Speech Hearing Res.,
in press.

Goldstein, M.H. and Proctor, A. (1985). Tactile aids
for profoundly deaf children. J. Acoust. Soc. Am.,
77, 258-265.

Henderson, D., Salvi, R., Pavek, G., and Hamernik, R.
(1984). Amplitude modulation thresholds in
chinchillas with high-frequency hearing loss. J.
Acoust. Soc. Am., 75, 1177-1183.

Lamore, P.J.J., Verweij, C., and Brocaar, M.P.
(1984). Reliability of auditory function tests in
severely hearing-impaired and deaf subjects.
Audiology, 23, 453-466.

Long, G.R. and Clark, W.W. (1984). Detection of
frequency and rate modulation by the chinchilla.
J. Acoust. Soc. Am., 75, 1184-1190.

Miller, G.A. and Taylor, W.G. (1948). The perception
of repeated bursts of noise. J. Acoust. Soc. Am.,
20, 171-182.

Patterson, R.D. (1977). Comments, in Psychophysics and
Physiology of Hearing, E.F. Evans and J.P. Wilson,
eds., Academic, London, p. 438.

Patterson, R.D., Johnson-Davies, D. and Milroy, R.
(1978). Amplitude-modulated noise: The detection
of modulation versus the detection of modulation
rate. J. Acoust. Soc. Am. 63, 1904-1911.

Rodenburg, M. (1977). Investigation of temporal
effects with amplitude modulated signals,
Psychophysics and Physiology of Hearing, E.F. Evans
and J.P. Wilson, eds., Academic, London, pp. 429-
437.

Viemeister, N.F. (1977). Temporal factors in
audition: A systems analysis approach,
Psychophysics and Physiology of Hearing, E.F. Evans
and J.P. Wilson, eds., Academic, London, pp. 419-
428.

Viemeister, N.F. (1979). Temporal modulation transfer
functions based upon modulation thresholds. J.
Acoust. Soc. Am., 66, 1365-1380.

van Zanten, G.A. (1980). Temporal modulation transfer
functions for intensity modulated noise bands,
Psychophysical, Physiological and Behavioral
Studies in Hearing, G. van den Brink and F.A.
Bilsen, eds., Delft University Press, Delft, The
Netherlands, pp. 206-209.

On Creating a Precedent for Binaural Patterns: When Is an Echo an Echo?

Pierre L. Divenyi
Speech and Hearing Research, Veterans Administration
Medical Center, Martinez, California, and University of
California, Santa Barbara, California
and
Jens Blauert
Lehrstuhl für Allgemeine Elektrotechnik und Akustik,
Ruhr-Universität, Bochum, Federal Republic of Germany

Previous studies on the precedence effect (e.g.,
Zurek, JASA 67, 952-964 [1980]) demonstrated that a
brief diotic sound, called the conditioner,
suppressed its spatially displaced "echo", i.e., a
brief dichotic probe presented a few ms later, when
the spectral composition of both stimuli was identical.   In our experiments we used various unfiltered and filtered (high-pass, low-pass, band-pass,
and band-reject) brief sounds (noise bursts and
clicks) for the conditioner and the probe.
Suppression of the probe was seen in all conditions
where the conditioner and the probe were identical
in their spectra, but coherence between conditioner
and probe waveforms was not required in order for
echo suppression to occur.   Some suppression was
also seen when the probe had its energy concentrated in regions above the spectrum of the conditioner.   On the other hand no suppression was seen
for probes with spectra below the conditioner.   Our
findings indicate that echo suppression may occur
whenever we can infer a significant overlap between
the monaural excitation patterns generated by the
conditioner and the probe, suggesting that binaural
interaction is subsequent to, and may be based on,
monaural frequency analysis.

INTRODUCTION

The famous conductor, the late Thomas Beecham, is
credited with the bon mot that Royal Albert Hall in London was the only place in the world where works of contemporary British composers could be heard more than
once.   The true causticity of this remark is understood
by those who know that Sir Thomas referred to the

147

problematic acoustics -- i.e., the long and multiple reverberations of the concert hall in question. However, echoes are present in every concert hall and theater, in those judged to be acoustically satisfying just as well as in those which performers and public unanimously dislike. Actually, reverberation gives to the sound a dimension of spaciousness without which the listener's experience becomes less satisfying (Lehmann, 1980). Only those echoes that are of the order of 50 to more than 100 milliseconds will be judged as interfering with the desired degree of spatiousness (Barron, 1971); at very brief delays (approximately 10 ms or less) the echo does not even disturb localization of the primary sound source, for the simple reason that it is not heard. The "precedence effect", "Haas effect", or "Law of the first wavefront" (Wallach et al., 1949; Haas, 1951) refers to the phenomenon whereby a stimulus originating at one point of the auditory space has the capacity of suppressing the percept of its echo having a different spatial locus. Recently, this phenomenon has received renewed attention (Zurek, 1980; Gaskell, 1983; Blauert, 1984). These studies have shown that the precedence effect is a potent factor in binaural signal processing: Echo suppression is considered to be the effect of the disruption of sound localization as a whole as well as the two major underlying binaural processes, namely, interaural time- and interaural intensity discrimination.

In a natural, everyday setting echo suppression must be a process of great complexity. For example, in a concert hall during performance many different primary sounds co-occur together with first- and higher-order reflections, thereby creating a situation in which the auditory system is required to make continuous decisions as to whether a given sound was an echo (and, therefore, should be suppressed) or whether it was a primary sound (and, therefore, to be processed). Furthermore, depending on the acoustic absorbancy of the walls, echoes of complex primary sounds may have markedly altered spectra. The question of what sound may be accepted as an echo by the auditory system, however, remains unanswered. First of all, it is not clear whether echo suppression is restricted to the frequency band of the primary sound or whether its effect transcends across bands. In other words, we should ask if a sound that was first localized will suppress the perception of only a delayed copy of itself or whether it will also block out the spatial percept of another sound arriving later from a different spatial position. A second point of

148

interest is whether, in order for the echo to be suppressed, it is required to be a true, coherent copy of the primary sound or whether it is sufficient that it only <u>resembles</u> the primary sound in some characteristics, e.g., envelope shape and/or power spectrum. The present study represents an effort to elucidate these questions.

METHODS

Our investigation of echo suppression was based on the following rationale: (1) If the echo following a primary sound presented at a 0° azimuth after a delay of τ ms is not suppressed, then the listener should be able to discriminate between an echo arriving from a 0° azimuth location and one arriving from an angle of X° in the horizontal half plane. (2) If such a discrimination is not possible for any azimuth X, then we consider the echo to be fully suppressed. (3) In order to be able to focus on the suppression of "fake echoes" (i.e., on situations in which the primary sound and the echo are different), one first needs to find a certain delay τ at which a given primary sound would suppress an identical echo. Only after such a delay is found that one may ask the question whether the primary sound will also suppress echoes that are different.

Thus, the study had to contain two parts: Identification of the delay range in which suppression exists and experiments on the discrimination of echoes differing in location. The study was conducted with dichotic stimuli delivered through earphones (Sennheiser Model HD-414). Movement in the horizontal plane was emulated by introducing interaural time delays (ITD) favoring the right ear, ranging from 0 (frontal location) to a maximum of 466 μs (90° right azimuth). In all experiments reported below the stimulus consisted of a brief conditioner sound (CD) (=the primary sound) that was followed by a brief probe (PR) (=the echo) after a separation of τ ms. The CD was always diotic. All stimuli were generated digitally (DEC PDP 11/34 computer) and delivered in synchrony through a pair of 16-bit D/A converters (Charybdis Analog I/O System) at a 33.33 kHz sampling rate. The level of stimuli at peak voltage corresponded to 75 dB SPL. One subject was tested at a time in a single-walled IAC sound-treated chamber. Three trained listeners participated.

RESULTS

1. Identification of the Echo Suppression Delay

When the CD and the PR are identical sounds for
what temporal separations is there echo suppression?
For a diotic CD and a dichotic PR with a fixed ITD (say,
200 vs) but the separation τ between the CD and the PR
is gradually increased, experienced listeners easily
identify three perceptual regions. First (I), at very
short separations (typically less than 2 ms for very
brief to between 3 and 8 ms for 5-10 ms sounds), the
listeners hear only one compact image which appears at
the midline. As the separation τ increases, the image
still remains fused but it is more and more lateralized
to the side of the leading ear (II). Finally, at even
larger separations the CD and the PR will be heard as
two individual images, with the CD appearing at the midline and the PR clearly lateralized at the leading ear
side (III). Thus, echo suppression, complete or partial, may occur only for echo delays that give rise to
the first two kinds of percept. Unfortunately, the precise limits of the categories depend on the sound(s)
that constitute the CD and the PR and, in the absence of
a theory that would account for the phenomenon, can only
be empirically determined. In the first series of experiments we attempted to identify, for a given sound, a
region of τ at which no split percept was elicited --
i.e., a PR delay below the category boundary between
perceptual regions II and III. The method we employed to
determine these regions was the one widely used in
speech perception research for the definition of
phonemic categories.

The stimulus consisted of a CR and a PR of identical envelope and spectrum (though not necessarily two
identical sounds). The ITD was fixed at 200 us, whereas
the separation τ between CR and PR varied from trial to
trial. At each trial any one of ten values of τ could
appear with equal probability. The listener was
instructed to press one of two keys if he heard only one
image and the other if he heard two. We found that making this distinction required little practice and each
listener quickly adopted rather firm criteria. More
surprisingly, as Fig. 1 illustrates, the category boundary established by two listeners for a given CR-PR pair
(3-ms bursts of white noise band-pass filtered at 4.5
kHz) almost exactly overlapped. (As a matter of
interest, we also display the not-too-conclusive results
for the categorical distinction between Percepts I and

II, i.e., the "Compact" - "Diffuse" categories.)

For each sound tested we conservatively identified one PR delay at which no more (but often considerably less) than 50 per cent "SPLIT" judgments were given by any subject. We used this value to generate the stimuli used in the second series of experiments.

2. Experiments on Interaural Time Difference Discrimination in Probe Sounds with Preceding Conditioning Sounds

In these experiments CD and PR were no longer necessarily identical. For each CD-PR pair we used one value of probe delay τ and attempted to determine a threshold (75 per cent correct) ITD -- whenever this was possible. The listeners' task was to discriminate, in a multiple-level two-alternative forced-choice paradigm, a stimulus with a non-zero and one with a zero ITD. Each threshold estimate, whenever it could be determined, was based on at least 480 trials.

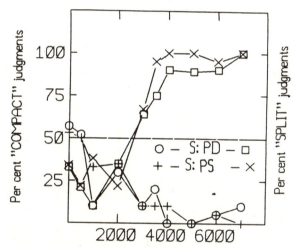

Figure 1. Categorical perception of CD-PR pairs as a function of PR delay. Results of two subjects. The "S"-shaped curves were obtained for the distinction "SPLIT" - "NO SPLIT" percepts, whereas the other two curves for the "COMPACT" - "DIFFUSE" categories.

a. Experiments with band-pass noise bursts.

In these experiments the stimuli were filtered and unfiltered noise bursts. In order to test the notion that the CD and the PR did not need to be identical as long as they bore resemblance to each other in their spectra and envelopes, CD and PR were always independent noise samples. The first experiment in this series replicated one key condition of Zurek's (1980) study in which the CD and the PR were independent 1-ms broad-band noise bursts with a 3-ms echo delay. In agreement with Zurek, we could find no evidence for probe lateralization -- i.e., at a 3-ms τ there was echo suppression.

In the experiments that followed the stimuli were generated by passing the noise through Critical-Band filters and shaping the output with a Gaussian time window. The rms power of all stimuli was held constant. Three center frequencies were tested: 500 Hz (with a 5 ms window length), 1.5 kHz (3 ms), and 4.5 kHz (2 ms). When both the CD and the PR were 1.5-kHz bursts, there was some lateralization at long (6-ms) echo delays but not enough to reach the threshold at any ITD for two subjects. When the PR was a 4.5-kHz burst lateralization of the echo was completely suppressed with either a 4.5-kHz or a 1.5-kHz CD. However, lateralization was measurable with a 0.5-kHz CD. Some lateralization could also be observed when the CD was a 1-ms unfiltered click. Interestingly however, clear lateralization was found when the CD was a high- (4.5-kHz) and the PR a lower-frequency (1.5-kHz) burst. Data of one of two subjects are shown in Fig. 2; those of the other were nearly identical. These data suggest that if the probe has spectral energy not contained in the conditioner, the echo will not be suppressed, unless the energy of the CD is concentrated in a region of the spectrum just below that of the PR. This is to say that echo suppression spreads upward in the spectrum, just as masking does.

b. Experiments with comb-filtered and band-pass/band-reject noise bursts.

The effect of spectral commonality can be best studied with noise stimuli having periodic spectra (comb-filtered white noise) -- a type of spectral structure that arises naturally in a reverberant environment (Zurek, 1980). In particular, we investigated one extreme case in which both the CD and the PR were (independent) noise bursts having spectra with the same

152

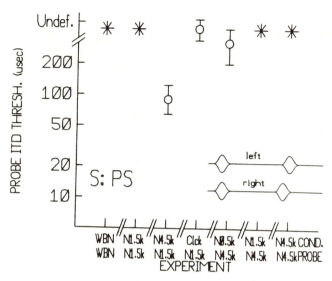

Figure 2. Interaural time difference thresholds (in vs) of the probe (PR) for various combinations of conditioner (CD) and probe. "Undef." signifies that the psychometric function did not reach 75 per cent correct for any ITD value and, therefore, the threshold remained undefined. Both CD and PR are bandpass-filtered noise bursts shaped with a Gaussian envelope. The stimuli (CD or PR) making up the conditions shown on the abscissa were: WBN: CD and PR 1-ms bursts of broad-band white noise, N0.5K: 5-ms burst of white noise filtered at 0.5 kHz, N1.5K: 3-ms burst of white noise filtered at 1.5 kHz, N4.5K: 2-ms burst of white noise filtered at 4.5 kHz, Clck: 1-ms unfiltered square pulse. The probe delays (τ) for the various pairs were: WBN-WBN: 3 ms, N1.5k-N1.5k: 6 ms, N4.5k-N1.5k: 2 ms, Clck-N1.5k: 3 ms, N0.5k-N1.5k: 6 ms, N1.5k-N4.5k: - ms, N4.5k-N4.5k: 2 ms. Results of two subjects.

period, except that one of them was harmonic and the other inharmonic. Since spectral peaks in the CD correspond to notches in the PR and vice versa, we expected to find no echo suppression in this condition and our data confirmed this expectation. When, however, we high-pass filtered both the CD and the PR above 2.5 kHz, lateralization was obliterated. These results strongly suggest that a lack of spectral coherence of the CD and the PR will allow the echo to be perceived only if the spectral singularities of each sound can be peripherally resolved. A further evidence stressing the importance of peripheral frequency analysis in echo suppression was offered by another experiment in which the CD was a brief (10-ms) band-reject white noise burst with a steep spectral notch between 0.5 and 3.5 kHz. When the PR was a band-pass noise with energy between 2.5 and 3.5 kHz, clear lateralization was observed: The threshold obtained was about identical (60 to 95 us) to that observed for the probe burst without the diotic conditioner present. When, on the other hand, the PR center frequency was shifted to 1.3 kHz, the lateralization threshold, albeit still measurable (about 150 us), was much higher than the less than 33-us threshold obtained when the PR was presented alone. Results of one of two subjects are shown in Fig. 3; those of the other subject were essentially identical.

DISCUSSION

Our results indicate that the precedence effect persists as long as there is a spectral overlap between the first sound and the echo. However, the data also make it clear that the spectral overlap is not to be interpreted in the physical sense but, rather, in terms of frequency selectivity in the peripheral auditory system. Spectral singularities not shared by the conditioner and the echo will allow the echo to be detected but only if these singularities can be resolved. Further, suppression of an echo appears to possess features similar to masking in that it spreads upwards but not downwards.

A similar dependence of binaural interaction on peripheral frequency analysis has been reported for binaural fusion (Scharf et al., 1976; Ebata and Sone, 1968) and for saturation effects in lateralization (Hafter and Buell, 1985). From the point of view of the auditory system, such a dependence makes a profound sense: An echo should be suppressed only if in reality it is the reflection of a sound that has been first heard directly. It is also comforting to see that a broad-band sound object will be more effective in suppressing higher-frequency (transient) echoes which could best interfere with the perceived direct source of the sound (Blauert 1984). While one could feel tempted to assign suppression to monaural forward masking, we

154

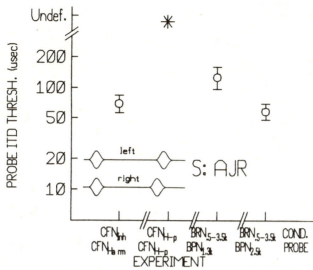

Figure 3. As in Fig. 2, except that in the two
leftmost conditions both CD and PR are comb-
filtered noise bursts shaped with a Gaussian envelope, whereas in the two other conditions the
CD is a burst of white noise with a steep notch
in its spectrum between 0.5 and 3.5 kHz and the
PR is a sharp bandpass-filtered noise burst.
The precise stimuli (CD or PR) were: CFN_{Harm}:
5-ms comb-filtered noise burst with a cosine
spectral envelope having the filter poles at
harmonics of 1.5 kHz, CFN_{Inh}: Same but with a
spectral envelope having the filter zeroes at
harmonics of 1.5 kHz, CFN_{H-p}: CD and PR as before but both harmonic and inharmonic comb-
filtered noise bursts high-pass filtered at 2.5
kHz, $BRN_{.5-3.5k}$: 10-ms white noise with a spectral notch between .5 and 3.5 kHz, $BPN_{1.3k}$: 3-ms
white noise 1/3-octave bandpass filtered at 1.3
kHz, $BPN_{2.5k}$: 2-ms white noise 1/3-octave
bandpass filtered at 2.5 kHz. The probe delays
(τ) for the various pairs were: $CFN_{Harm}-CFN_{Inh}$:
4 ms, CFN_{H-p}(Harm)$-CFN_{H-p}$(Inharm): 3 ms, $BRN_{.5-}$
$_{3.5k}-BPN_{1.3k}$: 6 ms, $BRN_{.5-3.5k}-BPN_{2.5k}$: 4 ms.

were unable to find evidence of temporal masking in control tests where the conditioner and the probe were
presented monaurally. Thus, echo suppression is a
situation in which the <u>presence</u> of the probe is clearly
detectable but its spatial position cannot be

155

recognized. Thus, if we were to propose that masking accounts for echo suppression, then it would become imperative to expand the definition of peripheral temporal masking.

While the present data are preliminary in nature, they clearly point to the necessity to re-evaluate contemporary models of binaural interaction in a way consistent with peripheral processing of signals rather than with their raw physical reality.

ACKNOWLEDGMENTS

This research has been supported by the Veterans Administration, the Deutsche Forschungsgemeinschaft, and by Travel Fellowship No. 413/85/TT-A6 from NATO.

REFERENCES

Barron, M. (1971). The subjective effects of first reflections in concert halls -- the need for lateral reflections. J. Sound Vibr., 15, 475-494.
Blauert, J. (1984). Spatial hearing. Cambridge, Mass.: MIT Press.
Ebata, M., & Sone, N. (1968). Binaural fusion of tone bursts different in frequency. Proc. Sixth Intern. Congr. Acoust. (Tokyo) , A-3-7.
Gaskell, H. (1983). The precedence effect. Hear. Res., 11, 277-305.
Haas, H. (1951). Ueber den Einfluss eines Einfachechos an die Hoersamkeit von Sprache. Acustica, 1, 49-58.
Hafter, E. R., & Buell, T. N. (1985). The importance of transients for maintaining the separation of signals in auditory space. In O. Marin & M. Posner (Eds.), Attention and performance (vol. XI, pp. 337-354). Hillsdale, NJ: L. Erlbaum.
Lehmann, P., & Wilkens, H. (1980). Zusammenhang subjektiver Beurteilungen von Konzertsälen mit raumakustischer Kriterien. Acustica, 45, 256-268.
Scharf, B., Florentine, M., & Meiselman, C. H. (1976). Critical band in auditory lateralization. Sens. Proc., 1, 109-126.
Wallach, H., Newman, E. B., & Rosenzweig, M. R. (1949). The precedence effect in sound localization. Am. J. Psychol., 57, 315-336.
Zurek, P. M. (1980). Measurement of binaural echo suppression. J. Acoust. Soc. Amer., 66, 1750-1757.

GESTALT PRINCIPLES AND MUSIC PERCEPTION

Ernst Terhardt
Institute for Electroacoustics, Technische Universität,
P.O.Box 202420, D-8000 München 2, F.R. Germany

Retracing the views of early Gestalt psychologists, a
concept of Gestalt perception is suggested that is more
stringent and coherent than approaches utilized to date.
In particular, the contrast between "cognitive psychology" and "psychophysics" disappears in the concept, which
is called Hierarchical Processing of Categories (HPC).
Its main assumptions are: (1) that Gestalt perception is
entirely depent on contourized and categorized sensory
representations of external objects; and (2) that perception is organized in hierarchical layers in each of
which basically one and the same type of processing goes
on, i.e., (re-)categorization. With regard to auditory
perception, it is pointed out that on the most peripheral level it is the spectral pitches which are analogous
to primary visual contours, while virtual pitches are
equivalent to "secondary", or "illusory" visual contours. Perception of musical tones, chords, and melodies
is discussed in the light of the HPC concept.

INTRODUCTION

For the scientific study of complex sound perception
music appears to be a particularly promising type of auditory stimulus, for the following reasons:
(1) Music can be supposed to be intuitively created
and performed to appeal to several (or even many) principles of audititory perception that are more or less
general and universal.
(2) Tonal music essentially is made up of relatively
simple and well-defined acoustic signals (i.e., the
tones of musical instruments, and the human voice),
which for theoretical purposes can be idealized as simple periodic sound waves with well-defined oscillation
frequencies; therefore, studying the perception of tonal
music is well suited to cover and reconcile both the
psychoacoustic and cognitive aspects of perception.
(3) With tonal music, there exist a wealth of practical and conceptual experiences as well as theoretical

157

concepts that provide many useful hints to general principles of perception.

To date there is a wide conceptual gap between "psychophysics" and "cognititive psychology"; so there is no easy way to the reconciliation mentioned. Therefore this paper is concerned with developing a concept of perception that provides a framework both to the psychophysical and the cognitive types of perception. That concept is based on the classical Gestalt approach. The Gestalt pioneers were clearly aware of the impact of musical structures on Gestalt perception (e.g., Ehrenfels, 1890; Köhler, 1933). So the present paper actually just picks up a line of development which already had existed decades ago, introducing some recent aspects and concepts such as that of information.

THE HPC CONCEPT OF GESTALT PERCEPTION

To reduce the vagueness that to date is in the Gestalt approach, we may begin with asking "What is particular about Gestalt perception as opposed to sensory perception in general?" As it turns out, the answer to that question is a key to a concept which indeed unifies "psychophysics" and "cognitive psychology". That miracle is achieved by remembering that, at least in vision, "Gestalts" are associated with, and dependent on, contours. We ordinarily call a perceptual process "Gestalt perception", if the perceived sensory object on a most peripheral level already is represented in a contourized manner. Indeed, the most prominent function of the peripheral visual system is contourization.

The next thing to be recalled is that contourization is equivalent to discretization which includes a decision process. Contourization may even be regarded as an essential element of categorization, in particular when the latter is understood in an implicit sense, i.e., without explicit labeling. Here it becomes apparent how the Gestalt approach gets its unifying effect: Instead of conceptualizing categorization as a "central", phenomenon, the stringent Gestalt approach suggested here implies that categorization (in a generalized sense of the term) is a phenomenon that can be observed on a most peripheral (i.e., "low") level of perceptual processing, and on higher levels anyway, of course. The message of that concept is, that "cognition begins at the very periphery".

From that conclusion it is only a little step to the next, i.e., that Gestalt perception basically is just a series of hierarchically ordered operations that are of one and the same basic type, namely, categorization. The "model" of Gestalt perception such specified has one well defined input, i.e., the stimulus, but many outputs on different levels of processing. This in fact appears to be a realistic feature of the hypothetical system. Fig.1 illustrates the concept, which may be called the HPC-concept: Hierarchical Processing of Categories.

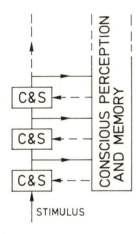

Figure 1. Concept of Gestalt perception: Hierarchical Processing of Categories (HPC). C&S = contourization & synthesis = categorization.

Figure 2. Illustration of categorization on three levels: (1) parts of flower; (2) flower; (3) female face.

Fig.2 illustrates the contourization-plus-synthesis effect in three different layers: On the lowest level, black lines are seen as contours, although the lines as such have a finite width, i.e., are two-dimensional; synthesis on that level yields perception of the stalk, leaves, etc., i.e. parts of a flower. On the next level, the units just mentioned are organized, i.e., "contourized and synthesized" into the Gestalt of a flower. Finally, on the third level, the same units as before are "contourized and synthesized" in an even more abstract manner, yielding a female face.

Gestalt perception is more or less equivalent to "finding out what a particular stimulus means". Therefore, the HPC concept is particularly attractive from the aspect of information acquisition. Information essentially is dependent on decision processes; and decisions are equivalent to discretization and categorization. In other words, discretization and categorization on any level are equivalent to acquisition of information. Contourization, discretization, and categorization are elementary steps of abstraction. Therefore we may say as well that abstraction begins at the very periphery. Let us in the following sections throw a glance on the processing of music in various C&S layers, beginning with the lowest one.

SPECTRAL PITCHES AND VIRTUAL PITCHES:
THE PRIMARY AND SECONDARY CONTOURS IN HEARING

Application of the HPC concept to hearing, in particular hearing of music, requires a solid concept of what auditory parameters play the role that corresponds to primary visual contour. The answer is: It is the spectral pitches (i.e., pitches directly corresponding to spectral components) which are equivalent to primary visual contours. While in the virtual-pitch theory the spectral pitches have been shown already many years ago to play a key role in pitch perception of complex signals (Terhardt, 1972; 1974), it was only recently that the definite conclusion emerged that the spectral pitches play a much more universal role, i.e., that of "primary auditory contours" (Terhardt, 1986a). That conclusion is based, among others, on the following arguments:

(1) Spectral pitches are not obtained "just by Fourier analysis" but are extracted from a sound spectrum which is continuous both in frequency and time; i.e., spectral-pitch formation requires a decision process (cf. Terhardt, 1986a,b).

(2) Spectral pitches show perceptual effects similar to visual contour perception, in particular, dependence of conscious perception on stimulus contrast, and subjective aftereffects (Zwicker, 1964; Viemeister, 1980; Summerfield et al., 1984).

(3) By appropriately simulating auditory extraction of spectral pitches from speech and music, one can show that the information conveyed by the stimuli is to a large extent represented by the spectral-pitch pattern alone (Heinbach, 1986).

Virtual pitches have been explained as a product of "inference" from spectral pitches (Terhardt, 1972; 1974). That conclusion fits perfectly into the HPC concept: While the first C&S step (cf. Fig.1) is spectral-pitch formation, virtual-pitch formation is the second. Virtual pitch can readily be understood as an auditory equivalent of "illusory contour" (cf., e.g., Petry & Meyer, 1986. The term "virtual contour" would appear more appropriate, by the way).

STEADY UNITS OF MUSIC: TONES AND CHORDS

A musical "flow", consisting of successive tones and harmonies, is "contourized" into subunits such as melodic phrases, rhythm patterns, and, on the lowest level of temporal segmentation, tones and chords. Obviously, the HPC concept enables appropriate description of these aspects. Rhythmic contourization, i.e. segmentation into individual quasi-steady elements, follows to a large extent simple laws which can be modeled in a "psychophysical" sense (Terhardt & Schütte, 1976; Morton et al., 1976; Köhlmann, 1985). Here again it becomes apparent that the HPC concept readily unifies "psychophysical" and "cognitive" sensory performances.

Since a musical tone ordinarily includes a number of spectral components which can be heard as individual spectral pitches (on the lowest C&S level, cf. Fig.1), and moreover produces a number of virtual pitches (on the next higher level), a single, isolated musical tone is far from being an indivisible elementary unit but rather perceptually is a complex Gestalt, formed by "primary" as well as "secondary contours" (spectral and virtual pitches). Fig.3 shows a recent experimental verification of that type of Gestalt. The ordinate of each diagram shows the relative number of pitch matches falling into a small frequency interval whose center frequency is at the abscissa. Pure tones were matched in pitch to harmonic complex tones with fundamental frequency f_b (For details see Terhardt et al., 1986). The

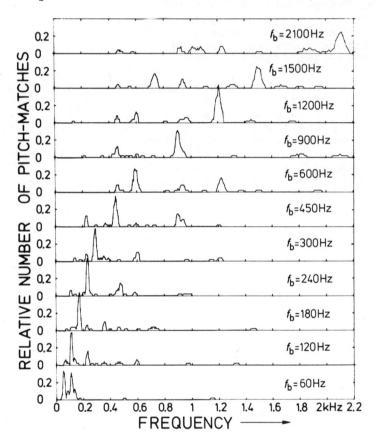

Figure 3. Pitch-matching histograms of harmonic complex tones with fundamental frequencies f_b (from Terhardt et al., 1986). Abscissa: frequency of matching tone (pure tone).

histogram maxima indicate perceived pitches, while no
distinction is made between spectral and virtual pitches.

AMBIGUITY, SIMILARITY, AND HARMONY

The pitch ambiguity of musical tones which becomes
apparent on the corresponding C&S level is a key phenomenon for understanding the basic musical phenomenon of
tonal affinity (octave equivalence, fifth- and fourth
similarity). On that basis, the similarity of tones
whose fundamental frequencies are in a ratio of small
integers is readily explained by the identity of some of
the pitches included in the respective pitch patterns.

On the C&S levels of spectral and virtual pitches,
the HPC model accounts for the Gestalt percept of any
steady tonal stimulus and therefore includes musical
chords as well. In particular, perception of "roots" is
readily explained (Terhardt, 1974; 1978). Since the root
effect and tonal affinity are just two main aspects of
musical harmony, one can say that the present Gestalt
view provides a promising basis to the understanding of
those complex phenomena of tonal music (cf. Terhardt et
al., 1986; Parncutt, 1986).

DISTORTION

On the basis of Gestalt representation of musical
tones, it is moreover easy to understand and evaluate
the impacts of the so-called pitch-shifts (cf. Terhardt,
1972; 1974). In the HPC concept, those shifts (that are
assigned to mutual interaction of spectral components in
the peripheral ear) can be seen as just an auditory
example of "distortion", i.e., a kind of artifact of the
peripheral sensory system. Visual examples of that type
of distortion are seen in "geometric illusions", i.e.,
discrepancies in apparent length of lines, bending of
contours that actually are straight, etc. With respect
to music perception, it is apparent that pitch shifts
should significantly affect intonation. In the virtual-
pitch theory, in particular the intonation of the octave
interval is explained as a consequence of the pitch
shifts (for details, see Terhardt, 1978). The present
HPC concept naturally incorporates that explanation but

163

provides a more general frame to it. Since the explanation is based on individual learning effects (which determine the kind of contourization and synthesis in each HPC-layer), one should expect that the magnitudes of pitch shift and of octave enlargement that can be measured in completely independent experiments, should be individually correlated.

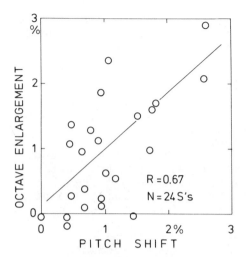

Figure 4. Statistical relationship between individual octave enlargement and pitch shift effects (the latter induced by partially masking low-pass noise), in 24 Ss. Note significant correlation of the two effects.

We have recently carried out systematic measurements with 10 subjects, to test that hypothesis. Fig.4 shows the results. While we were not able to find a straight functional relationship between the two phenomena, there is however a highly significant statistical correlation that supports the theoretical interpretations mentioned.

MUSIC PERCEPTION ON HIGHER LEVELS

While description of isolated tones and chords requires the first two C&S layers, the next higher level of complexity is attained when a melodic phrase is perceived. This requires taking into account the role of time as another Gestalt dimension, and of short-term memory. Dowling & Fujitani (1971) have pointed out that in melody perception pitch plays a role in two different ways: First, the sequence of pitches defines a "pitch contour" (in the sense of ups and downs through time); second, the precise musical intervals of pitch are significant, as well.

The above finding that musical tones are represented by pitch patterns rather than single pitches somewhat modifies that description, as illustrated in Fig.5. The simple melody (CDEFGEFDC) composed of harmonic complex tones is shown. The most prominent pitch of each tone, corresponding to its fundamental frequency, is shown by large dots, while the most prominent other pitches are represented by smaller dots. In a sense, that sequence of pitch patterns is analogous to the flower shown in Fig.2: As the flower is made up of "sub-Gestalts" (stalk, leaves, etc.), the melody is made up of pitch patterns. Those pitch patterns, and their temporal arrangement, provide a "psychophysical" basis for extraction of the essential higher-level components of melody, namely, pitch-pattern contour, harmony, and rhythm.

An excellent survey on most aspects of music perception is provided by Deutsch (1982).

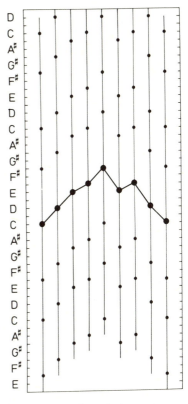

Figure 5. Simplified pitch-pattern-contour of the melody CDEFGEFDC, composed of harmonic complex tones. Large dots: main pitches; small dots: alternative pitches. Note similarity of pitch patterns having pitches in common (e.g. C and G).

REFERENCES

Deutsch, D. (1982). The Psychology of Music. Academic Press, New York, London.
Dowling, W.J., and Fujitani, D.A. (1971). Contour, interval and pitch recognition in memory for melodies. J. Acoust. Soc. Am., 49, 524-531.

Terhardt   -   Gestalt Principles

Ehrenfels, C. (1890). Über Gestaltqualitäten. Viertel-
jahresschrift für wissenschaftliche Philosophie, 14.
Heinbach, W. (1986). Untersuchung einer gehörbezogenen
Spektralanalyse mittels Resynthese, in: DAGA 86,
Fortschritte der Akustik, Bad Honnef, 453-456.
Köhler, W. (1933). Gestalt Psychology. New York.
Köhlmann, M. (1985). Rhythmische Segmentierung von
Sprach- und Musiksignalen und ihre Nachbildung mit
einem Funktionsschema. Acustica, 56, 193-204.
Morton,J., Marcus, S., and Frankish, C. (1976). Percep-
tual centers. Psychol. Rev., 83, 405-408.
Parncutt, R. (1986). Sensory bases of harmony in Western
music. Dissertation, Univ. of New England, Dept. of
Psychol., Armidale, N.S.W., Australia.
Petry, S. and Meyer, G.E. (1986). Adelphi International
Conference on Illusory Contours: A Report on the
Conference. Perception & Psychophysics, 39, 210-221.
Summerfield, Q., Haggard, M., Foster, J., and Gray, S.
(1984). Perceiving vowels from uniform spectra: Pho-
netic exploration of an auditory aftereffect.
Perception & Psychophysics, 35, 203-213.
Terhardt, E. (1972). Zur Tonhöhenwahrnehmung von Klängen
I/II. Acustica, 26, 173-199.
Terhardt, E. (1974). Pitch, consonance, and harmony.
J. Acoust. Soc. Am., 55, 1061-1069.
Terhardt, E. (1978). Psychoacoustic evaluation of musi-
cal sounds. Perception & Psychophysics, 23, 483-492.
Terhardt, E. (1986a). Psychophysics of audio signal pro-
cessing and the role of pitch in speech, in: Work-
shop on the Psychophysics of Speech Perception,
Inst. Phonetics, University of Utrecht, Utrecht, NL.
Terhardt, E. (1986b). Pitch perception and frequency
analysis, in: 6th FASE Symposium, Sopron, Hungary.
Terhardt, E. & Schütte, H. (1976). Akustische Rhythmus-
wahrnehmung: Subjektive Gleichmäßigkeit. Acustica,
35, 122-126.
Terhardt, E., Stoll, G., Schermbach, R., and Parncutt,
R. (1986). Tonhöhenmehrdeutigkeit, Tonverwandt-
schaft und Identifikation von Sukzessivintervallen.
Acustica, in print.
Viemeister, N. (1980). Adaptation of masking, in: G. van
den Brink & F. A. Bilsen, eds., Psychophysical, Phy-
siological, and Behavioural Studies in Hearing,
Delft University Press (Netherlands).
Zwicker, E. (1964). "Negative afterimage" in hearing.
J. Acoust. Soc. Am., 36, 2413-2415.

A PULSE RIBBON MODEL OF PERIPHERAL AUDITORY PROCESSING

Roy D. Patterson
MRC Applied Psychology Unit, 15 Chaucer Road,
    Cambridge CB2 2EF, England

This paper outlines a 'pulse ribbon' model of
hearing that attempts to provide a bridge between the
output of the cochlea as observed in single fibers of
animals and the sensations that humans hear when
stimulated by complex sounds. The first two stages
simulate the operation of the cochlea with a 24-channel
filter bank and 24 pulse generators. Together they
convert a sound into a set of 24 pulse streams, collectively referred to as a pulse ribbon. The remaining three
stages transform the initial pulse ribbon into 'aligned',
'spiral' and 'cylindrical' pulse ribbons. The transformations are intended to characterise phase perception,
pitch perception and timbre perception, respectively.
Together they illustrate the kind of neural processing
required to convert the output of the cochlea into
auditory sensations. A set of experiments on monaural
phase perception was performed to determine the
appropriate properties for the phase transformation.
They show that we hear between-channel phase changes as
well as within-channel envelope changes.

COCHLEA SIMULATION

The operation of the model is illustrated in Fig. 1
with the aid of a periodic sound consisting of 31 equal-
amplitude harmonics of 125 Hz. Successive harmonics are
phase shifted by an ever decreasing amount to produce a
'monotonic-phase' wave (Fig. 1a) in which some of the
low-frequency energy arrives before the main pulse and
some of the high-frequency energy arrives after the main
pulse. The remaining five subfigures show the products
of the five stages of the model operating on this
monotonic-phase wave. The first stage performs a
spectral analysis using a 24-channel filter bank and the
Roex(p) auditory-filter shape of Patterson et al (1982).
The outputs of six channels are shown in Fig. 1b. The
second stage simulates the neural transduction process by
converting the waves into pulse streams -- one for each
channel. Together these stages simulate the operation

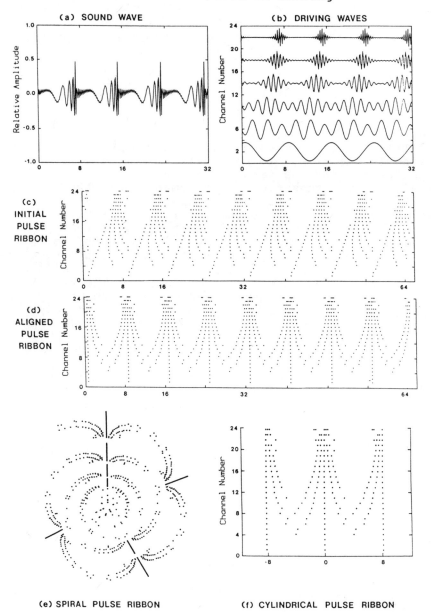

Figure 1. Transforming a monotonic-phase wave(a) into aligned(d), spiral(e) and cylindrical(f) pulse ribbons to simulate phase, pitch and timbre perception.

of the cochlea. In response to a sound they produce an
ordered set of 24 pulse streams referred to as the
'initial pulse ribbon' (Fig. 1c).

The filter outputs are referred to as driving waves
because they determine the temporal pattern of the pulses
in the pulse streams. The driving waves flowing from
filters centred in the region of the first three harmonics are essentially sinusoidal in shape but those
flowing from filters centred above the third harmonic are
more like amplitude modulated sinusoids. The 'carrier'
frequency is approximately the centre frequency of the
filter and the 'modulation' frequency is the repetition
rate of the input signal. The modulation depth increases
with centre frequency as the filter broadens and the
attenuation of adjacent harmonics decreases. For the
moment, the phase-lag introduced by the cochlea is
ignored. The progressive delay in the peak of the
modulator from channel to channel reflects the phase
spectrum of the stimulus rather than the phase characteristic of the cochlea. Phase-locked auditory-nerve fibers
generate streams of pulses that preserve information
concerning the times between the positive peaks in the
wave. For the moment, the stochastic properties of
neural transduction are ignored. Sinusoidal driving
waves like those in the lower portion of Fig. 1b are
converted into regular pulse streams with one pulse per
cycle as shown at the bottom of Fig. 1c. Modulated
driving waves like those at the top of Fig. 1b are
converted into modulated pulse streams in which bursts of
pulses are regularly separated by gaps as shown at the
top of Fig. 1c. The period of the carrier frequency is
equal to the time between pulses within a burst and the
period of the modulation frequency is equal to the time
between corresponding pulses in successive bursts.

Collectively, the 24 pulse streams are referred to
as the 'initial pulse ribbon' and it provides an overview
of the information flowing up the auditory system from
the cochlea. The horizontal dimension of the ribbon is
'time since the sound reached the eardrum'; the vertical
dimension is filter centre frequency on a roughly logarithmic frequency scale. If the brightness of each
channel were varied to reflect its current amplitude, the
initial pulse ribbon would be like a spectrogram with an
expanded time scale. For a periodic sound, the pattern
repeats on the ribbon and the rate of repetition corresponds to the pitch of the sound. Timbre is assumed to

correspond to the pattern of pulses within the cycle. The pattern has a spectral dimension (vertical) as in traditional hearing models, but it also has a temporal dimension and this added dimension enables the ribbon to represent phase-related timbre changes. The initial pulse ribbon, then, is a device for presenting the temporal information and the phase information of the auditory nerve, in a form where we can better appreciate the patterns of information generated by complex sounds. It is not intended to be new or controversial but rather to provide a highly simplified simulation of cochlear processing. The main purpose of the model is to characterise the operations required to convert the initial pulse ribbon into something more like auditory sensations. In the paper it is argued that we only need three transformations -- one for phase alignment, one for pitch extraction and one for timbre stabilisation -- and that each of the transformations is essentially just a mapping of the initial pulse ribbon.

PHASE ALIGNMENT

In 1947 Mathes and Miller showed that we are sensitive to changes in the envelopes of sounds with high harmonics and so proved that the auditory system is not phase deaf. In one sense, this is not surprising; the phase changes that produce audible timbre changes produce changes in the initial pulse ribbon. On the other hand, there are many phase changes that produce changes in the initial pulse ribbon which do not produce timbre changes. The monotonic-phase wave of Fig. 1 is a case in point; it sounds like a pulse train even though the wave has a relatively low peak factor and the initial pulse ribbon has a pronounced slant. This illustrates the double-sided problem that a phase model must solve; it must remove variations in the initial pulse ribbon that we do not hear while preserving those that we do hear, and some form of this problem exists for any model that uses the pattern as well as the rate of neural activity in the auditory nerve. Broadly speaking, the existing data suggest that we hear a phase change if it produces a significant change in the envelope of one or more of the driving waves, and we do not hear a phase change if it only produces a shift of one driving wave relative to another in time. For convenience, a change in the envelope of a particular driving wave is referred to as a 'within-channel' phase change and a change in the

170

relative phase of two driving waves is referred to as a
'between-channel' phase change. A series of experiments
was performed to determine the limits of monaural phase
perception and to see if it could be sensibly described
in terms of pulse ribbons. The stimuli were sets of 31
equal-amplitude harmonics of a fundamental, F; all that
varied within or across experiments was the phase spectrum of the stimulus. When all of the components start
in cosine phase the wave is a pulse train. It has a
characteristic buzzy timbre and the listeners' task was
to discriminate the cosine-phase wave from one with a
different phase spectrum on the basis of a change in
timbre. Pitch and loudness were randomised over a small
range to ensure a timbre judgement.

A. Within-Channel Envelope Changes: 'Alternating-
phase' waves were used to introduce a small bump in the
driving wave envelope near its minimum while at the same
time preserving the alignment of envelope peaks across
channels. All of the odd harmonics were in zero phase
while all of the even harmonics were in some other fixed
phase, D. Figure 2a shows the alternating-phase wave
when D is 40 degrees; when D is 0 the wave is a cosine-
phase wave. As D increases the secondary peak in the
middle of the cycle grows. The wave in Fig. 2a is just
discriminable from a cosine-phase wave when the
fundamental, F, is 125 Hz and the level, L, is 45
dB/component. In the mid- to high-frequency channels of
the filter bank, the secondary peak in the sound wave
causes a local maximum in the envelope of the driving
wave midway between the main envelope peaks (Fig. 2b) and
the size of the local maximum increases with D. When D
is large, the local maxima cause the pulse stream
generators to produce an extra column of pulses in the
initial pulse ribbon and it is these pulses that are
assumed to produce the timbre change. When D is small,
the local maxima do not excite the pulse stream
generators, the pulse ribbon is like that for a cosine-
phase wave, and we do not hear a timbre difference. When
setting up the model, then, the sustained firing rates
were adjusted so that the column of pulses appears in the
ribbon just as D reaches 40 degrees.

When the F is lowered by an octave, the period of
the wave doubles. In this case, the pulse generators
have effectively twice as many pulses to assign to each
cycle of the driving wave and the local maxima appear in
the pulse ribbon at a lower D value. Thus, the model

171

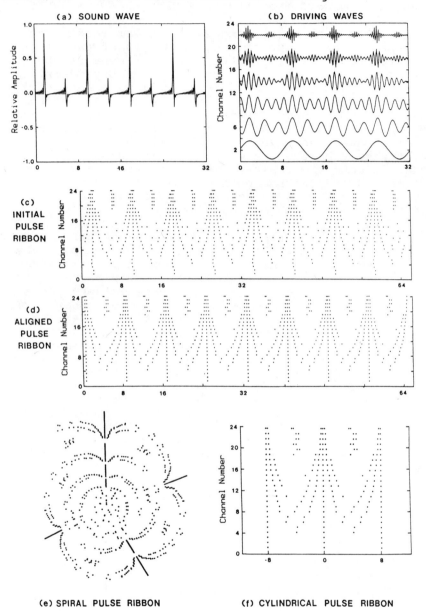

Figure 2. Transforming alternating-phase wave(a) into
aligned(d), spiral(e) and cylindrical(f) pulse ribbons to simulate phase, pitch and timbre perception.

predicts that phase-discrimination threshold will decrease with the pitch of the stimulus, and indeed, we find that fundamentals of 62.5, 125, and 250 Hz produce thresholds of 25, 40, and 51 degrees, respectively. Beyond 250 Hz the discrimination becomes increasingly difficult and above about 400 Hz it is impossible for most listeners. The sustained firing rates of auditory nerve fibers increase with stimulus level which suggests that the sustained rates of the pulse generators in the model should vary with stimulus level. Increasing the model rates causes the local maxima in the driving waves to appear in the pulse ribbon at a lower D value and so the model predicts that phase-discrimination threshold will vary inversely with stimulus level. We found that levels of 25, 45 and 65 dB/component produce thresholds of 64, 45, and 24 degrees when F is 125 Hz and thresholds of 52, 25 and 13 degrees when F is 62.5 Hz. Thus, it would appear that a pulse ribbon model can describe the timbre changes associated with envelope changes in terms of the firing rates of the pulse stream generators.

B. Between-Channel Phase Shifts: The second set of experiments was performed to determine whether the auditory system is indeed deaf to between-channel phase changes. The stimuli were monotonic-phase waves which produce large between-channel phase shifts with minimal envelope changes. The phase spectrum of the starting stimulus was created by calculating the number of auditory-filter bandwidths between one harmonic and the next and rotating the phase of the upper harmonic by 180 degrees for each filter bandwidth (bandwidths from Moore and Glasberg, 1983). The result is a monotonically increasing phase spectrum that decelerates as frequency increases. The remaining stimuli were produced by multiplying the phase spectrum times a scalar that ranged from 1/32 to 32; in the former case the stimulus resembles a cosine-phase wave and in the latter case it is like a random-phase wave. The scalar for the wave in Fig. 1a is 1/2 and it is not discriminable from a cosine-phase wave when F is 125 Hz and L is 45 dB/component. If the scalar is less than about 4, the driving waves associated with monotonic-phase waves have simple envelopes like those of the cosine-phase wave. But there is a progressive delay of the envelope peak from channel to channel as frequency increases, and since the rate of change of phase is inversely related to filter bandwidth, the delay is roughly constant from channel to channel. This is seen most clearly in the initial pulse ribbon (Fig. 1c) where

the slant of the pattern shows the progressive delay.
These stimuli enable us, then, to present a controlled
between-channel phase change with minimal envelope
changes. When L is 45 dB/component, threshold occurs at
scalar values of 0.4, 0.65, and 1.4 for fundamentals of
62.5, 125, and 250 Hz, respectively. When the scalar is
two or less the driving waves produced by monotonic- and
cosine-phase waves are virtually indistinguishable, which
suggests that the auditory system is sensitive to
between-channel phase changes. For a given scalar value,
the slope of the pattern on the initial pulse ribbon is
inversely proportional to F. The threshold slope values
are, respectively, .43, .35, and .38 ms/channel for the
three funamentals; that is, the slope value at threshold
is essentially independent of the pitch. Increasing the
stimulus level of the monotonic-phase waves from 45 to 65
dB/component does not affect threshold; decreasing the
level to 25 dB/component raises threshold by a factor of
2. Overall, however, the data give the impression that
threshold for between-channel phase changes is rather
insensitive to level as well as pitch. There are about
five channels per octave in the filter bank of the model
and so, as a rule of thumb, one can say that we hear
between-channel phase changes as a timbre change when the
slope of the pattern on the pulse ribbon exceeds about 2
ms/octave or about 0.4 ms/channel.

C. A Channel-Alignment Phase Mechanism: One can
remove the pulse ribbon differences associated with
between-channel phase changes that we do not hear, by
aligning the peaks in the driving waves across channels.
In the auditory system this would be a post-cochlear
process and so in the current model it is the pulse
streams rather than the driving waves that are aligned.
For each channel, the times of the envelope peaks are
estimated by locating clusters of pulses in the pulse
stream; the peak time is taken to be the time of the
pulse closest to the midpoint of the cluster. The pulse
streams can then be shifted horizontally to align the
envelope peaks across channels up to a maximum of 2
ms/octave. Despite its simplicity, this channel alignment mechanism characterises the existing data on phase
perception reasonably well. When channel alignment is
applied to the initial pulse ribbon of the monotonic-
phase wave it is converted into the aligned pulse ribbon
shown in Fig. 1d. This is also the pattern produced by a
pulse train before, or after, alignment. So channel
alignment is successful in removing some of the phase

174

changes that we do not hear from the initial pulse
ribbon. The aligned pulse ribbon for the alternating-
phase wave with D equal 40 degrees is shown in Fig. 2c.
No amount of alignment can restore the simple pattern of
the cosine-phase wave when there is more than one cluster
of pulses per period. Some of the pulses have to fall in
the area between the main ribs of the pattern. So
channel alignment is also successful in the sense that it
leaves a phase related change in the pulse ribbon when we
do hear a timbre change.

    D. The Phase-Lag of the Cochlea: Now consider the
implications of channel-phase alignment for perceptual
modelling. When constructing a spectro-temporal model of
hearing, one has to decide what to do about the fact that
low frequencies are delayed in the cochlea. The propa-
gation delay corresponds to a monotonic, decelerating
phase function similar to that of a monotonic-phase wave
with a scalar of unity. Thus, the phase changes
introduced by the cochlea are primarily between-channel
phase changes that tilt the initial pulse ribbon about
twice as much as shown in Fig. 1c. What we would like to
know, then, is whether there are any perceptual
correlates of the phase changes introduced by the
cochlea. That is, 'Does the auditory system compensate
for its phase lag and, if so, how?'. To put the problem
another way: A pulse train causes high-frequency fibers
in the cochlea to fire before low-frequency fibers. If
the auditory system does not compensate for the cochlea's
phase characteristic, then it should be possible to make
a 'super pulse train' by sending the low-frequency energy
into the ear a little ahead of the high frequency energy
and causing all the fibers to fire at the same time.

    The monotonic-phase waves were originally designed
to explore these questions. When the scalar is positive,
low frequencies appear before the pulse in the wave and
high frequencies follow it. When the scalar is negative,
the high frequencies preceed and the low frequencies
follow the pulse. The positive scalar makes the initial
pulse ribbon slope to the right and the negative scalar
makes it slope to the left. The positive scalar produces
waves that tend to cancel the cochlear phase delay and so
we might expect one of them to produce a super pulse
train. The negative-scalar waves accentuate the phase
delay of the cochlea and so they might be expected to
sound less like a pulse-train. The monotonic-phase
experiments were run with both positive and negative

scalar values and there was essentially no difference in phase-discrimination threshold; they both sound like pulse trains until the slope induced by the stimulus is greater than about 2 ms/octave and the direction of the slope does not matter. This suggests that the sensitivity of the auditory system to between-channel phase differences might be characterised by a channel-alignment mechanism which (a) begins by shifting channels to compensate for the phase lag introduced by the cochlea, and (b) goes on to remove between-channel differences introduced by the stimulus up to 2 ms/octave in either direction. Between-channel shifts greater than this are heard as timbre changes. If, in the longer term, this operation proves to be a reasonable interpretation of phase perception, then we can simply omit the phase characteristic of the cochlea in models of auditory perception.

PITCH EXTRACTION AND TIMBRE STABILISATION

A. Pitch Extraction: Periodic sounds produce a repeating pattern on the initial pulse ribbon and, although the frequency information in the stimulus is encoded in both dimensions of the pulse ribbon, the characteristic that corresponds most directly to the pitch of the sound is the repetition rate of the pattern on the ribbon. The periodic sounds of everyday life (e.g. the voiced parts of speech and the notes of music) are like the monotonic- and alternating-phase waves in that they typically contain many harmonically related components and they are rarely simple sinusoids. The components of everyday sounds vary widely in amplitude and phase. Nevertheless, it remains the case that most of the pulse streams associated with everyday periodic sounds are modulated pulse streams, and they typically come in correlated sets, or ribbons. In the current model the purpose of the pitch extractor is to determine the period of the pattern on the pulse ribbon. Place models of pitch perception ignore the timing information in the pulse streams and restrict themselves to the overall rate of activity in each frequency channel. Spectro-temporal models analyse the temporal information to extract both the carrier and the envelope frequencies which are combined to provide the pitch estimate. The envelope frequency also indicates which channels should be combined when analysing sounds with multiple sources since driving waves that come from the same source will have the same envelope frequency. In a spectro-temporal

176

model, then, there is a stage of frequency analysis
beyond that provided by the cochlea -- a temporal
frequency analysis in which the carrier and envelope
frequencies are detected and separated. In any given
channel, the frequency of the carrier ranges over about
an octave from half an octave below to half an octave
above the centre frequency of the channel. The envelope
frequency ranges from the centre frequency of the channel
down to around 5 percent of the centre frequency. Thus,
the periodicity extraction mechanism associated with a
mid-frequency channel must be able to cope with a 4-5
octave range of periods. At the same time, the
individual detectors need to be selective to support
discrimination.

B. The Spiral Processor: One attempt to solve the
problem of temporal frequency analysis is the 'spiral
processor' suggested by Patterson (1985). Briefly, the
temporal regularity observed in the pulse ribbons of
periodic sounds can be converted into position information if the pulse ribbon is wrapped into a logarithmic
spiral, base 2. The spiral processor is described in
detail in Patterson (1986) and Patterson and Nimmo-Smith
(1986); the former includes a description of the implications for the scales and harmony of Western music, the
latter provides a description of the detectors at the
heart of the spiral processor. The following is a brief
description of the processor intended to illustrate how a
spiral mapping of the pulse ribbon can be used to extract
the period of the sound as the pulses flow up the auditory pathway. If, for convenience, we assume that the
temporal window on which the periodicity mechanism
operates is 72 ms in duration, then it will contain 9
cycles of the pulse ribbon shown in Fig. 1d at any one
moment. If this pulse ribbon is wrapped into a spiral on
which duration doubles as the spiral completes each successive circuit, the result is the 9-cycle spiral ribbon
shown in Fig. 1e. The individual time lines in Fig. 1,
that is the threads of the aligned pulse ribbon, become a
set of concentric spirals which are omitted in Fig. 1e to
avoid clutter. The outer strand of the spiral ribbon
contains the regular pulse stream from the filter centred
just below the fundamental of the sound. The inner
strand contains the modulated pulse stream from the 24-th
channel of the filter bank.

The pulses appear at the centre of the spiral as
they are generated and flow along the spiral as time

progresses, dropping off at the outer end 72 ms after
appearing. So time itself does the bookkeeping while the
pulses are being correlated with their neighbours in time
and space. At the moment shown, four of the vertical
bars that mark cycles on the aligned pulse ribbon are
themselves lined up on one spoke of the spiral -- the
vertical spoke emanating from the centre of the spiral.
A unit monitoring this spoke would note above average
activity at this instant and so serve as a detector for
125 Hz. The angles between the spokes are the same no
matter what the note; it is only the orientation of the
spoke pattern that changes when the pitch is altered. As
we raise the pitch of the note, the peaks in the wave,
and the pulses in the streams, get closer together, with
the result that the spokes on the spiral rotate clockwise
as a unit. The pattern completes one full revolution as
the pitch rises an octave. Thus, a set of secondary
units checking for this pattern of spokes at different
orientations would serve to detect and classify the
periodicity of incoming sounds.

C. Timbre Stabilisation: The pulse patterns produced by successive cycles of a periodic wave are highly
correlated. The timbre of the sound is coded in the
pulse pattern and so to obtain the best estimate of the
timbre in the statistical sense one should somehow bring
these successive estimates together and 'average' them.
In the pulse ribbon model, once the pitch of the source
is known, a stabilised timbre pattern can be constructed
by wrapping the aligned pulse ribbon around a cylinder
whose circumference is the period of the original sound.
In this case, successive cycles of the ribbon fall on top
of each other. In a stochastic version of the model,
where some of the pulses are omitted on each cycle, the
cylindrical mapping generates a summary, or average,
pattern that provides a 'best estimate' of the timbre of
the sound. The timbre pattern for the alternating-phase
wave is shown in Fig. 2f. For convenience, a planar
display is used as if the cylindrical ribbon had been
slit down the back and flattened out. A complete cycle
is shown both to the left and right of the moment of
coalescence to make the cyclic aspect of the pattern
readily apparent. The column of pulses midway through
the cycle is assumed to give the sound its distinctive
timbre. A place model that integrates across the
temporal dimension of the ribbon would obscure this
feature.

178

If the current pitch estimate from the spiral processor is fed forward to control the diameter of the
cylinder and cause it to expand and contract as the pitch
falls and rises, then the timbre pattern will remain
stable as the pitch varies over a limited range. The
image shrinks or expands with the period of the sound but
the pattern does not vary. The timbre patterns emerge
and fade on the cylindrical pulse ribbon as the sound
proceeds. If the sound is only stationary for a few
cycles the timbre pattern will only appear for a moment
and it will be blurred. If the sound is stationary for a
longer period the definition of the pattern will improve
over time up to about 70 ms. Thus, the cylindrical pulse
ribbon can be expected to exhibit a reasonable form of
temporal integration. Finally, with regard to speech
perception, the pulse ribbon model suggests that pitch is
not just one of many speech features. Rather, it is a
key feature that makes it possible to stabilise the
timbre of the voiced parts of speech and so extract the
speech features more effectively.

REFERENCES

Mathes, R.C., and Miller, R.L. (1947). Phase effects in
    monaural perception, J. Acoust. Soc. Am., 18, 780-
    797.
Moore, B.C.J., and Glasberg, B.R. (1983). Suggested
    formulae for calculating auditory-filter bandwidths
    and excitation patterns, J. Acoust. Soc. Am., 74,
    750-753.
Patterson, R.D. (1985). A temporal model of pitch
    perception based on spiral periodicity detection, J.
    Acoust. Soc. Am., 77, S50.
Patterson, R.D. (1986). Spiral detection of periodicity
    and the spiral form of musical scales, Psychology of
    Music, 14, 44-61.
Patterson, R.D., Nimmo-Smith, I., Weber, D.L. and Milroy,
    R. (1982). The deterioration of hearing with age:
    Frequency selectivity, the critical ratio, the
    audiogram, and speech threshold, J. Acoust. Soc.
    Am., 72, 1788-1803.
Patterson, R.D., and Nimmo-Smith, I. (1986). Thinning
    periodicity detectors for modulated pulse streams,
    in: Auditory Frequency Selectivity, B.C.J. Moore and
    R.D. Patterson, eds., Plenum, New York.

THE PERCEPTION OF INHARMONIC COMPLEX TONES

Brian C. J. Moore
Department of Experimental Psychology, University of
Cambridge, Downing Street, Cambridge CB2 3EB, U.K.

When a single low partial in a harmonic complex
tone is shifted progressively in frequency from its
harmonic value, the pitch of the whole complex (residue
pitch) shifts with it, in a proportional manner, until
the shift exceeds a certain value. Beyond that, the
pitch shift is less than proportional and eventually
declines. The mechanism determining the pitch of
complex tones apparently rejects components which are
sufficiently mistuned. A component which is
sufficiently mistuned also tends to be heard as a
separate component, standing out from the complex as a
whole. The present paper considers whether these two
perceptual effects reflect the same underlying process.
Thresholds for hearing a mistuned harmonic as standing
out from a complex tone decrease as the duration of the
stimulus increases. The degree to which a partial can
be mistuned before it makes a reduced contribution to
residue pitch also decreases with increasing duration,
but not to the same extent. For long-duration tones
and for moderate degrees of mistuning (3-4%) the
mistuned harmonic is clearly heard as a separate tone,
but at the same time it can make a strong contribution
to the pitch of the complex as a whole, indicating a
form of "duplex perception". Finally, it is
demonstrated that, when subjects compare the pitches of
complex tones with common harmonics, they do not simply
compare the pitches of individual components; rather,
judgements are made on the basis of residue pitch.

INTRODUCTION

When a low partial in a harmonic complex tone is
shifted in frequency from its harmonic value, the pitch
of the whole tone (residue pitch) shifts slightly in
the same direction as the shift in frequency of the
partial (Moore et al., 1985a). For complex tones 410
ms in duration, the shift in residue pitch is almost
directly proportional to the shift in the frequency of
the partial for shifts up to about 3%, but for shifts
greater than about 4% the shift in residue pitch

180

usually declines. This is illustrated in fig. 1, which shows the sum of the pitch shifts for the first six harmonics, averaged for three subjects and three fundamental frequencies (fo = 100, 200 and 400 Hz).

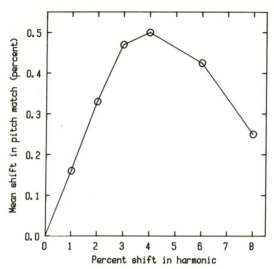

Figure 1. The shift in residue pitch produced by shifting the frequency of a single harmonic, as a function of the percent shift in the harmonic, summed for the first six harmonics.

The detailed pattern of results can vary considerably from one subject to another, and from one harmonic to another. Moore et al. (1985a) suggested that, when the nth harmonic (with frequency fn) is shifted, the initial slope in a plot like that of fig. 1 gives a measure of the pitch dominance or weight, Wn, of that harmonic. For a given complex tone, several harmonics make a significant contribution to the pitch of the complex, but the dominant harmonics usually lie within the first six. Notice that, for shifts up to 3%, the sum of the shifts in residue pitch is almost equal to the percentage shift in each harmonic (see fig. 1), i.e. the sum of the weights, Wn, is one. This suggests that the residue pitch, P, of an m-component complex sound can be predicted as a weighted sum of information derived from the individual components:

$$P = \sum_{n=1}^{n=m} Wn fn/n$$

181

A comparison of the pitch-dominance results with those of an earlier experiment (Moore et al., 1984) revealed that the dominant harmonics were those whose frequency DLs were smallest when presented within the context of the complex tone. This leads to an explanation for why the dominant harmonics usually lie around 3-5 times the fundamental frequency for fundamentals in the range 100-400 Hz. For sinusoids in isolation, frequency DLs, expressed as a proportion of center frequency, improve as frequency increases up to about 2 kHz (Moore, 1973). However, for individual harmonics within complex tones, frequency DLs worsen markedly when the harmonics are no longer resolvable, i.e., when the harmonic number exceeds about six (Moore et al., 1984). Hence, the dominant harmonics are the highest ones which are well resolved, i.e., the third to fifth.

The pattern of results illustrated in fig. 1 suggests that the pitch mechanism has a way of rejecting components which are sufficiently mistuned. This could be achieved by a "harmonic sieve" of the type proposed by Duifhuis et al. (1982), or by modified versions of the pitch theories of Terhardt (1979) or Goldstein (1973) in which the central processor is "told" to "expect" more than one complex tone. Finally, it would be possible to account for the rejection of mistuned harmonics with a time-place model of the type proposed by Moore (1982) and Moore and Glasberg (1986). In this model, a central processor searches for common neural inter-spike intervals (ISIs) across neurons with different characteristic frequencies. The ISIs have some variability, but, for a harmonic complex, many ISIs will be grouped around the period of the fundamental component. The pitch of the complex is assumed to be based on some measure of the center of the distribution (for example, the mean, the median or the mode). When a single low partial is mistuned, the ISIs evoked by that partial around the fundamental period will shift, and, if the mistuning is sufficiently large, the ISIs will form a separate distribution. The mistuned component will then no longer contribute to the pitch of the complex.

A second perceptual effect associated with mistuning a low partial is that, when the mistuning is sufficiently large, the mistuned component "pops out" as a separate tone. This leads to the question: is the same mechanism involved in rejecting a mistuned component from the computation of pitch and in the formation of perceptual streams? If so, we would expect, on the basis of fig. 1, that a mistuned component would first be heard as a separate tone when it was mistuned by 3-4%, the point at which it ceases to make its full contribution to the pitch of the complex. In the next section we consider whether this is a valid hypothesis.

THRESHOLDS FOR HEARING MISTUNED COMPONENTS AS SEPARATE TONES

Moore et al. (1986) determined the extent to which mistuning a single partial in a complex tone increases the tendency for it to be heard as a separate tone in comparison with the case where all harmonics are at harmonic frequencies. They used a single-interval task, in which half of the stimuli were harmonic complexes and half contained a mistuned partial. Subjects were asked to say whether they heard a single sound with one pitch or two sounds - a complex tone and a component with a pure-tone quality not "belonging" to the complex. An adaptive procedure was used to track the degree of mistuning required to achieve a d' of 1. Results were similar for fo's of 100, 200 and 400 Hz. Fig. 2 shows mean results of four subjects, for fo = 200 Hz and for a tone containing harmonics 1 - 12, varying in duration from 50 to 1610 ms.

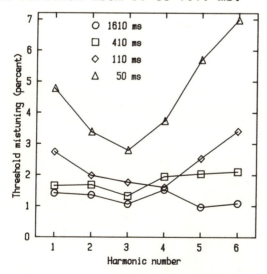

Figure 2. The degree of mistuning required for a partial to be heard as a separate tone.

For a duration of 410 ms, the same as used to obtain the data in fig. 1, thresholds are between 1.5 and 2% of the harmonic frequency. These thresholds are somewhat greater than those required to detect the mistuning using any available cue (Moore et al., 1985b), but are still less than the limit of 3-4% beyond which a component ceases to make its full contribution to the pitch of the complex. Apparently a component can be heard as a separate tone while still contributing to residue pitch, a form of "duplex perception" (Bregman, 1986). However, the data in fig. 1 (see also figs 3 and 4 below) suggest that the mechanism rejecting a mistuned component from the computation of pitch does not have an all-or-none character. Rather a component may be weighted less and less in the pitch determining process as it becomes more and more mistuned. At the same time the component becomes progressively more audible as a separate tone.

Fig. 2 shows that the degree of mistuning required for a partial to be heard as a separate tone varies with duration. The effect becomes marked as the duration decreases below 100 ms. We can interpret this as a competition between two principles of perceptual organization: 1) components of sounds which vary in a coherent way (e.g., which start and stop together) tend to form a single perceptual stream, whereas components with a long steady-state portion and which do not change together tend to split into separate streams (Bregman, 1978); 2) components in a harmonic series tend to fuse, while inharmonic components tend to form separate perceptual streams. Principle 1) tends to offset the effects of principle 2) at short durations.

If the pitch mechanism is involved in the formation of perceptual streams, the data in fig. 2 lead us to expect that the point at which a mistuned component ceases to contribute to residue pitch should vary with duration. This is considered next.

EFFECTS OF DURATION ON THE PITCH OF INHARMONIC COMPLEX TONES

The method used was similar to that described in Moore et al. (1985a). Briefly, the test stimulus was a complex tone composed of 12 equal-amplitude components (60 dB SPL per component). Eleven of the components were harmonics of a 200-Hz fo, while the remaining

component was slightly mistuned from its harmonic value
(five times upwards and five times downwards within a
block of ten pitch matches). The mistuned component
was chosen for each subject so as to be one of the most
dominant. It was the second harmonic for two of the
subjects and the fourth harmonic for the other two.
Subjects were required to adjust a comparison complex
tone so that its pitch matched that of the test tone,
and the fo of the comparison tone was taken as an
estimate of the pitch of the test tone. Results
averaged across the four subjects are shown in fig.3,
for durations of 50 ms and 410 ms.

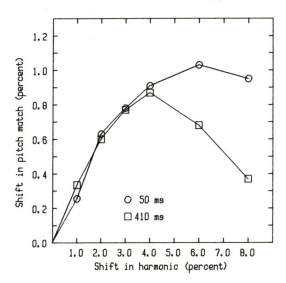

Figure 3. The shift in pitch of a complex tone
produced by shifting the frequency of a single
harmonic, as a function of the mistuning of the
harmonic, for two durations: 50 ms and 410 ms.

The results for the 410-ms duration are similar in
form to those shown in fig. 1 . However, for the 50-ms
duration, the mistuned component has an increasing
effect on the pitch of the complex for mistunings up to
6%, and the pitch shift is still large for a mistuning
of 8%. An analysis of variance showed a significant
effect of duration ($p < 0.01$) and a significant
interaction of duration and degree of mistuning
($p < 0.05$). The pitch shift was significantly greater
for the 50-ms than for the 410-ms duration for mistunings of 6% and 8% ($p < 0.01$), but not for other mis-

tunings. These results indicate that the tolerance of the pitch mechanism for accepting mistuned partials increases with decreasing duration. However, the peaks of the two functions in fig. 3 differ only by about a factor of 1.5, whereas thresholds for hearing a mistuned partial as a separate tone increase by more than a factor of 2 as duration is decreased from 410 to 50 ms. Thus, changes in the tolerance of the pitch mechanism with duration do not correspond exactly with changes in the threshold for hearing a mistuned partial as a separate tone.

One important implication of the results in fig. 3 is that the pitch of inharmonic complex tones may depend on duration. For example, a partial mistuned by 8% might make a strong contribution to the pitch of a 50-ms tone, but only a weak contribution to the pitch of a 410-ms tone. I know of no pitch model which can account for this effect.

RESIDUE MATCHING OR COMPONENT MATCHING

Faulkner (1985) has suggested that, when subjects are comparing or discriminating complex tones with corresponding harmonics, they compare the pitches of individual components, rather than the residue pitches of the sounds. If this were true, it would have serious implications for our experiments on pitch discrimination of complex tones (Moore et al., 1984) as well as for the pitch-matching experiments described above. To test this idea, we conducted a pitch-matching experiment like that described above, but using two different comparison tones. The comparison tone either contained 12 equal-amplitude harmonics (the same as the test tone, except that one partial was mistuned in the test tone), or it contained only 11 harmonics; the harmonic corresponding to the mistuned partial was omitted. If subjects match the pitches of individual components, then in the latter case there should be no pitch shifts; the components in the test and comparison stimulus can be matched exactly. However, if the subjects match on the basis of residue pitch, the pitch shifts should be similar for the two comparison stimuli. Results are shown in fig. 4.

It is clear that substantial pitch shifts occur for the comparison tone with the harmonic absent, indicating that subjects do not just match the pitches

186

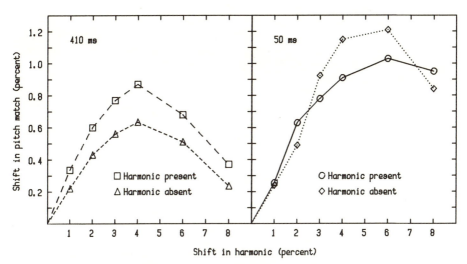

Figure 4. Results of an experiment in which a complex
        tone containing a single mistuned harmonic was
        matched with two different comparison tones. One
        had harmonics corresponding to those of the test
        tone. For the other, the mistuned harmonic was
        absent. Results are shown for two durations of
        the test and comparison tones.

of components. An analysis of variance showed no
significant overall effect of the presence or absence
of the harmonic, but there was a significant
interaction of presence or absence with duration
($p < 0.05$). The nature of this interaction can be seen
in fig. 4; pitch shifts tend to be slightly smaller
when the harmonic is absent at the longer duration but
not at the shorter duration. This effect is largely
due to the results of one subject who consistently
produced smaller pitch shifts when the harmonic was
absent at the longer duration. Overall, the results
suggest that subjects primarily match residue pitches
rather than the pitches of individual components.

    Although the results presented here pertain only
to pitch matching, it is likely that the pitch discrimination of complex tones with corresponding harmonics
is also usually based on judgements of residue pitch.
Pitch matching can be viewed as a series of pitch
discriminations; the subject tries to decide whether
the pitch of the comparison stimulus is higher or lower
than that of the test stimulus, and adjusts the compar-

ison stimulus accordingly. Thus, our earlier conclusion also stands: the pitch discrimination of complex tones can be predicted from the discriminability of the frequencies of the individual partials without assuming an additional internal noise (Moore et al., 1984). The discrimination of complex tones with non-corresponding harmonics (Faulkner, 1985) is worse than expected on this basis, probably because the marked difference in timbre between the tones makes it difficult for the subject to pay attention only to their relative pitch.

SUMMARY AND CONCLUSIONS

The pitch of complex tones can be predicted as a weighted sum of information derived from the lower components. The pitch mechanism has a certain tolerance for accepting non-harmonic components, but components which are sufficiently mistuned cease to contribute to residue pitch. The mechanism for rejecting mistuned components works in a gradual rather than an all-or-none way. The tolerance of the pitch mechanism decreases with increasing duration. Thus, the pitches of inharmonic complex tones may vary with duration.

A component which is sufficiently mistuned tends to be heard out from a complex tone, sounding like a separate tone. The threshold for this to occur decreases with increasing duration. This suggests a link with the operation of the pitch mechanism in rejecting mistuned components. However, under some conditions a mistuned component can be heard as a separate tone while still contributing to residue pitch.

When subjects compare the pitches of complex tones with corresponding harmonics they do not simply compare the pitches of individual harmonics; rather they seem primarily to compare residue pitches.

ACKNOWLEDGEMENTS

This work was supported by the Medical Research Council (U.K.). I thank Brian Glasberg, Roy Patterson, Robert Peters, Brian Roberts, Greg Schooneveldt and Michael Shailer for helpful comments. Brian Glasberg, Russell Newton and Damian Brassington helped to obtain the data shown in figs. 3 and 4.

REFERENCES

Bregman, A. S. (1978). The formation of auditory
    streams, in: Attention and Performance, Vol. 7,
    J. Requin, ed., Erlbaum, New Jersey.
Bregman, A.S. (1986). The meaning of duplex percep-
    tion: sounds as transparent objects, in:
    Psychophysics and Speech Perception, M.E.H.
    Schouten, ed., Nijhoff, Netherlands.
Duifhuis, H., Willems, L.F. and Sluyter, R.J. (1982).
    Measurement of pitch in speech: An implementation
    of Goldstein's theory of pitch perception, J.
    Acoust. Soc. Am., 71, 1568-1580.
Faulkner, A. (1985). Pitch discrimination of harmonic
    complex signals: Residue pitch or multiple
    component discriminations, J. Acoust. Soc. Am.,
    78, 1993-2004.
Goldstein, J. L. (1973). An optimum processor theory
    for the central formation of the pitch of complex
    tones, J. Acoust. Soc. Am., 54, 1496-1516.
Moore, B. C. J. (1973). Frequency difference limens for
    short-duration tones, J. Acoust. Soc. Am., 54,
    610-619.
Moore, B. C. J. (1982). An Introduction to the
    Psychology of Hearing, Academic Press, New York.
Moore, B. C. J., Glasberg, B.R. and Shailer, M.J.
    (1984). Frequency and intensity difference limens
    for harmonics within complex tones, J. Acoust.
    Soc. Am., 75, 550-561.
Moore, B.C.J., Glasberg, B. R. and Peters, R. W.
    (1985a). Relative dominance of individual
    partials in determining the pitch of complex
    tones, J. Acoust. Soc. Am., 77, 1853-1860.
Moore, B. C. J., Peters, R. W. and Glasberg, B.R.
    (1985b). Thresholds for the detection of
    inharmonicity in complex tones, J. Acoust. Soc.
    Am., 77, 1861-1867.
Moore, B. C. J., Glasberg, B. R. and Peters, R. W.
    (1986). Thresholds for hearing mistuned partials
    as separate tones in harmonic complexes, J.
    Acoust. Soc. Am., 80, 479-483.
Moore, B. C. J. and Glasberg, B. R. (1986). The role of
    frequency selectivity in the perception of
    loudness, pitch and time, in Frequency Selectivity
    in Hearing, B. C. J. Moore, ed., Academic Press,
    London.
Terhardt, E. (1979). Calculating virtual pitch, Hear.
    Res., 1, 155-182.

Complex Spectral Patterns with Interaural Differences:
Dichotic Pitch and the 'Central Spectrum'

William A. Yost, P.J. Harder, and R.H. Dye
Parmly Hearing Institute
Loyola University
Chicago, IL

A complex sound's amplitude and phase spectra are
likely to be different at one ear relative to the other
ear when the sound arrives at the two ears. This chapter
describes experiments involving broadband stimuli in
which narrow bands are presented with interaural
differences of amplitude or phase. Listeners perceive a
pitch for these stimuli that corresponds to the spectral
location of the band of interaurally shifted components.
These stimuli produce a version of the Cramer-Huggins
dichotic pitch. A psychophysical procedure was developed
to estimate the salience of the dichotic pitches for a
variety of stimulus conditions. The results are described
in terms of a 'Central Spectrum' and are discussed in
relationship to conditions that yield binaural masking-
level differences (BMLD).

INTRODUCTION

In most acoustic environments, the sound
arriving at one ear is different from that arriving at
the other ear. The classic Duplex Theory of Localization
defines the interaural differences of time and amplitude
as important interaural cues for locating the source of a
sound. For a complex sound these interaural differences
of time and amplitude will often vary as a function of
spectral region. That is, due to the characteristics of
the environment and the head, the interaural differences
in one region of the spectrum may be different from those
measured in other spectral regions. In 1958 Cramer and
Huggins described a dichotic complex stimulus generated
with an all-pass filter. The amplitude spectra at the two
ears was identical. The phase spectra at the ears was the
same except for a narrow-band region where the phase at
one ear was shifted through 360º relative to the phase at
the other ear. Thus, the filter generated a stimulus with
a interaural phase shift in a narrow band. This stimulus
is described in Fig. 1a. Cramer and Huggins (1958)
reported that they perceived a pitch with this dichotic
presentation and that it was approximately equal to the
frequencies where the interaural phase shifted from 0º to
360º. Other investigators have generated complex dichotic

stimuli with interaural differences that varied across the spectrum of the sound. Examples of some of these stimuli are described in Figs. 1a-d.

For all of the stimuli shown in Fig. 1 listeners perceive a pitch in the context of the noisy timbre of these complex stimuli. For many conditions the stimulus is perceived as if a narrow-band stimulus (i.e. a tone) was added to a broadband noise. The frequency of the pitch can be estimated by obtaining the difference between the two stimuli delivered to the two ears. These difference spectra are shown on the right of Fig. 1e-h. Subtraction of the inputs at the two ears from one another is the major assumption of the Durlach Equalization/Cancellation (EC) model (1972) used to account for many binaural phenomena. The difference spectrum describes a 'central spectrum' from which the pitch of the binaural inputs can be determined (Bilsen, 1977).

PRESENT RESEARCH

The major purpose of our research to date has been to estimate: 1) the spectral region over which these pitches exist, and 2) the range of interaural values of time (phase) and intensity that yield these dichotic pitches. The stimulus for these experiments was a broadband noise generated with a 16384 point FFT so that every component up to 8192 was present in the stimulus. The noise was generated with a flat amplitude spectrum and a random (rectangularly distributed) phase spectrum. Either a constant phase shift or a decrease in level was introduced to the stimulus delivered to the right ear, while the original stimulus was delivered to the left ear. Thus, these stimuli produced either an interaural level difference or an interaural phase shift in a particular spectral region. The variables in the study

Figure 1 (next page). Figs. 1a-d show interaural differences produced in the cited studies (the spectra were identical at the ears except for the difference shown). Fig 1a-Cramer and Huggins (1958), Fig. 1b-Klein and Hartmann (1981), Fig. 1c-Kubovy et al (1974), Fig. 1d-Raatgever and Bilsen (1986). Figs. 1e-h depict the difference spectra for the stimuli shown on the left. Fig. 1i and 1j show the stimulus conditions used in the present study.

191

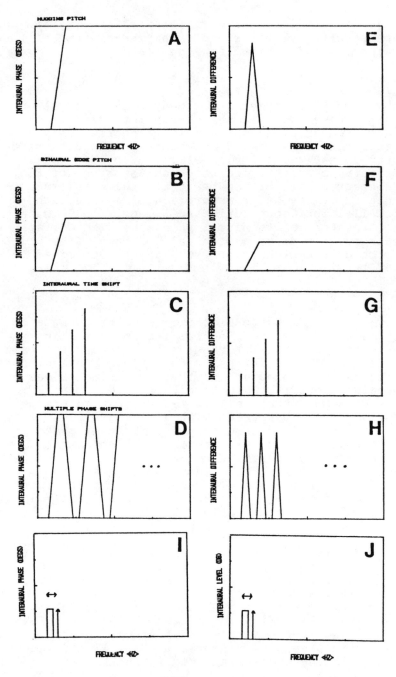

were the bandwidth over which the level decrement or
phase shift was introduced and the size of the level
decrease or phase shift. The spectra Fig. 1i and 1j
depict these stimulus conditions.

An 11-second stimulus was constructed by generating
10, 500-msec. samples of the stimulus described above.
The 10 samples differed in the frequency region over
which the interaural level difference or phase shift was
generated. The center frequency of the spectral region
increased logarithmically from 221 Hz to 4035 Hz. The
amount of the phase shift or level difference remained
the same for all 10 samples, and the bandwidth over which
the interaural difference was produced was proportional
(1% and 20%) to the center frequency of the spectral
region containing the interaural difference. Each of the
10 samples was preceded by 500 msec. of random noise
presented with no interaural differences (a diotic
filler), with the last sample being followed by 500 msecs
of the diotic filler and the first sample being preceded
by one second of the diotic filler. The spectrum level of
the noise was 35 dB SPL. The entire 11-second stimulus,
therefore, contained 10 opportunities for a listener to
report hearing a dichotic pitch with the pitch ascending
in a logarithmic order.

During each presentation of a dichotic sample
(containing a possible dichotic pitch), a number from 1
to 10 appeared on the listener's response console (a
Tandy Model 100 computer). The listener's task was to
indicate on the keyboard which of the 10 presentations
(coinciding with the 10 samples) contained a pitch. The
listener recorded the answer after five repetitions of
the 11-second stimulus. The interaural differences were
always presented in the same order, but the center
frequency at which the order began was chosen at random
for each trial. For instance, on a trial the order might
start with pitch number 3, followed by pitch numbers
4,5,6,7,8,9,10,1,2. For the this example, the listener
might respond that pitches were heard during samples
1,2,3,4,5,9,10 and the computer would indicate that the
listener reported hearing a pitch when the interaural
differences were presented with center frequencies at 221
(e.g. when the number 9 appeared on the console, the
listener reported hearing a pitch which would have been
pitch '1' at a center frequency of 221 Hz), 305, 421,
582, 803, 1110 and 1531 Hz (see the legend on Figs. 2-7
for the center frequencies of each pitch).

193

Twelve listeners with normal hearing participated in the study. The results were tabulated as the percent of total times the listeners reported hearing a dichotic pitch at a particular center frequency. Figures 2 and 3 show the results for the major part of the study. Figs. 2 are for interaural differences of phase, and Figs. 3 are for interaural differences of level.

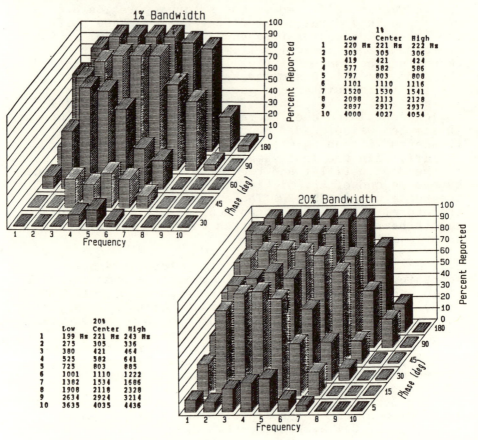

Figure 2. Each Figure shows the proportion of times the listeners reported a pitch for each of the ten center frequencies at which an interaural difference was presented. The amount of the interaural phase shift is plotted on the 'z' axis. The center frequency and band width over which the interaural phase shift was presented is shown in the legend. Figs. 2a-c are for the three bandwidth conditions.

194

The data shown in Figs. 2 and 3 indicate a variety of interesting findings: 1) there is a spectral region between approximately 300 and 1500 Hz where the pitches appear to be most salient (the existence region for dichotic pitch), 2) this existence region appears to be about the same when either interaural phase or interaural level was varied, 3) the existence region is approximately the same for all three bandwidth conditions, and 4) pitches were perceived by some listeners for phase shifts as small as 3º and level differences as small as 1 dB.

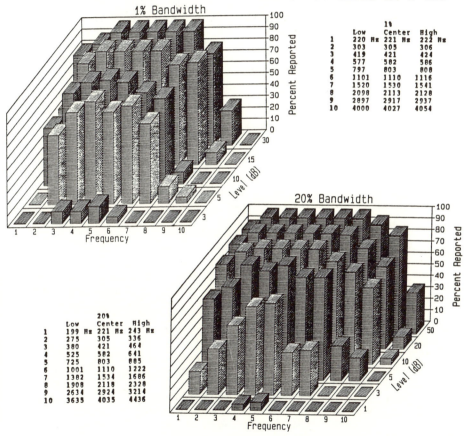

Figure 3. The same format as was used in Fig. 2. Results for changes in interaural level.

An exception to the second observation made above may be seen for the reported pitches in Fig. 3c. For this condition when the interaural level difference was 50 dB and the bandwidth was 20%, listeners reported pitches above the 1534 Hz spectral region (pitch position 7) suggested as the upper bound of the dichotic pitch existence region. However, in these conditions a large 2-3 dB interaural level difference exists for the entire spectral complex, in that 20% of the spectrum has a 50 dB interaural level difference. For this condition there was a noticeable shift in the lateral position of the entire stimulus. It is highly likely that some listeners registered this image shift as if it were a pitch occurrence because the image shift appeared in rhythm with the pitches that the listener may actually have heard. Additional investigation suggested that reports of pitches at these higher frequencies are probably artifactual.

When the dichotic pitch is perceived, it is often reported as being at a lateral position inside the head away from midline. The noisy timbre of the stimulus out of which the pitch is heard appears always to be in the center of the head. To estimate the relative lateral location of the perceived pitches and the noisy background, a five-point rating scale was used in which 1 meant left ear, 3 midline, and 5 right ear. After the listener was presented the five repetitions of the 11-second stimulus for judging the presence of the dichotic pitches, the same 11-second stimulus was presented twice more, once for the subject to judge the lateral location of the pitches and once to judge the lateral location of the noisy-timbred background.

For all listeners and conditions the noisy background received a mean lateral location rating of 3.01 (indicating the background noise was in the middle of the head). For all conditions involving interaural level differences the listeners perceived the location of the lateral image of the pitches to be toward the ear receiving the greater level (mean rating of 1.4). The lateral location of the pitches produced with interaural phase differences depended on the stimulus condition. For large values of interaural phase shifts (phase shifts greater than 45°), listeners indicated that the pitch was toward either the right or the left ear (an ambiguous location). For smaller interaural phase shifts the

pitches were lateralized toward the right ear, the ear
leading in phase.

In addition to perceiving a pitch with a particular
lateral location, listeners often reported that the pitch
appeared to warble much like the amplitude modulation of
a narrow band noise. Although no accurate estimate of the
warble was obtained in this study, listeners' reports
suggest that the warble was greatest for large values of
interaural phase shifts when the bandwidth was 5% of the
center frequency. However, a warbling pitch was reported
for many other conditions.

Although these dichotic pitches can be predicted by
calculating the difference between the inputs to the
ears, a simple subtraction does not completely describe
the perception of these dichotic stimuli. A simple
subtraction cannot account for the noisy timbre of the
sounds, the lateral location of the perceived pitch, or
the warble perceived in some stimulus conditions. In the
E-C model, the subtraction (cancellation) is a noisy
subtraction, in that interaurally-uncorrelated,
multiplicative noise is introduced before the
cancellation stage (at the equalization stage). The
multiplicative noise means that subtraction is not
complete and that a residual noise will remain after
subtraction. Thus, a model with internal multiplicative
noise may help account for the noisy timbre of these
dichotic sounds.

In order to test the multiplicative, internal noise
assumption, uncorrelated noise (equal level for the two
inputs) was multiplied by the two inputs that made up the
dichotic stimuli. The multiplicative noise simulated the
assumed internal noise. The inputs were then subtracted
and presented to both ears as the _variable diotic
stimulus_. The stimuli without the multiplicative noise
were presented, as in the first part of the experiment,
as the _dichotic standard stimulus_. For these tests, the
listener adjusted the amount of multiplicative noise
until a match was achieved between the diotic variable
and the dichotic standard stimulus. The stimulus
consisted of interaural differences produced at three
center frequencies: 529 Hz, followed by 595 Hz and 668
Hz. The same 500 msec durations and filler noises used in
the first part of the study were used in these tests.
The level of the multiplicative noise required for a
match was divided by the level of the original noise to

estimate the internal noise-to-external noise ratio. The average estimated internal noise-to-external noise ratio remained fairly constant at - 4 to - 6 dB for the six conditions tested. The fact that the estimates remain about the same for various stimulus conditions supports a noisy subtraction hypothesis. The listeners also reported, with one exception, that the diotic stimulus formed by combining interaurally-uncorrelated noise with the original noise produces a pitch sensation identical to that produced by the dichotic noise. The exception is that the pitches and the background noise in the diotic condition were both lateralized at midline, while the pitches in the dichotic stimulus were lateralized off midline away from the noise background.

In the formalization of the E-C model the amount of internal noise increases with increasing frequency. In this case the internal noise would eliminate a spectral peak in the central spectrum at some upper frequency independent of whether or not an interaural level difference or an interaural phase shift was used to form the central spectrum. The fact that the existence region for the dichotic pitches is the same for conditions involving both level and phase differences is consistent with the assumption of a frequency-dependent internal noise. Also the absence of pitches above 1500 Hz is consistent with the amount of internal noise originally assumed by the E-C model.

Although the above arguments may indicate that the E-C model is a good one for modeling these data, it cannot (in its basic form) account for the lateral position of the reported pitches or for the warble sensation associated with some of the stimulus conditions. Bilsen and his colleagues (1986a and 1986b) have proposed a cross-correlation model (Central Activation Pattern, CAP model) to account for the pitch and lateral location of the dichotic pitches. The data from the present study involving interaural phase shifts are consistent with this model. Although the cross-correlation model does not attempt to account for the perception of the noisy timbre out of which the pitches are heard, the addition of a frequency-dependent internal noise would probably achieve the same success as it did for the E-C model. The reported work on the cross-correlation model has not yet dealt with conditions involving interaural level differences.

198

In studies of the binaural masking-level difference (BMLD, see Green and Yost 1975), a tonal signal is usually added to a noise masker such that either the signal or the masker is presented with interaural differences of phase or level. Therefore, the resulting spectrum of the sound presented to the ears is such that the spectral region at the frequency of the tone has a different interaural configuration from the rest of the broadband spectrum. In these cases the spectra are very similar to those described above. However, the addition of the signal in the BMLD conditions also means that there is additional energy in the broadband stimulus at the signal frequency. Most descriptions of the BMLDs (Colburn and Durlach, 1978 and Durlach and Colburn, 1978) assume binaural processing releases the signal from masking (hence, the concept of binaural release from masking).

The observations described in this paper suggest another interpretation for the BMLD. Although there is a slight increment in the level at the signal frequency, it is very small. Rather than conceiving that the interaural differences in the spectrum releases the small signal increment from masking, the observations of this paper suggest that the signal supplies a great enough interaural difference at its frequency for the 'central spectrum' to have a sufficiently large difference spectrum peak for a listener to perceive the pitch associated with the signal. The simple E-C model would suggest that when both interaural differences (time and level) are present, they might: 1) either supplement one another producing a greater difference spectrum (central spectrum) than either interaural difference alone could produce or 2) cancel each other in their abilities to produce a difference spectrum. However, the values of these interaural differences are random variables and, thus, impossible to control in the standard BMLD conditions. A large number of coherent signal and masker studies (see Robinson, Langford and Yost, 1974) have been conducted to study the individual roles of the two interaural variables. In these coherent masking studies the signal and masker spectra are identical, which is not the case for the typical BMLD conditions. The stimulus paradigm described in this paper separates the interaural variables similar to the way they occur in studies of the BMLD and, thus, it might allow for studying the roles of the two interaural variables in the production of BMLDs.

In conclusion, this chapter describes a type of dichotic configuration that produces binaurally generated pitches. The results suggest that a 'central spectrum' is calculated and the peaks in the central spectrum predict the reported pitch. The laterality and temporal warble of the pitch are additional attributes of dichotic pitch which require careful consideration in any comprehensive model of dichotic pitch. The paradigm allows for careful control of the interaural variables of phase and level in stimulus conditions similar to the ones used in BMLD studies.

ACKNOWLEDGMENT-This work was supported by grants from the National Science Foundation, National Institutes of Health (NINCDS) and the Air Force Office of Scientific Research (Life Sciences).

REFERENCES

Bilsen, F. A. (1977). "Pitch of Noise Signals: Evidence for a `Central Spectrum'," J. Acoust. Soc. Am. 61, 150-159.

Colburn, H. S., and Durlach, N. I. (1978). "Models of Binaural Interaction," in Handbook of Perception: Hearing, edited by E. C. Carterette and M. P. Friedman (Academic Press, New York).

Cramer, E. M., and Huggins, W. H. (1958). "Creation of Pitch through Binaural Interaction," J. Acoust. Soc. Am. 30, 412-417.

Durlach, N. I. (1972). "Binaural Signal Detection: Equalization and Cancellation Theory," in Foundations of Modern Auditory Theory, edited by J.T. Tobias (Academic Press, New York).

Durlach, N. I., and Colburn, H. S. (1978). "Binaural Phenomena," in Handbook of Perception, VIV, Hearing, edited by E. C. Carterette and M. P. Friedman (Academic Press, New York).

Frijns, J. H. M., Raatgever, J., and Bilsen, F. A. (1986). "A Central Spectrum Theory of Binaural Processing. The Binaural Edge Pitch revisited," J. Acoust. Am. Soc. 80, 442-452.

Green, D. M., and Yost, W. A. (1975). "Binaural Analysis," in Handbook of Sensory Physiology: Hearing, edited by Keidel and Neff (Springer-Verlag, Netherlands).

Kubovy, M., Cutting, J. E., and McGuire, R. M. (1974). "Hearing with the Third Ear: Dichotic Perception of a Melody without Monaural Familiarity Cues," Science 186, 272-274.

Klein, M.A., and Hartmann, W.M. (1981) "Binaural Edge Pitch", J. Acoust. Am. Soc. 70, 51-61.

Raatgever, J., and Bilsen, F. A. (1986). "A Central Spectrum Theory of Binaural Processing. Evidence for Dichotic Pitch," J. Acoust. Soc. Am. 80, 429-441.

Robinson, D. E., Langford, T. L., and Yost, W. A. (1974). "Tone-on-Tone and Noise-in-Noise Binaural Masking," Per. Psych. 15, 159-168.

Comparative Aspects of Complex Acoustic Perception

Stewart H. Hulse
Department of Psychology   Johns Hopkins University
Baltimore, MD 21218   U.S.A.

The research compares the ability of human and nonhuman animals (songbirds) to process serial acoustic patterns. Stimuli are sound patterns that vary in absolute or relative pitch or in temporal (rhythmic) structure. In contrast with humans, who are primarily relative pitch processors, songbirds depend extensively upon absolute pitch to discriminate serial pitch patterns. They fail, for example, to generalize a discrimination between rising and falling pitch patterns to new absolute frequencies outside the range of frequencies used to train them. However, although they remain sensitive to absolute pitch, songbirds can generalize pitch relationships to new frequencies if the novel frequencies occur in a familiar range. Furthermore, within the boundaries established by this absolute pitch range constraint, songbirds discriminate pitch contour and other aspects of serial pitch processing quite well.

Songbirds share with humans the ability to process rhythmic structures on a relational basis. They readily discriminate rhythmic structures and generalize the discrimination across ratio changes in the duration of pattern components.

The comparative approach adopted by the research tells us how songbirds process complex acoustic information. Perhaps more important, however, the contrast between human and nonhuman animals highlights those features of complex acoustic perception that are uniquely human and those that are not. As a consequence new research paths for complex acoustic perception in all species may appear -- encouraged by the broadened perspective that the comparative approach affords.

INTRODUCTION

Human beings, when faced with the task of learning and remembering a melodic line or a rhythmic pattern, generally encode how tones or temporal units are related to one another, not their absolute properties. We remember the ups and downs -- the contour -- of a melody in its tonal context, for example, not the

absolute frequencies of the sounds involved (Deutsch,
1982; Dowling, 1982). Furthermore, once having encoded
the necessary relations, we readily generalize them
to new stimuli along the same dimension. That is,
we easily recognize a melodic contour or a rhythmic
structure transposed to new frequencies on a log scale
of frequency, or to new temporal units on a log scale
of time. Musicians, of course, are familiar with
these facts. More generally, they have been studied
in a more abstract form by those interested in how
organisms organize serial patterns -- not only those
based on musical or other acoustic stimuli, but also
those constructed from visual, spatial, or other forms
of stimulus information (Bower & Winzenz, 1969; Deutsch
& Feroe, 1982; Garner, 1974; Jones, 1978; Lashley,
1951; Restle, 1970; Simon & Kotovsky, 1963). The combination of theories associated with serial pattern
learning and human music perception constitutes two
of the three organizing principles of the present
research.

The third principle comes from the study of how
nonhuman animals respond to serially-organized stimuli
(Hulse, Cynx, & Humpal, 1985). Many species must
learn and remember how events occur serially in time
or place. The comparative approach to this issue
can tell us a lot about the capacities of any given
animal, and the commonalities and differences in the
skills of all species. The comparative approach offers
a perspective that can highlight hitherto unrealized
perceptual capacities.

PROCEDURES

In order to build the foregoing three areas into
a meaningful research program, experiments have been
undertaken with serial acoustic patterns based on principles drawn from human pitch and rhythm perception;
to date, most of the work has dealt with pitch perception. Mimicking songbirds have been used as subjects
because of their putative ability to process arbitrary,
nonnatural sound patterns.

In a typical experiment (e.g. Hulse, Cynx, &
Humpal, 1984), starlings (_Sturnus_ _vulgaris_) are first
trained to discriminate two sound patterns. Then,
the patterns are changed in a series of transfer or
probe trials to determine which pattern features control the birds' discrimination performance. Thus,
baseline discrimination training begins by teaching
the birds with food reward to peck at disks on a wall

in a sound shielded chamber. Sound stimuli are com-
puter-controlled patterns of sinetones delivered to
a speaker mounted over the birds' head. With a GO/NOGO
procedure use in most experiments, the birds start a
trial by pecking on one disk that turns on a stimulus
pattern for a preset listening period usually 4 seconds
long. Then a second disk comes into play, and the
birds must peck rapidly at that disk (the GO response)
when stimulus pattern A occurs for a food reward,
and withhold a peck for 4 seconds (the NOGO response)
when stimulus pattern B occurs. If the bird pecks
before 4 seconds on a NOGO trial, mild punishment is
administered by darkening the chamber for a 10-second
"timeout." The discrimination emerges as short-latency
responses begin to occur to pattern A, and long-latency
responses occur to pattern B. Subsequent transfer
tests probe for the features controlling the discrimination by changing pattern structure in some prede-
termined fashion. The procedure is based on the assumption that changes which produce significant impairment of discrimination performance are critical
for the baseline discrimination, while those that do
not are functionally neutral. In the latter case,
no claim is made that the birds fail to <u>notice</u> the
change; it is just that the altered stimuli still
contain sufficient information to maintain accurate
performance.
     Experiments on rhythm discrimination use a modifi-
cation of the GO/NOGO task that creates a two-alternative, forced-choice (2AFC) procedure. After the
trial-starting peck, the birds must peck on disk 1
if pattern A appears, and disk 2 if pattern B appears.
Error data are typically recorded.
RHYTHM PERCEPTION
     Research began on birds' perception of rhythmic
structure by teaching them to discriminate with the
2AFC procedure one of two forms of temporally-organized
2000-Hz sinetone patterns from an arrhythmic, unorganized pattern (Hulse, Humpal, & Cynx, 1984). The
stimulus patterns appear in Figure 1; the birds heard
one pattern type on a trial. Following initial training, the <u>tempo</u> of the patterns was changed by multiplying the intervals involved by constants covering
a range that both doubled and halved the baseline
tempo. If birds responded like humans, they should
maintain the discrimination across tempo changes --
showing perceptual constancy for constant <u>relative</u>
durations in the stimulus patterns.

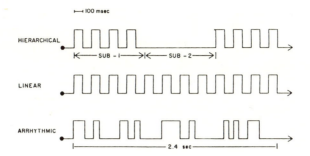

Figure 1.   Samples of rhythmic and arrhythmic 2000-
    Hz patterns.   The hierarchical pattern contains
    two subpatterns consisting of a 4-tone sequence
    and a pause of equal duration.   For the arrhythmic
    pattern the computer sampled continuously from
    a list of tone and intertone durations varying
    from 30 to 300 msec.

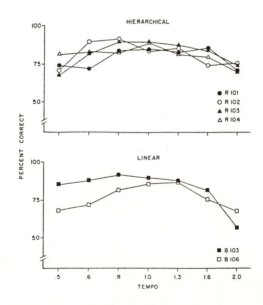

Figure 2.   Results of discrimination and tempo trans-
    fers of a rhythmic/arrhythmic discrimination by
    starlings.   Data appear for the original discrim-
    ination at the baseline (1.0) tempo and for trans-
    fer tests across a range that doubled (0.5) and
    halved (2.0) the baseline tempo.

205

The birds learned the original discriminations
easily and transferred them readily to new tempos.
Figure 2 shows the results of original training and
the transfer tests for the hierarchical and linear
rhythmic patterns. Data for the baseline tempo for
4 starlings are shown at 1.0 on the abscissa. Data
for other tempos range from 0.5 to 2.0 (twice and half
the baseline tempo, respectively). There was some loss
in discrimination accuracy at extreme tempo changes,
but in all case, performance was well above chance.
The birds showed excellent perceptual constancy for
a constant-ratio tempo change.

In another transfer test, the birds maintained
excellent discrimination performance when they were
shifted from the hierarchical to the linear rhythmic
pattern or vice versa. Apparently, starlings acquire
the capacity to generalize the discrimination on the
more general basis of whether the stimulus patterns
are structured or not.

To summarize, starlings readily learn a discrimination between rhythmic and arrhythmic sound patterns,
and they readily generalize that discrimination on a
relational basis. In every respect tested thus far,
they appear to process complex temporal patterns just
like humans do.

PITCH PERCEPTION

Our initial research on avian pitch pattern perception was again guided by basic questions stemming
directly from human pitch processing. The first
question asked was whether songbirds could discriminate
two patterns that were differentiated by a relational
rule, namely, whether they rose or fell in pitch.
The next, related, question was whether that discrimination would generalize to new frequencies an octave
away from than the range in which the birds first
learned the discrimination (Hulse, Cynx, & Humpal,
1984; Hulse & Cynx, 1985, in press). Humans readily
generalize such discriminations. They do so whenever
they remember a melody and recognize it with a change
in key (Deutsch, 1982). Apparently, humans process
melodic information based on constant ratios among
sequences of tone frequencies. Do songbirds?

The first experiment used the GO/NOGO task and
the stimulus patterns appearing in Figure 3. On any
trial, the birds heard one of the set of 8 stimuli
for 4 sec, and their task was then to peck (GO) for
a pattern that fell in frequency and to withhold pecking (NOGO) for a pattern that rose in frequency.

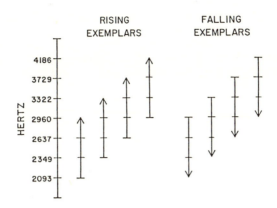

Figure 3.   Frequencies of sinetones in the four rising
    and falling patterns that starlings learned to
    discriminate initially.   Tone and intertone inter-
    vals were each 100 msec, and each pattern repe-
    tition was separated by an 800 msec pause.

    After initial training with baseline frequencies,
the birds were transferred to 4-tone rising and falling
patterns an octave lower in frequency.   Then they were
returned briefly to baseline frequencies and shifted
to patterns an octave higher in frequency.   Finally,
in this experiment, they were tested with occasional
probe patterns that were created from novel frequencies
within the original baseline range.   The respective
frequencies involved in each of these transfers appear
in Table I.

Table I.   Frequencies (Hz) of 4-tone patterns in
transfer tests for relative pitch discrimination.

Baseline	Lower	Higher	Within
4186	2093	8372	3951
3729	1864	7458	3520
3322	1661	6644	3136
2960	1480	5920	2793
2637	1318	5274	2489
2349	1174	4698	2128
2093	1046	4186	

The starlings readily learned the baseline ris-
ing/falling discrimination in from 3 to 6 weeks of
daily 30-m to 1-hr sessions. The relevant data at
asymptote appear in Figure 4 at points (-3, -2, -1)
for three days prior to the transfer day (T). Latencies for falling (GO) patterns are all less than 1 sec,
while those for rising (NOGO) patterns are close to
the 4-sec maximum.

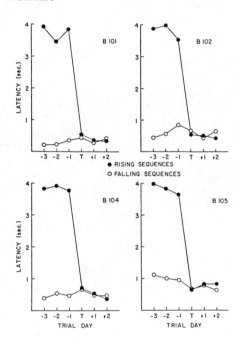

Figure 4.   Latency data for the last three days of
baseline training (-3, -2, -1), the day of transfer to a lower octave (T), and for two days
(+1, +2) following the transfer.

When the birds were transferred to the lower
octave, they lost the rising/falling discrimination
immediately, as Figure 4 shows, and relearned it slowly
over a period of time not substantially different
from original baseline training. In other words,
there was no transfer of the relational, rising/falling
discrimination at all. However, the birds recovered

208

the original baseline discrimination immediately when
returned to baseline frequencies -- only to lose it
again (and relearn it slowly) when transferred to
frequencies an octave higher than baseline. When
the birds were tested with novel frequencies within
the familiar baseline training range, on the other
hand, they generalized the discrimination readily.
Apparently, unlike humans, songbirds (we have obtained
identical data from cowbirds and a mockingbird) can
process relative pitch information, but they can do
so only in a range of __absolute__ frequencies with which
they are familiar. We have explored this phenomenon
in detail (e.g., Hulse & Cynx, 1985, in press), and
it is quite general. More to the point, it suggests
that birds process complex acoustic patterns as much
on the basis of absolute pitch as relative pitch.

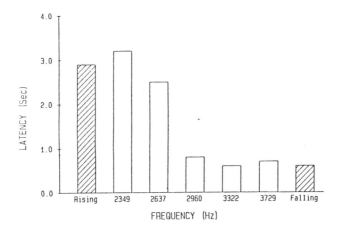

Figure 5. Response latencies from a test in which the
        birds heard just the repeated initial frequency
        of 4-tone rising or falling exemplars. Baseline
        data for 4-tone sequences that did rise or fall
        in frequency are shown at the left and right
        of the figure.

        To this end, we have eliminated relative pitch
information from 4-tone patterns, after baseline training just like that described, by introducing probe
trials in which a pattern consists of 4 tones of identical frequency. Under these circumstances, we obtained
data appearing in Figure 5. As frequencies move from
the low (NOGO) end of the range to the high (GO) end

209

of the range, latencies grow progressively shorter.
This suggests that in 4-tone rising or falling patterns, birds may be paying attention as much to the
absolute frequency of the initial tone, say, of each
pattern as to frequency relations within patterns.
They do not do so exclusively because we have tested
with patterns that begin near one edge of the baseline
range and "go the wrong way," that is, violate the
rule that rising, NOGO patterns begin a low frequencies
in the range. Under these circumstances, birds maintain the relative pitch discrimination.

In retrospect, however, (no doubt because of
our homocentric viewpoint!) we did not consider the
possibility of absolute pitch processing sufficiently
in designing the original baseline patterns. Although
they contain frequencies that overlap extensively
across patterns, the initial (or terminal) frequencies
distinguish uniquely all but those patterns beginning
on 2960 Hz. We are currently exploring intensively
the interplay between relative and absolute pitch
processing.

SUMMARY

In any case, humans and songbirds differ substantially in at least one mechanism by which they
perceive complex pitch structures. Humans are heavily
biased toward relative pitch; most, as a matter of
fact, have very little ability to learn and remember
the absolute pitch of a given sound. Songbirds, on
the other hand, perceive many absolute features of
sound patterns that are otherwise constructed according
to relational pitch rules. In contrast to their perception of temporal structure, which does seem to
parallel human relational perception, songbirds are
locked far more to absolute features of the complex
sounds they hear.

Of course, we have thus far sampled a rather
limited set of the animal kingdom. At this point,
for example, we do not know whether songbirds or humans
are aberrant with respect to hearing animals as a
whole. Given our human predilection to assign relations and rule-based organization to our perceptual
world, we may overestimate the prevalence of that
process in the animal kingdom. Perhaps the norm is
to encode information by placing great emphasis on
the absolute features of complex acoustic sounds.

REFERENCES

Bower, G. & Winzenz, D.   (1969).   Group structure, coding, anbd memory for serial digits. <u>Journal of Experimental Psychology Monographs</u>. <u>80</u>, Part 2, 1-17.

Deutsch, D. (Ed.)   (1982).   <u>The psychology of music</u>. New York: Academic Press.

Deutsch, D., & Feroe, J.   (1981).   The internal representations of pitch sequences in tonal music. <u>Psychological Review</u>, <u>88</u>, 503-522.

Dowling, W. J.   (1982).   Melodic information processing and its development.   In D. Deutsch (Ed.), <u>The psychology of music</u> (pp.413-430).   New York: Academic Press.

Garner, W. R.   (1974).   <u>The processing of information and structure</u>.   Hillsdale, NJ: Erlbaum.

Hulse, S. H., Cynx, J., & Humpal, J.   (1985).   Pitch context and pitch discrimination by birds.   In P. D. Balsam and A. Tomie (Eds.)   <u>Context and learning</u>.   (pp.273-293).   Hillsdale, NJ: Erlbaum.

Hulse, S. H., Cynx, J., & Humpal, J.   (1984).   Absolute and relative discrimination in serial pitch perception by birds.   <u>Journal of Experiment Psychology: General</u>, <u>113</u>, 38-54.

Hulse, S. H., Humpal, J., & Cynx, J.   (1984).   Discrimination and generalization of rhythmic and arrythmic sound patterns by European Starlings (<u>Sturnus vulgaris</u>).   <u>Music Perception</u>, <u>1</u>, 442-464.

Hulse, S. H., & Cynx, J.   (1985).   Relative pitch perception is constrained by absolute pitch in songbirds (<u>Mimus</u>, <u>Molothrus</u>, <u>Sturnus</u>).   <u>Journal of Comparative Psychology</u>, <u>99</u>, 176-196.

Jones, M. R.   (1978).   Auditory patterns: Studies in the perception of structure.   In E. C. Carterette and M. P. Friedman (Eds.), <u>Handbook of perception</u>, Vol. 8.   New York: Academic Press.

Lashley, K. S.   (1951).   The problem of serial order in behavior.   In L. H. Jeffress (Ed.), <u>Cerebral mechanisms in behavior</u>.   New York: Wiley.

Restle, F.   (1970).   Theory of serial pattern learning: Structural trees. <u>Psychological Review</u>, <u>77</u>, 481-495.

Simon, H. A., & Kotovsky, K.   (1963).   Human acquisition of concepts for sequential patterns. <u>Psychological Review</u>, <u>70</u>, 534-546.

Rate Coding in the Auditory-Nerve

R. L. Winslow[*], P. E. Barta[+], and M. B. Sachs[+]
Institute for Biomedical Computing[*]
Washington University, St. Louis, MO 63110
Department of Biomedical Engineering[+]
The Johns Hopkins University School of Medicine, Baltimore, MD 21205

We review the properties of rate-place representations of single tone frequency and intensity in backgrounds of quiet and broadband noise. Special emphasis is placed on statistical analysis of auditory-nerve rate responses, the role of low spontaneous rate fibers, and effects of efferent stimulation. Rate-place profiles encode tone frequency and intensity over a wide range of tone and noise levels if the properties of low spontaneous rate fibers are taken into account. Efferent input to the cochlea may improve rate-place representations in noise backgrounds. The experimental data show that selective weighting of the responses of low versus high threshold fibers is crucial if rate-place representations are to remain robust over a wide range of stimulus levels. We suggest a simple neural circuit that may be capable of performing this weighting.

INTRODUCTION

An important focus of auditory neuroscience has been to understand which features of auditory-nerve discharge patterns encode spectral information. Two general theories have been proposed. The rate-place theory (Kiang and Moxon, 1974; Sachs and Young, 1979) states that this information is represented by the distribution of average discharge rate across fiber best frequency (BF); the temporal-place theory states that spectral information is represented by the distribution of phase-locked response across BF (Young and Sachs, 1979). Temporal-place representations maintain the spectral features of steady-state vowels and single-tones even at stimulus and masker noise levels high enough to produce significant degradation of rate-place representations derived from the responses of the majority of auditory-nerve fibers (Young and Sachs, 1979; Sachs et al., 1983; Costalupes, 1985). These robust properties suggest that it is the temporal responses of auditory-nerve fibers which are most important in the perception of complex sounds. However, as we have repeatedly emphasized, we must be very cautious in this interpretation (Sachs and Young, 1979; Sachs et al., 1986).

It is now clear, for example, that there are significant differences in the rate-response properties of auditory-nerve fibers with different spontaneous rates (Sachs and Abbas, 1974; Liberman, 1978; Evans and Palmer, 1980; Schalk and Sachs, 1980). Some important differences are that fibers with spontaneous rate (SR) less than 1 spike per second can exhibit much higher rate-response thresholds (Liberman, 1978), broader dynamic ranges (Evans and Palmer, 1980; Sachs and Abbas, 1974; Schalk and Sachs, 1980), and give significantly larger rate responses to tones in high-level noise (Young and Barta, 1985; Costalupes, 1985; Costalupes et al., 1984) than do high SR fibers. Low SR fibers may therefore play an important role in sound perception at both high stimulus levels and in the presence of masking noise. Furthermore, carefull analysis of the statistical properties of rate responses has shown that stimulus features may be extracted in situations where the rate representation seems poor on casual examination (Sachs et al., 1986; Barta, 1985; Young and Barta, 1985; Winslow, 1985). Finally, stimulation of cochlear efferents has recently been shown to enhance the rate response of auditory-nerve fibers in noise (Winslow and Sachs, 1986a). This chapter will review our current understanding of the adequacy as well as the limitations of rate-place representations of acoustic stimuli in light of these considerations. Emphasis will be placed on the role of low SR fibers, efferent stimulation, and statistical analysis of auditory-nerve discharge patterns.

DYNAMIC RANGE AND INTENSITY DISCRIMINATION

Human subjects are capable of performing fine intensity discriminations over a wide range of tone levels in backgrounds of quiet (Jesteadt et al., 1977) despite the fact that most auditory-nerve fibers have rate-response thresholds which are clustered within a 20 dB range of levels (Liberman, 1978) and have dynamic ranges in response to BF tones of less than 40 dB (Schalk and Sachs, 1980; Evans, 1981). It is in fact not necessary that the rate-responses of auditory-nerve fibers exhibit broader dynamic ranges in order to account for pure tone intensity discrimination at high stimulus levels; at such levels performance may be mediated by the rate-responses of unsaturated fibers with BF's different from the stimulus frequency (Siebert, 1965; Siebert, 1968). However, such spread of excitation is unlikely to mediate discrimination in those situations where narrowband signals are presented simultaneously with broadband masking noise. Viemeister (1983) studied the ability of human subjects to detect differences in the intensity of bandpass noise bursts under such conditions, and concluded that the rate responses of auditory-nerve fibers projecting from relatively restricted regions of the basilar membrane could account for behavioral performance over a wide range of stimulus levels. In order to support this hypothesis, he showed that optimal processing of the rate-responses of a small number of high threshold low SR fibers would be sufficient to account for performance at the highest signal and noise levels studied. Other investigators have reached similar conclusions concerning the ability of individual fibers to signal small intensity changes in terms of discharge rate. Intensity difference limens (DL's) based on optimal processing of single fiber rate responses can be as small as 1.0 dB (Colburn unpublished results; Winslow and Sachs, 1986b; Delgutte, 1986), and optimal processing of the rate responses of fibers projecting from as few as 10 inner hair cells centered at the 8.0 kHz place can account for pure-tone intensity discrimination performance at 8.0 kHz over a 70 dB range of tone levels (Winslow and Sachs, 1986b). An even greater dynamic range is needed, however, because human subjects can detect differences in the intensity of 1.0 kHz tones as small as 1.1 dB over a range of at least 100 dB SPL (Viemeister, 1983). Liberman (1978) has reported that a small percentage of low SR fiber rate-thresholds are 40-70 dB higher than those of high SR fibers. It is possible that the rate responses of this very small population could extend dynamic range to the high stimulus levels mentioned above. The alternative is that pure-tone intensity discrimination at these very high levels must be mediated by spread of excitation.

DYNAMIC RANGE AND PURE-TONE FREQUENCY DISCRIMINATION

Evans (1981) has noted that rate-place profiles of responses to high frequency tones maintain a clear peak of activity centered at the tone frequency over a wide range of stimulus levels. The maintenance of this peak results primarily from the very steep high-frequency slopes of auditory-nerve fiber tuning curves. Fibers with BF much below the stimulus frequency simply don't respond. At low tone levels, rate-place profiles of responses to low frequency tones also show a peak of activity centered at the tone frequency. However, increases in tone level produce a flattening of these profiles until no clear peak is discernible in the rate responses of at least the high SR fibers (Kim and Molnar, 1979). This spread of activity results primarily from the low-frequency tails (Kiang and Moxon, 1974) as well as the limited dynamic range of the high SR fibers.

The results described in the previous section have shown that the rate responses of high threshold low SR fibers may be of great importance in extending the dynamic range of the peripheral auditory system. Shofner and Sachs (1986) have addressed the issue of whether or not a precise representation of a low frequency tone is maintained in the rate responses of this population at high stimulus levels. Figure 1 summarizes their findings. Each panel of Fig. 1 shows a moving window average of discharge rate in response to a 1.5 kHz tone plotted as a function of BF across the population of auditory-nerve fibers. The rate responses of high, medium, and low SR fibers were averaged separately and are shown in each panel by the solid, dashed, and dotted lines, respectively. Panels A and E show that at low stimulus levels, rate-place profiles derived from the responses of all three spontaneous rate populations maintain peaks of activity centered at the stimulus frequency. As tone intensity is increased, rate-place profiles derived from the responses of high SR fibers become flattened and show no evidence of a distinct peak. In contrast, rate-place profiles derived from the responses of low SR fibers (and in experiment 2/21/85, medium SR fibers) maintain a distinct peak at all tone levels studied. These data show that the frequency of low frequency tones may

214

be encoded by rate-place profiles over a wide range of tone levels extending to nearly 90 dB.

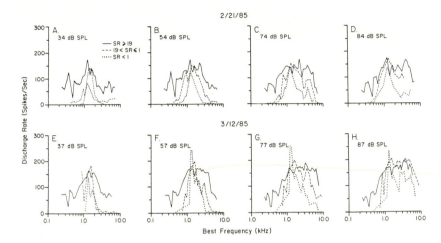

Fig. 1. Moving window averages of discharge rate in response to 1.5 kHz tones of the indicated level as a function of BF for experiments 2/21/85 and 3/12/85 (Shofner and Sachs, 1986).

TONE DETECTION IN NOISE BASED ON AVERAGE RATE

The previous sections have considered whether or not rate-place representations of acoustic stimuli are limited by a lack of dynamic range. A second possible limitation of rate-place representations is their apparent degradation in the presence of masking noise. The following sections will address this issue.

The affects of broadband noise on auditory-nerve rate responses have been studied extensively by Costalupes et al. (1984). Data similar to theirs is shown in Fig. 2. This figure shows BF tone rate-level functions for a low SR fiber. The solid line is a rate-level function measured in a background of quiet; the dotted and dashed lines are rate-level functions measured in the presence of background noise of the indicated spectral level. One effect of noise is to shift the dynamic range of this fiber to higher sound levels. This upward shift of dynamic range is believed to be a result of two-tone suppression (Costalupes et al., 1984), and can prevent noise energy from saturating fiber rate response. Increases in noise level also produce increases in low level rate, and decreases in saturation rate. Increases in low-level rate reflect fiber response to the background noise, whereas decreases in saturation rate are a result of rate adaptation (Smith and Brachman, 1980) produced by the background noise. The net result of these two effects is a compression of rate-level functions in noise.

215

In order to test the statistical significance of the remaining rate changes, Young and Barta (1985) computed estimates of the rate response thresholds of single auditory-nerve fibers to BF tones in noise and compared these estimates to behavioral masked thresholds at similar noise levels in cats (Costalupes, 1983).

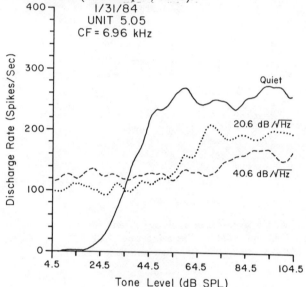

Fig. 2. BF tone rate-level functions for a low SR fiber measured in backgrounds of quiet (solid line) and in broadband noise with spectral level 20.6 (dotted line) and 40.6 (dashed line) db per $\sqrt{Hz}$ (Winslow, 1985).

Their data are summarized in Fig. 3. Panels A, B, and C show scaled rate-level functions in response to BF tones presented in three levels of background noise. Rate-level functions were computed separately for low, medium, and high SR fibers. These scaled rate-level functions are plots of rate to the tone plus noise minus rate to the noise divided by the standard deviation of rate (ordinate) as a function of tone level (abscissa). Panels D, E, and F show scaled rate-level functions for each of the three spontaneous rate populations at the indicated noise levels. The arrows show behavioral masked threshold at each noise level. At the lowest noise level (-10 dB), behavioral threshold is near the statistical threshold (the tone level at which the ordinate value D=1) of single low, medium, or high SR fibers. At the highest noise level (30 dB), low SR fibers have the lowest statistical threshold with high SR fibers showing very little rate change. These data imply that optimal use of the rate responses of a relatively small number of auditory-nerve fibers can account for behavioral detection thresholds in cats over a wide range of noise levels.

216

At the highest noise levels, tone detection is probably mediated by the rate responses of low SR fibers (Costalupes, 1985).

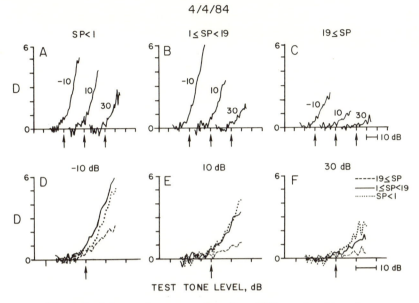

Fig. 3. Scaled rate-change as a function of BF tone level in noise. Arrows show behavioral masked thresholds in cats from Costalupes (1983). Data from Young and Barta, 1985.

A similar conclusion has been reached by Fay and Coombs (1983), who found close correspondence between behavioral and rate thresholds for tones in noise in the saccular nerve of the goldfish; phase-locking thresholds were significantly lower.

FREQUENCY DISCRIMINATION IN NOISE BASED ON AVERAGE RATE

Dye and Hafter (1980) studied the abilty of human subjects to detect changes in the frequency of single tones in the presence of masking noise. Frequency DL's were measured as a function of tone level at constant signal-to-noise-ratio. They were found to vary both with tone level and frequency. At low frequencies (.5 and 1.0 kHz), frequency DL's decrease with increasing tone level, whereas at higher frequencies (3.0 and 4.0 kHz), DL's increase with increasing tone level. These different trends with level for low and high frequency tones led Dye and Hafter to suggest that discrimination of tone frequency is based on temporal responses of auditory-nerve fibers at low frequencies, and on rate responses at higher frequencies.

217

Barta (1985) measured temporal-place and rate-place profiles in response to 1.0 and 3.0 kHz tones in noise at signal-to-noise ratios comparable to those used in the studies of Dye and Hafter. Optimal processor performance in the frequency discrimination task was evaluated as a function of tone level using both rate-place and temporal-place profiles and the results are shown in Fig. 4.

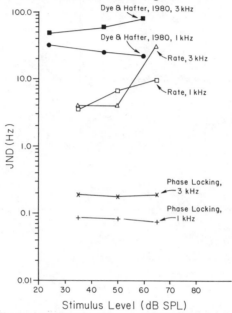

Fig. 4. The just-noticeable-difference (JND) in frequency (ordinate) versus tone level (abscissa) at constant signal-to-noise ratio from Dye and Hafter (1980; filled symbols), predicted using rate-place profiles (open symbols), and predicted using temporal-place profiles (x and +). From Barta, 1985.

Model estimates of frequency DL's based on either rate or temporal-place profiles exceed the psychophysical performance reported by Dye and Hafter at tone frequencies of 1.0 and 3.0 kHz. At 3.0 kHz, frequency DL's based on rate-place profiles show an increase at the highest tone level studied whereas those based on temporal place profiles remain essentially constant. This apparent level dependent behaviour of frequency DL's predicted using rate-place profiles is consistent with the trend in the psychophysical data at 3.0 kHz. However, model performance was based only on the responses of high and medium SR fibers. Rate-place profiles derived from the responses of high threshold low SR fibers maintain a peak of activity centered at the tone frequency at higher levels than do high SR fibers (Barta, 1985; Costalupes, 1985). Therefore, it is not clear

218

that frequency DL's based on rate-place profiles will increase at high stimulus levels if model estimates are expanded to include the responses of low SR fibers (Barta, 1985). At 1.0 kHz, frequency DL's based on rate-place profiles increase with tone level, whereas performance based on temporal-place profiles decreases slightly. Therefore, both rate-place and temporal-place profiles contain sufficient information to more than account for frequency DL's over the range of tone and noise levels studied by Dye and Hafter. Predicted frequency DL's exhibit the same dependence on tone level as do the psychophysical data if processing is based on rate-place profiles at 3.0 kHz, and temporal-place profiles at 1.0 kHz.

EFFECTS OF EFFERENT STIMULATION ON RATE RESPONSES IN NOISE

The cochlea receives efferent innervation from two distinct regions of the brainstem (Guinan et al., 1983). Fibers of the lateral olivocochlear system (LOCS) innervate almost exclusively the dendrites of auditory-nerve fibers in the inner hair cell region and project primarily to the ipsilateral cochlea. Fibers of the medial olivocochlear system (MOCS) project predominantly to outer hair cells in the contralateral cochlea. That set of efferent fibers which cross the brainstem to innervate the contralateral cochlea is known as the crossed olivocochlear bundle (COCB). Lesions of the COCB primarily disrupt innervation of the cochlea by the MOCS (Guinan et al., 1983). Dewson (1968) presented evidence that such lesions impair the abilities of monkeys to discriminate the vowel sounds /i/ and /u/ in the presence of masking noise but have no affect on the performance of this task in quiet. Other studies have shown that lesions of the COCB have no significant affect on tone detection threshold in backgrounds of quiet and masking noise (Trahiotis and Elliot, 1970; Igarashi et al., 1972), or on pure-tone intensity discrimination (Igarashi et al., 1979). One interpretation of these psychophysical data is that a function of the MOCS is to enhance the discrimination of above threshold signals in noise. Although fibers of the MOCS are active in the anesthetized cat preparation which is used in most studies of auditory-nerve responses (Liberman and Brown, 1985), it is unlikely that they function as they do in conscious, behaving animals. For these reasons, we have investigated the effects of electrical stimulation of the COCB on auditory-nerve rate responses to tones in noise (Winslow and Sachs, 1986a).

The effects of COCB stimulation on rate-level functions in broadband noise are shown in Fig. 5. The solid lines show rate-level functions for BF tones in noise backgrounds in the absence of COCB stimulation. In each case BF tones produce little rate change. Considerable rate changes do occur in the presence of 400 per second electrical shocks to the COCB (dashed lines). These data suggest that efferent input to the cochlea may function to restore rate-place representations of stimuli in noise and thereby enhance their discrimination. Effects of COCB stimulation are known to be largest on fibers with high BF (Wiederhold, 1970; Winslow and Sachs, 1986a). Thus, COCB induced restoration of rate-change in noise may be greatest in precisely that population of afferent fibers which must convey information to the CNS using rate-coding schemes.

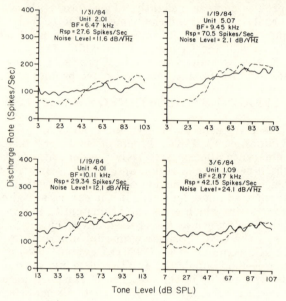

Fig. 5. BF tone rate-level functions measured in noise backgrounds of the indicated spectral level in the absence (solid lines) and presence (dashed lines) of 400 per second COCB shocks (Winslow and Sachs, 1986a).

DISCUSSION

We have considered recent results concerning rate-place representations of the frequency and intensity of single tones in backgrounds of quiet and noise. These results suggest that rate-place codes maintain these spectral features over a wide range of tone and noise levels if the properties of low spontaneous rate high threshold fibers are taken into account. We have also reviewed evidence which shows that efferent input to the cochlea may function to improve rate-place representations of signals in noise. An important implication of the data reviewed here is that the rate responses of fibers projecting from restricted regions of the basilar membrane can encode single tone intensity and frequency over a wide range of stimulus levels if there exists a mechanism for selectively weighting the rate responses of fibers from different SR populations so as to emphasize the low SR population at high stimulus levels. This selective weighting is also implicit in the form of the optimal intensity discrimination rule (Siebert, 1968; Viemeister, 1983; Winslow and Sachs, 1986b; also see Delgutte, 1982).

We have hypothesized a simple neural circuit which may be capable of performing this level dependent weighting of auditory-nerve fiber rate responses (Winslow, 1985; Winslow and Sachs, 1986b). The circuit is based on the principle of direct path inhibition which has been suggested as a possible synaptic mechanism underlying the directional selectivity of retinal ganglion cells (Koch et al., 1982). Assume that high SR fibers with BF near a frequency f kHz form excitatory synapses at distal locations within the dendritic tree of a second order neuron, and that high threshold low SR fibers with similar BF form excitatory synapses closer to the soma. Also assume that high SR off-BF fibers project to interneurons which in turn form inhibitory synapses on the direct path that current must take when flowing from the distal extremities of the dendritic tree to the soma. Finally, assume that the equilibrium potential of the ion(s) mediating inhibition are near the resting potential of the second order cell (shunting inhibition). We have speculated that at stimulus levels producing little spread of excitation, the rate responses of this second order neuron to an f kHz tone will be qualitatively similar to those of high SR fibers with BF near f kHz because the low SR fibers will be below threshold. However, as stimulus level increases, spread of excitation will activate high SR off-BF fibers which indirectly inhibit this second order neuron. Direct path shunting inhibition is very effective in preventing current from distal locations from reaching the soma, but can have little affect on synaptic current due to changes in membrane conductance at more proximal locations (Koch et al., 1982). Thus, at stimulus levels high enough to activate off-BF high SR fibers, synaptic current generated by conductance changes at distal locations in the dendritic tree will short circuit across the cell membrane at the sites of inhibition, allowing synaptic current due to excitatory input at more proximal locations from high threshold low SR fibers with BF near f kHz to drive the responses of this cell. Such a circuit thus achieves the desired selective weighting. We have noted that chopper cells in the ventral cochlear nucleus (VCN) exhibit many of the response properties required of such a second order neuron (Winslow, 1985; Winslow and Sachs, 1986b). It is especially interesting that the rate responses of these cells may maintain a stable rate-place representation of steady-state vowel spectra at stimulus levels which are high enough to cause saturation of rate response in the population of high SR fibers (Blackburn and Sachs, personal communication).

While there appears to be a rough correspondence between what we believe are the characteristics of the model described above and the response properties of VCN chopper cells, it is clear that there are alternative hypotheses concerning membrane mechanisms which may

221

produce the apparent wide dynamic range in response to steady-state vowels observed in these cells (Young, 1986). It is equally clear that a lack of quantitative models renders it impossible to decide which hypothesis is most consistent with existing data. The process of formulating such models in order to test hypotheses concerning the receptive field and response properties of cochlear nucleus neurons should prove to be of great value in understanding those aspects of auditory-nerve responses which are important in the perception of complex sounds.

REFERENCES

Barta, P. (1985). "Testing stimulus encoding in the auditory nerve," Ph. D. dissertation, Dept. Biomed. Eng., The Johns Hopkins University, Baltimore, Md.

Costalupes, J. A. (1983). "Broadband masking noise and behavioral pure tone thresholds in cats," J. Acoust. Soc. Am. 74, 758-764.

Costalupes, J. A., Young, E. D., and Gibson, D. J. (1984). "Effects of continuous noise backgrounds on rate response of auditory-nerve fibers in cat," J. Neurophysiol. 51, 1326-1344.

Costalupes, J. A. (1985). "Representation of tones in noise in the responses of auditory nerve fibers in cats: I. Comparison with detection thresholds," J. Neurosci., 5, 3261-3269.

Delgutte, B (1982). "Some correlates of phonetic distinctions at the level of the auditory nerve," in: The Representation of Speech in the Peripheral Auditory System, R. Carlson and B. Granstrom, eds., Elsevier Biomedical Press, Amsterdam.

Delgutte, B. (1986). "Peripheral auditory processing of speech information: implications from a physiological study of intensity discrimination, " NATO Advanced Research Workshop on the Psychophysics of Speech Perception, Utrecht University, the Netherlands, in press.

Dewson, J. H. (1968). "Efferent olivocochlear bundle: some relationships to stimulus discrimination in noise," J. Acoust. Soc. Am., 34, 122-130.

Dye, R. H., and Hafter, E. R. (1980). "Just-noticeable differences of frequency for masked tones," J. Acoust. Soc. Am., 67, 1746-1753.

Evans, E. F., and Palmer, A. R. (1980). "Relationship between dynamic range of cochlear nerve fibers and their spontaneous activity," Exp. Brain Res., 40, 115-118.

Evans, E. F. (1981). "The dynamic range problem: place and time coding at the level of cochlear nerve and nucleus," in: Neuronal Mechanisms of Hearing, J. Syka and L. Aitkin, eds., Plenum Press, New York.

Fay, R. R., and Coombs, S. (1983). "Neural mechanisms in sound detection and temporal summation," Hearing Res. 10, 69-92.

Guinan, J. J., Warr, W. B., and Norris, B. E. (1983). "Differential olivocochlear projections from lateral versus medial zones of the superior olivary complex," J. Comp. Neurol., 221, 358-370.

Igarashi, M., Alford, B., Nakai, Y., and Gordon, W. (1972). "Behavioral auditory function after transection of crossed olivocochlear bundle in the cat. I. Pure-tone threshold and perceptual signal to noise ratio," Acta Otolaryngol. 73, 455-466.

Igarashi, M., Cranford, J. L., Atler, E., and Alford, B. R. (1979). "Behavioral function after transection of crossed olivocochlear bundle in the cat. V. Pure-tone intensity discrimination," Acta Otolaryngol., 87, 429-433.

Jesteadt, W., Wier, C. C., and Green, D. M. (1977). "Intensity discrimination as a function of frequency and sensation level," J. Acoust. Soc. Am. 61, 169-177.

Kiang, N. Y. S., and Moxon, E. C. (1974). "Tails of tuning curves of auditory-nerve fibers," J. Acoust. Soc. Am., 55, 620-630.

Kim, D. O., and Molnar, C. E. (1979). "A population study of cochlear nerve fibers: comparison of spatial distributions of average-rate and phase-locking measures of responses to single tones, " J. Neurophysiol., 42, 16-30.

Koch, C., Poggio, T., and Torre, V. (1982). "Retinal ganglion cells: a functional interpretation of dendritic morphology," Phil. Trans. R. Soc. Lond. B 298, 227-264.

Liberman, M. C. (1978). "Auditory-nerve response from cats raised in a low-noise chamber," J. Acoust. Soc. Am. 63, 447-455.

Liberman, M. C., and Brown, M. C. (1985). "Intracellular labeling of olivocochlear efferents near the anastomosis of Oort in cats, 8th Midwinter Res. Meeting Assoc. Res. Otolaryngol., Clearwater Beach, FL, 13-14.

Sachs. M. B., and Abbas, P. J. (1974). "Rate versus level functions for auditory-nerve fibers in cats: tone burst stimuli," J. Acoust. Soc. Am. 56, 1835-1847.

Sachs, M. B., and Young, E. D. (1979). "Encoding of steady-state vowels in the auditory-nerve: representation in terms of discharge rate," J. Acoust. Soc. Am. 66, 470-479.

Sachs, M. B., Voigt, H. F., and Young, E. D. (1983). "Auditory nerve representation of vowels in background noise," J. Neurophysiol., 50, 27-45.

Sachs, M. B., Winslow, R. L., and Blackburn, C. C. (1986). "Representation of speech in the auditory periphery," in: Functions of the Auditory System, S. Hassler, ed., John Wiley and Sons, Inc., New York.

Schalk, T., and Sachs, M. B. (1980). "Nonlinearities in auditory-nerve fiber response to bandlimited noise," J. Acoust. Soc. Am. 67, 903-913.

Shofner, W. P., and Sachs, M. B. (1986). "Representation of a low-frequency tone in the discharge rate of populations of auditory nerve fibers, ", Hearing Res., 21, 91-95.

Siebert, W. M. (1965). "Some implications of the stochastic behaviour of primary auditory neurons," Kybernetik 2, 206-215.

Siebert, W. M. (1968). "Stimulus transformations in the peripheral auditory system," in: Recognizing Patterns, P. A. Kolers and M. Eden, eds., MIT Press, Cambridge, MA.

Smith, R. L., and Brachman, M. (1980). "Operating range and maximum response of single auditory-nerve fibers, " Brain Res. 183, 499-505.

Trahiotis, C., and Elliot, D. N.(1970). "Behavioral investigation of some possible effects of sectioning the crossed olivocochlear bundle," J. Acoust. Soc. Am. 47, 592-596.

Viemeister, N. F. (1983). "Auditory intensity discrimination at high frequencies in the presence of noise," Science 221, 1206-1207.

Wiederhold, M. L. (1970). "Variations in the effects of electric stimulation of the crossed olivocochlear bundle on cat single auditory-nerve-fiber responses to tone bursts," J. Acoust. Soc. Am., 48, 966-977.

Winslow, R. L. (1985). "A quantitative analysis of rate-coding in the auditory-nerve," Ph. D. dissertation, Dept. Biomed. Eng., The Johns Hopkins University, Baltimore, MD.

Winslow, R. L., and Sachs, M. B. (1986a). "The effects of electrical stimulation of the crossed olivocochlear bundle on auditory-nerve fiber rate responses to tones in noise," J. Neurophysiol., in press.

Winslow, R. L., and Sachs, M. B. (1986b). "A statistical study of intensity discrimination based on auditory-nerve fiber rate-level functions, " J. Acoust. Soc. Am., submitted.

Young, E. D., and Sachs, M. B. (1979). "Representation of steady-state vowels in the temporal aspects of the discharge patterns of populations of auditory-nerve fibers," J. Acoust. Soc. Am. 66, 1381-1403.

Young, E. D., and Barta, P. E. (1985). "Rate responses of auditory-nerve fibers to tones in noise near masked threshold," J. Acoust. Soc. Am. 79, 426-442.

Young, E. D. (1986). " Organization of the cochlear nucleus for information processing," NATO Advanced Research Workshop on the Psychophysics of Speech Perception, Utrecht University, the Netherlands, in press.

Periodicity Coding in Cochlear Nerve and Ventral Cochlear Nucleus

Steven Greenberg and William S. Rhode
Department of Neurophysiology
University of Wisconsin
Madison, WI   53706

     Neurons in the cochlear nerve and ventral cochlear nucleus encode within their temporal firing patterns the periodicity of low-frequency (< 4 kHz) complex tones. Cochlear nerve fibers synchronize their discharge activity to a cochlear-filtered, half-wave-rectified (CFHWR) version of the signal's temporal-fine-structure. As a consequence, information relevant to the signal's low pitch is manifest in the autocorrelation of the unit's timing pattern when synchronized to a CFHWR reflecting the interaction of two or more contiguous spectral components. At the level of the ventral cochlear nucleus there occurs a diversification of cellular response patterns with respect to encoding waveform periodicity. Three physiological response classes may be distinguished: (1) "Primary-like" units (concentrated in the anteroventral cochlear nucleus) respond in a manner analogous to cochlear nerve fibers of comparable characteristic frequency and spontaneous rate. (2) "Chopper" units generally synchronize to the envelope of the CFHWR waveform, provided the signal's modulation frequency lies within the temporal bandpass characteristic of the neuron. (3) "Onset" neurons, under appropriate signal conditions, synchronize to the input signal's pitch period. Thus, at this relatively peripheral level of the auditory pathway, there occurs a functional diversification of physiological response patterns of potential relevance for encoding three distinct features of signal periodicity.

INTRODUCTION

     The low pitch of complex sounds has long been of interest to students of acoustics, music and hearing (Boring, 1942; de Boer, 1976; Greenberg, 1980). This interest stems, in part, from its peculiar perceptual properties, which provide a window with which to study the neural mechanisms underlying the integrative capabilities of the central auditory pathway (Greenberg, 1980).

     The spectral pattern recognition models of pitch [Goldstein (1973), Terhardt (1974) and Wightman (1973)] arose in response to the perceived inadequacies of the temporal-fine-structure model of Jan Schouten (1940) and his colleagues (1962). In particular, the association of a strong pitch with the lower, aurally resolved harmonics appeared inconsistent with a temporal mechanism. Frequencies separated by more than a "critical bandwidth" should not interact sufficiently to provide information about the waveform periodicity. The "dominance" of low harmonics implies that a salient sensation of pitch occurs only in the absence of significant cochlear interaction among components.

However, studies of the response of single cochlear nerve fibers to complex tones suggest that certain assumptions made by adherents of both the spectral and temporal approaches may be invalid. For example, Rose et al. (1969) found that the timing pattern of a cochlear fiber stimulated by a tone consisting of 800 and 1200 Hz does synchronize to a half-wave-rectified (HWR) version of the compound waveform produced by the interaction of the signal components. Such synchronization generates timing information which could be used to infer the frequency of the (missing) fundamental (400 Hz). Similar synchronization patterns have been observed by Rose et al. (1971), Arthur (1976), Evans (1978; 1986); Kim et al. (1980), Javel (1980) and Greenberg (1986b) in response to tones composed of harmonics below the rank of eight. Such temporal response patterns suggest that the components of a complex signal are not filtered in the cochlea as sharply as would be predicted on the basis of psychophysical measures of frequency selectivity.

The question arises as to the significance of these temporal responses for processing the pitch of complex signals. Evans (1978), Javel (1980), and Greenberg (1986b) have shown that, under certain conditions, information relevant to the "pseudo-period" of inharmonic signals is present in the interval statistics of single cochlear nerve fibers, and that the timing pattern of these fibers is relatively insensitive to manipulations of the signal's phase configuration.

METHODS

Sinusoidal signals were generated by a digital stimulus system (DSS) controlled by the Harris computer. The DSS permitted each sinusoid to be specified independently in terms of frequency, phase, duration and amplitude (Rhode, 1976).Stimuli in the present study were two-component signals, arithmetically centered in frequency around the characteristic frequency (CF) of low-frequency (< 4 kHz) cochlear nerve fibers. The frequencies of the signals always corresponded to either successive harmonics or successive odd harmonics of a common fundamental, in order to compare the response to a perfectly harmonic signal with that evoked by a signal in which there occurs a maximal dissociation between the waveform temporal-fine-structure and the envelope periodicity. Responses were typically recorded at amplitudes approximately 20 to 30 dB above the discharge rate threshold of the fiber.

The responses of cochlear nerve fibers and neurons in the ventral cochlear nucleus were analyzed in several ways. First, a half-wave-rectified version of the input signal was plotted over the period histogram in order to provide a rough estimate of the relationship between the stimulus waveform and the timing pattern of the unit. Second, the degree of neural synchronization to the waveform modulation envelope was measured using a variation of the vector strength metric popularized by Goldberg and Brown (1969). Third, the autocorrelation of the period histogram was computed to determine the intervals over which the fiber discharge activity displays a periodic pattern. Fourth, the ambiguity of the autocorrelation, in the vicinity of the modulation period, was determined by fitting a von Mises function (Mardia, 1972).

The surgical procedure (for the cochlear nerve) and details of the stimulus delivery and data collection systems are described in Greenberg et al.(1986). Surgical procedure for the cochlear nucleus exeriments is described in Rhode et al.(1983).

Experimental Signals

The spectrum and waveform of the signals used in the present study are illustrated in Figure 1. The upper left panel of Figure 1 shows the time-domain representation of a signal equivalent to the fourth and fifth harmonics of a common fundamental over an interval of two modulation periods. The signal's spectrum is shown in the lower center portion of the panel. The waveform of this signal is periodic, with a period equal to the modulation period.

In the lower left panel is illustrated the spectrum and waveform for the odd-harmonic signal. The period of this signal's waveform differs from the period of the temporal-fine-structure "envelope." The periodicity of the envelope is determined by the components' frequency separation f_2-f_1, which is the same for both signals. The TFS of the odd-harmonic signal repeats over two modulation periods rather than one. However, there are two intervals in the TFS which almost correspond to the modulation period. One of these "pseudo-periods" is approximately 10% longer than the modulation period, the other is about 10% shorter than the modulation period. This ambiguity in the TFS periodicity is manifest in the signal's autocorrelation which contains two maxima in the vicinity of the modulation period (PP 1 and PP 2).

A convenient mathematical characterization of these waveforms is obtained through their autocorrelation functions. The autocorrelation function is defined mathematically as:

(1)
$$c_{xx}(\tau) = 1/T \int_0^T x(t)\, x(t+\tau)\, dt$$

227

where T is the sampling interval and τ is the delay interval of the time-shifted signal. In the present analysis the resulting autocorrelation function was "normalized" by the average magnitude, thus becoming essentially equivalent to the autocovariance function (Glaser and Ruchkin, 1976).

In the right-hand panels of Figure 1 are illustrated the normalized autocorrelation functions (c_{norm}) for the two signals discussed above. The c_{norm} of the first signal contains a maximum at the waveform modulation period (P) and integral multiples thereof. In contrast, the c_{norm} of the other signal contains maxima which correspond to the pseudo-periods (PP 1 and PP 2) as well as to the actual period of the waveform, equivalent to two modulation periods.

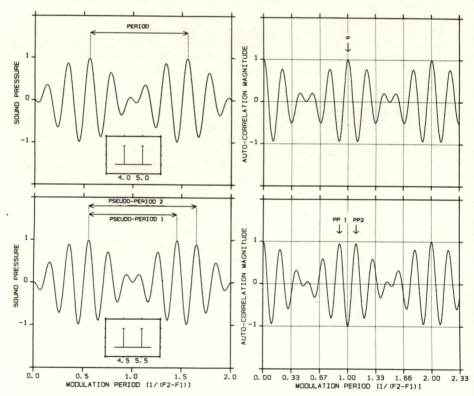

Figure 1. Schematized stimulus waveforms and their normalized autocorrelation functions. The waveform depicted in the upper left panel is equivalent to the fourth and fifth harmonics of a common fundamental. The lower left panel is the waveform of a signal equivalent to the ninth and eleventh harmonics of the fundamental.

The representation of the signal waveform in terms of the autocorrelation function is of interest because the pitch(es) to which the odd-harmonic signal are matched correspond closely to the reciprocal of the signal's pseudo-periods (de Boer, 1976; Smoorenburg, 1970).

RESULTS

Because there is no simple relationship between pitch and the waveform envelope periodicity, it is necessary to analyze the timing patterns of auditory neurons in a manner sensitive to phase locking to different features of the signal waveform. In particular, one should be careful to distinguish synchronization to the waveform modulation envelope from phase-locking to the temporal-fine-structure. Such timing patterns are distinguishable in the autocorrelation of the units' period histograms.

Cochlear Nerve

One means to distinguish the neural discharge activity synchronized to the waveform modulation characteristics from those associated with the waveform TFS is to compare the responses to signals composed of successive harmonics (of a common fundamental) to those evoked by successive odd-harmonics of roughly equivalent frequency spacing. For such stimuli, the modulation frequencies are virtually identical, although the temporal-fine-structure periodicity differs significantly.

Figure 2 illustrates the response of a single cochlear nerve fiber to a set of two-component signals analogous to those shown in Figure 1. The left-hand panels show the period histograms for the responses of a cochlear nerve fiber (CF = 720 Hz) to the two-component signals. The half-wave-rectified waveform of the input signal is plotted over the histogram. The waveform amplitude has been normalized to the histogram's maximum value. The HWR waveform has been time-shifted to provide the optimum fit (as ascertained by cross-correlation) with the period histogram. The time axis of the period histograms (and autocorrelations) has been normalized in this and subsequent figures to the modulation period of the input signal to facilitate comparison across a wide range of input frequencies. The actual time scale can be derived from the signal frequencies shown in the upper right corner of the histogram. The modulation period, τ_m, is given by the following equation:

$$(2) \qquad \qquad \tau_m = 1/(f_2-f_1)$$

Thus, the modulation period of the harmonic signal is 6.25 msec and that of the inharmonic signal is 6.94 msec.

The high correlation between the half-wave-rectified input signal and the period histogram makes it appear that the response of

229

the cochlear fiber is roughly linear for a sound pressure level of 30 dB [Although the cochlear nerve fiber response appears to be linear under many stimulus conditions, the transduction process is, itself, highly nonlinear. For discussion of this issue see Geisler and Greenberg (1986)].This seemingly linear response characteristic is typical of the majority of low-frequency cochlear nerve fibers provided that the components are arithmetically centered around the unit's characteristic frequency. The waveform fitting technique does not constitute a quantitative measure, but is merely intended to provide a rough idea of the relationship between a fiber's temporal response pattern and the input waveform.

The significance of the cochlear nerve fiber response to the input signal is evident from the responses' autocorrelation functions. The right-hand panels show the autocorrelation functions for the associated period histograms. The autocorrelation for the response to the harmonic signal has a maximum at the signal's period and at integral multiples of this interval. In contrast, the autocorrelation for the response to the inharmonic signal contains two maxima in the vicinity of the modulation period, one ten percent above, the other ten percent below this interval. These maxima

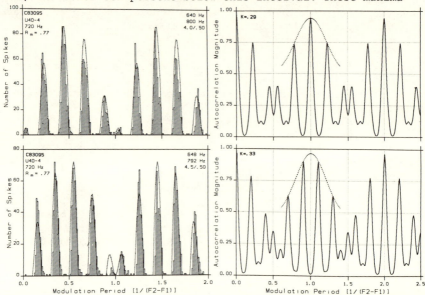

Figure 2. The period histograms and associated normalized autocorrelation functions for responses of a high-spontaneous cochlear nerve fiber to signals analogous to those illustrated in Fig. 1. The unit's CF is 720 Hz. Spontaneous rate of the fiber was 39 spikes/sec. Signals were presented 20 dB above the unit's rate threshold.

230

correspond to the pseudo-periods of the stimulus waveform. The primary pitch(es) associated with this type of signal correspond to intervals of the pseudo-periods. An additional maximum is observed in both autocorrelation functions at an interval equivalent to two modulation periods. For the response to the harmonic signal this peak merely reflects the periodic nature of the input waveform. For the response to the inharmonic signal, this interval corresponds to the signal's actual fundamental period. Occasionally, a low pitch corresponding to this fundamental may be heard (Patterson and Wightman, 1976; Gerson and Goldstein, 1978).

The response of the nerve fiber illustrated in Figure 2 is typical of low-frequency, high-spontaneous rate cochlear nerve fibers. Low- and medium-spontaneous rate fibers discharge over a more restricted portion of the modulation period in a fashion that enhances the periodicity coding properties of these units (Greenberg, 1986a).

Ventral Cochlear Nucleus

Frisina (1983) has shown that certain physiological response types within the ventral cochlear nucleus, the choppers and the onsets, are specialized to encode the periodicity of amplitude modulated signals and that most of these units synchronize most strongly to modulation frequencies between 50 and 500 Hz. Møller (1974) has also observed that the "modulation transfer functions" of most neurons in the cochlear nucleus fall within this range.

However, in both studies, the center frequency of the majority of the signals was above the spectral existence region for low pitch [< 4 kHz - Ritsma, 1962]. In particular, it is unclear what potential choppers and onsets possess for encoding parameters of waveform periodicity relevant to low pitch.

Figure 3 illustrates a comparison of three basic ventral cochlear nucleus response classes to sinusoidal and to two-component signals, equivalent to the ninth and eleventh harmonics of a common fundamental.

Displayed are the post-stimulus time and interval histograms of responses to a sinusoidal signal (at the unit's characteristic frequency), as well as the period histogram (spanning two modulation periods) and the normalized autocorrelation for the response to the odd-harmonic signal (where the components are arithmetically centered around the unit's CF). The responses may be partitioned into the following classes:

(a) Fine-structure encoders: The top row displays the responses of a low-spontaneous rate primary-like unit. The response pattern is similar to that of cochlear nerve fibers of comparable CF and

231

spontaneous rate (Greenberg, 1986a). The unit is roughly synchronized to the half-wave rectified input signal, with the consequence that the pseudo-periods and true period are prominent in the histogram's autocorrelation (arrows). Note the presence of an additional maximum at the mean of the spectral frequencies.

(b) Envelope Encoders: In contrast, choppers rarely synchronize to the waveform's fine-structure. In response to sinusoidal signals, their discharge is modulated at a characteristic chopping frequency, which is typically between 100 and 600 Hz. Evidence of this chopping mode is observed in the interval histogram, which shows a symmetric, narrow, unimodal pattern. In response to the odd-harmonic signal, the unit synchronizes to the modulation envelope rather than to the fine-structure. As a consequence, the pseudo-periods are not represented in the autocorrelation. Rather, there is a broad maximum at the modulation period. In response to sinusoidal signals, onset units typically discharge with a high probability at stimulus initiation, and thereafter fire at a steady, if somewhat reduced rate [the average sustained discharge rate for onset units is 230 spikes/sec]. One class of onset response, the onset$_{chopper}$ has a slightly modulated pattern of discharge to a sinusoid. In response to the odd-harmonic signal, the unit is primarily synchronized to the modulation envelope, although there appears to be a slight degree of synchronization to a segment of the fine-structure. The autocorrelation shows two rather small peaks in the vicinity of the pseudo-periods. However, the response is essentially synchronized to the waveform envelope.

(c) Pitch Period Encoders: The more common type of onset unit discharges only during a very restricted portion of the two-component signal's modulation period. Its firing pattern behaves as if each modulation cycle of a complex signal is a separate stimulus, capable of eliciting a spike. The consequence of such behavior is to encode information about the pseudo- and true periods of the waveform. Note the absence of information in the autocorrelation pertaining to the spectral frequencies of the input signal.

DISCUSSION

Although most complex sounds are spectrally richer than those used in the present study, the response of cochlear fibers (and most ventral cochlear nucleus units) tuned to the pitch-relevant, aurally resolved portion of the spectrum would be expected to be driven by either one or two components. Thus, the timing patterns generated by spectrally simple signals may be utilized to infer the temporal discharge activity produced by broader bandwidth signals at a

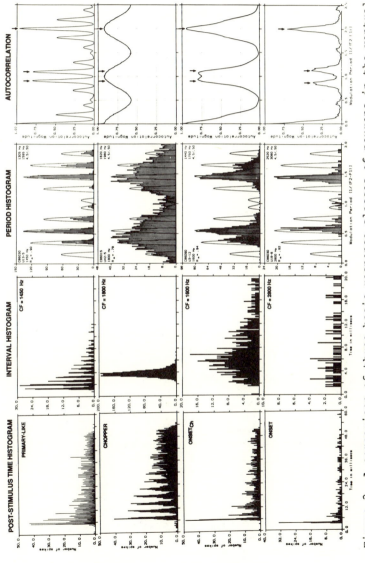

Figure 3. A comparison of three basic response classes of neurons in the ventral cochlear nucleus to sinusoidal and to two-component signals, equivalent to the ninth and eleventh harmonics of a common fundamental. Displayed are the post-stimulus time and interval histograms of responses to a pure tone (at the unit's characteristic frequency), as well as the period histogram (spanning two modulation periods) and the normalized autocorrelation for the response to the odd-harmonic signal.

specific tonotopic location. Those units driven by a single harmonic reflect the system's ability to "resolve" individual spectral components. Neurons responsive to the interaction between contiguous components provide a means with which to infer the input signal's periodicity.

Pattern recognition models of pitch require that the input signal be subjected to some form of peripheral frequency analysis prior to computation of waveform periodicity. However, the data presented in the present study suggest that frequency analysis, *per se*, is not essential for periodicity extraction, but may rather be a by-product of some more fundamental property of auditory signal processing (Greenberg, 1986b).

Cochlear nerve fibers, choppers, primary-like and onset units are all capable of encoding information about waveform periodicity within their timing patterns. Of the four unit response types, the onset cells provide the most direct means with which to encode information concerning the signal's pitch period. Neurons capable of measuring the temporal intervals between successive firings of these units would be capable of providing a fairly accurate estimate of the signal's pitch period.

The choppers appear to encode information relevant to the waveform modulation periodicity. Although the estimate of the signal's periodicity will be courser than that provided by the onset units, the chopper output could be useful in segregating simultaneously presented signals on the basis of discordant periodicity.

Cochlear nerve fibers and primary-like units encode information in their timing patterns relevant to both the pitch period(s) and the signal spectrum. Moreover, the information they encode concerning waveform periodicity is often ambiguous (as observed in the autocorrelation function of the period histograms), and parallels, in some instances, the sorts of perceptual ambiguity typical of musical pitch.

Together, the temporal response patterns of neurons in the auditory periphery provide a means for detailed analysis of complex sounds based on different features of waveform periodicity.

REFERENCES

Arthur, R. M. (1976). Harmonic analysis of two-tone discharge patterns in cochlear nerve fibers," Biol. Cybern. 22, 21-31.
Boer, E. de (1976). On the "residue" and auditory pitch perception, in: Handbook of Sensory Physiology V/3, W. D. Keidel and W. D. Neff, eds., Springer Verlag, Berlin.

Boring, E. (1942). Sensation and Perception in Experimental Psychology, Appleton-Century-Crofts, New York.

Evans, E. F. (1978). Place and time coding of frequency in the peripheral auditory system: Some physiological pros and cons, Audiology 17, 369-420

Evans, E. F. (1986). Cochlear nerve fiber temporal discharge patterns, cochlear frequency selectivity and the dominant region for pitch, in: NATO Advanced Research Workshop on Auditory Frequency Selectivity, B. Moore and R. Patterson, eds., Plenum, New York.

Frisina, R. F. (1983). Enhancement of responses to amplitude modulation in the gerbil cochlear nucleus: Single-unit recordings using an improved surgical approach, Institute for Sensory Research, Syracuse, N.Y. ISR-S-23.

Geisler, C. D. and Greenberg, S. (1986). A two-stage automatic gain control model predicts the temporal responses to two-tone signals, J. Acoust. Soc. Am., in press.

Gerson, and Goldstein, J. L. (1978). Evidence for a general template in central optimum processing for pitch of complex tones, J. Acoust. Soc. Am., 63, 498-510.

Glaser, E. and Ruchkin, D. (1976). Principles of Neurobiological Signal Analysis, New York, Academic Press.

Goldberg, J. and Brown, P. (1969). Response of binaural neurons of dog superior olivary complex to dichotic tonal stimuli: Some physiological mechanisms of sound localization, J. Neurophysiol., 32, 613-636.

Goldstein, J. L. (1973). An optimum processor theory for the central formation of the pitch of complex tones, J. Acoust. Soc. Am., 54, 1496-1505.

Greenberg, S. (1980) Neural Temporal Coding of Pitch and Timbre. UCLA Working Papers in Phonetics 52, Los Angeles, CA.

Greenberg, S. (1986a). Possible role of low and medium spontaneous rate cochlear nerve fibers in the encoding of waveform periodicity, in: NATO Advanced Research Workshop on Auditory Frequency Selectivity, B. Moore and R. Patterson, eds., Plenum, New York.

Greenberg, S. (1986b). Neural temporal coding of low pitch. II. Responses of single cochlear nerve fibers in the cat to two-component signals, in press.

Greenberg, S., Geisler, C. D. and Deng, L. (1986). Frequency selectivity of low-frequency cochlear nerve fibers based on the temporal response patterns of two-tone signals, J. Acoust. Soc. Am., 79, 1010-1019.

Javel, E. (1980). Coding of AM tones in the chinchilla auditory nerve: Implications for the pitch of complex tones, J. Acoust. Soc. Am., 68, 133-146.

Kim, D. O., Molnar, C. E. and Mathews, J. W. (1980). Cochlear mechanics: Nonlinear behavior in two tone responses as reflected in cochlear nerve fiber responses and in ear-canal sound pressure, J. Acoust. Soc. Am., 68, 1704-1721.

Mardia, K. V. (1972).Statistics of Directional Data, Academic Press, New York.

Møller, A. R. (1974). Responses of units in the cochlear nucleus to sinusoidally amplitude modulated tones, Exp. Neurol., 45, 104-117.

Patterson, R. D. and Wightman, F. L. (1976). Residue pitch as a function of component spacing, J. Acoust. Soc. Am., 59, 1450-1459.

Rhode, W. S. (1976). A digital system for auditory neurophysiological research, in: Current Computer Technology in Neurobiology, P. Brown, ed., Hemisphere Publishing Co., Washington, D.C., pp. 543-567.

Rhode, W. S., Smith, P. H. and Oertel, D. (1983) Physiological response properties of cells labeled intracellularly with horseradish peroxidase in cat dorsal cochlear nucleus, J. Comp. Neurol., 213, 426-427.

Ritsma, R. (1962). Existence region of the residue. I, J. Acoust. Soc. Am., 34, 1224-1229.

Rose, J. E., Brugge, J. E., Anderson, D. J. and Hind, J. E. (1969). Some possible neural correlates of combination tones, J. Neurophysiol., 32, 402-423.

Rose, J. E., Hind, J. E., Anderson, D. J. and Brugge, J. F. (1971). Some effects of stimulus intensity on response of auditory nerve fibers in the squirrel monkey, J. Neurophysiol., 34, 685-699.

Schouten, J. F. (1940). The perception of pitch, Phillips Tech. Rev., 5, 286-294.

Schouten, J. F., Ritsma, R. J. and Lopes Cardozo, B. (1962). Pitch of the residue, J. Acoust. Soc. Am., 34, 1418-1424.

Smoorenburg, G. F. (1970). Pitch perception of two-frequency stimuli, J. Acoust. Soc. Am., 48, 924-942.

Terhardt, E. (1974). Pitch, consonance and harmony, J. Acoust. Soc. Am., 55, 1061-1069.

Wightman, F. L. (1973). The pattern transformation model of pitch, J. Acoust. Soc. Am., 54, 407-416.

CODING OF COMPLEX TONES IN TEMPORAL RESPONSE PATTERNS
OF AUDITORY NERVE FIBERS

E. Javel, J. W. Horst, and G. R. Farley
Boys Town National Institute, Omaha, Nebraska 68131

The auditory system can determine the frequency
content of complex tones either by monitoring the
spatial distribution of cochlear activity or by
examining phase-locked responses of auditory neurons.
Psychophysical data suggest that the perceptual
apparatus uses both mechanisms. Using harmonic
complexes as stimuli, we investigated the ability of
cat auditory nerve fibers to encode spectral
information in their synchronized responses. Fibers
did this extremely well. Resolution of single
components greatly exceeded the human ear's ability
to do the same thing. At low intensities fiber
response spectra resembled acoustic signal spectra,
filtered by the fiber's tuning curve. Response
spectra behaved nonlinearly at high intensities.
Specifically, representations of spectral edges and
changes in amplitude or phase of single components
were enhanced for phase-coherent signals but not for
random-phase signals. Most features of responses to
harmonic complexes could be explained by considering
the effects of hair cells' compressive input-output
functions on waveform temporal fine structure.

INTRODUCTION

There are two mechanisms that the peripheral auditory
system can employ in assessing the frequency content of
complex tones. One mechanism is derived from the
mechanical waveform analysis performed by the inner ear.
This allows signal spectra to be represented as activity
distributed spatially in the cochlea. In this case
frequency (or, more accurately, pitch) is assigned by
determining the locus of peaks in the spatial excitation
pattern and applying weighting factors to ascertain the
position of the pattern's "center of gravity" (Zwicker,
1970). This type of analysis can account for many but
not all phenomena in direct masking and pitch perception.

The other mechanism, which is the one considered here,
is derived from a different aspect of cochlear mechanics.

It involves the synchronization or phase-locking of basilar membrane displacement to the instantaneous pressure fluctuations or temporal fine structure of acoustic waveforms, and it requires that hair cells exhibit directional sensitivity. This, however, is the case: Hair cells are depolarized when their stereocilia move in the direction of the longest hairs (Hudspeth, 1985), and neurotransmitter release increases only at those times. Consequently, the auditory nerve is excited only during unilateral basilar membrane deflections, imposing a type of rectification on the input waveform. The phase-locking of hair cell activity to basilar membrane vibrations allows stimulus fine structure, hence stimulus frequency, to be represented in temporal discharge cadences of auditory nerve fibers.

Synchronization in the auditory nerve and CNS has been studied thoroughly (Johnson, 1980; Brugge and Geisler, 1978), but its role in auditory perception is still unclear. Certain aspects of complex tone perception behave in virtually the same manner as neural synchronization in peripheral auditory nuclei, for example the frequency range over which complex tones possess low pitch (see Plomp, 1976). Also, it is likely that temporal cues underlie other aspects of hearing, for example pulsation thresholds (Houtgast, 1974), "roughness" perception (Fastl, 1977), and masking by complex tones (Zwicker, 1976) and narrowband noise (Buus, 1985). Finally, temporally based models can account for perceived pitch and pure-tone frequency discrimination relatively well (Goldstein and Srulovicz, 1977).

A question about the role temporal coding plays in complex tone perception arises from the observation that the human ear's ability to resolve individual components of complex tones is unexpectedly poor, that is, individual components cannot be "heard out" when they are spaced closer than 1.5 semitones or 10% (Plomp, 1976). This suggests that in these cases the cochlea transmits limited information about individual stimulus components and that frequency resolving power is determined by critical bandwidth. Neither limitation should exist temporally.

The purpose of the experiments described here was to investigate the degree to which synchronized auditory nerve fiber responses can provide information about the frequency spectra of complex tones. Studies similar to this one have been done, either using two-tone stimuli (see Greenberg, this volume) or synthesized speech (e.g., Delgutte, 1984). However, none of these were designed to address questions about temporal coding limits.

METHODS

Stimuli used in this study were harmonic complexes of the general type F = CF/N, where F is the fundamental frequency of the stimulus, CF is its center frequency, and N is an integer that defines component spacing and, therefore, signal complexity. As N increases, so does the number of components per unit bandwidth. Harmonic complexes are members of the same class of stimuli as speech vowels, but they have more restricted bandwidths and possess amplitude and phase spectra that are more easily controlled. We restricted signals to the octave band geometrically centered at CF, and signal CF was usually set to the fiber's characteristic frequency (i.e., the frequency to which the cell is most sensitive.) Calibration curves taken at the beginning of each experiment allowed us to equalize individual components during synthesis so that they possessed the desired acoustic intensities.

Examples of spectra and waveforms of some harmonic complexes are shown in Fig. 1. The parameter is the spacing factor N. One period of each waveform is shown. Because the periods vary with N, with period increasing as N increases, the time scales of the waveforms are unequal.

Responses of single auditory nerve fibers were obtained from anesthetized normal-hearing adult cats as CF, N, spectrum level and component starting phase

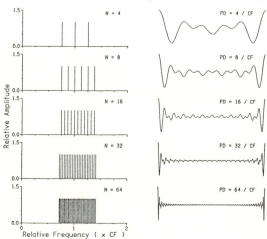

Figure 1. Spectra and waveforms for harmonic complexes of N=4, 8, 16, 32 and 64. Time scales are unequal.

were systematically varied. Analyses were based on
Fourier transforms of period histograms (PHs) and inter-
spike interval histograms (ISIHs). ISIHs were reflected
around t=0. This doubles the time over which the analysis
operates and improves resolution of individual components,
but it has no effect on the response spectrum. Fourier
coefficients were normalized by dividing by the DC value,
thereby removing the influence of overall discharge rate
and providing a measure of frequency information transfer
based entirely on discharge synchronization. Values of
normalized coefficients range from 0, indicating no phase-
locking at that frequency, to 1, indicating pinpoint
phase-locking. In practice, visually discernible phase-
locking in PHs and ISIHs produces values >0.1 .

RESULTS

Information about frequencies of individual signal
components was transmitted accurately in temporal response
spectra, even when components were spaced very closely.
An illustration of the analysis techniques we employed is
given in Fig. 2. The data in this figure are indicative
of those in our sample, and they also demonstrate the

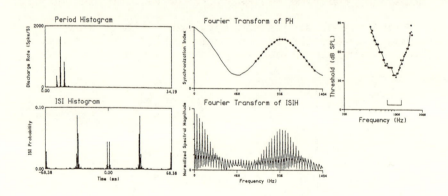

Figure 2. PHs and ISIHs (left) and normalized Fourier
    transforms (center) obtained at low intensity (35 dB
    SPL per component) for a cosine-phase harmonic complex
    of N=32. Neuron 84-H06-41 (CF=936 Hz, threshold for 20
    spike/s increase in discharge rate at CF (Thr)=35 dB
    SPL, ratio of center frequency to bandwidth at Thr+10
    dB SPL (Q10)=2.0, spontaneous rate (SR)=0.7 spikes/s.
    The fiber's tuning curve is shown at the right.

240

high precision by which frequency is signaled in temporal responses of auditory nerve fibers. The stimulus was a cosine-phase, octave-width harmonic complex of N=32. The signal possessed 23 frequencies, and its CF coincided with the fiber's CF. On the left are the PH and ISIH, and in the center are normalized Fourier transforms of the histograms. The filled symbols indicate the degree of phase-locking (synchronization index for the PH, normalized response magnitude for the ISIH) to frequencies present in the signal, and the lines indicate amounts of response to frequencies not present. The fiber's tuning curve is shown at the right. The correspondence between the shape of the tuning curve and the envelope of the response spectrum is evident, as is the squared relationship between Fourier transform values obtained from PHs and ISIHs.

Also notable in these data is the synchronization of activity to the (missing) fundamental. At higher fundamental frequencies, this frequency corresponds to the complex tone's perceived pitch. Data such as those shown in Fig. 2 indicate that auditory nerve fibers are capable of transmitting information about closely spaced frequencies and that their ability to do this exceeds the perceptual ability to resolve individual components of complex tones.

Responses of fibers with high spontaneous discharge rates (SRs) were similar to responses of fibers with low SRs, but high-SR fibers tended to transmit information about stimulus spectra less accurately, that is, widths of peaks in Fourier spectra of ISIHs were greater. Also, high-SR fibers tended to provide response spectra that possessed fewer components.

At low intensities response spectra resembled filtered versions of acoustic signal spectra. That is, the response spectrum was the linear product of the signal spectrum and the fiber's filter shape. Examples of this are shown in the top row of Fig. 3, which displays normalized Fourier transforms obtained for harmonic complexes with identical bandwidths but with variable numbers of stimulus components. At these intensities increasing the signal's spectral density merely delineates the fiber's filter shape more accurately.

Starting at about 30 dB above synchronization threshold and continuing for higher intensities, response spectra obtained for phase-coherent signals (i.e., all components in the same starting phase) differed from those obtained at lower intensities. That is, response behavior with increasing intensity was nonlinear, such that responses (1) became dominated by frequencies at the edges of the

241

stimulus spectrum, (2) occured at frequencies not present in the acoustic stimulus, and (3) were reduced at frequencies in the middle of the stimulus spectrum. These findings are illustrated by the data shown in the lower rows of Fig. 3.

The high-intensity "edge enhancement" disappeared when stimulus starting phase angles were randomized. An example is shown in Fig. 4, which displays response spectra obtained for stimuli with identical amplitude spectra but different phase spectra. On the left are shown responses obtained for stimuli with all components in cosine starting phase, and on the right are shown responses obtained from the same fiber for stimuli with components in random starting phase. The "edge enhancement" evident for cosine-phase signals is not seen for random-phase signals.

Another manipulation we performed was to vary the amplitude or phase of single stimulus components, typically the CF component. A representative series of stimuli and response spectra are shown in Fig. 5. At the top is the unmanipulated or "complete" octave-band harmonic complex and responses to it. Below that are stimuli and responses for complexes with the CF component deleted, phase-inverted, and increased in amplitude relative to the levels of the other components. The latter three signals are reminiscent of extremely simplified single-formant vowels. Response spectra obtained at low intensities were similar to those shown earlier in Figs. 2 and 3. That is, temporal response patterns signaled waveforms that were filtered versions of

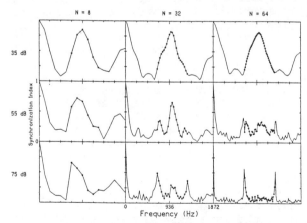

Figure 3. Normalized Fourier transforms obtained at three intensities using harmonic complexes of N=8, 16 and 64. Neuron 84-H06-41 (statistics given in legend to Fig. 2).

242

the input waveforms. Thus, when the CF component was deleted, the response spectrum showed no activity at the CF frequency; when the CF component was phase-inverted, the amplitude of that component in the response spectrum was unaffected (but phase shifted); and when the CF component was made more intense, the response spectrum reflected the emphasis to approximately the correct degree.

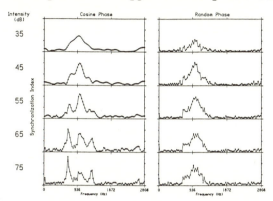

Figure 4. Normalized Fourier transforms obtained using signals with all components in cosine (left) and randomized starting phase (right). Neuron 84-H06-41 (statistics given in Fig. 2 legend).

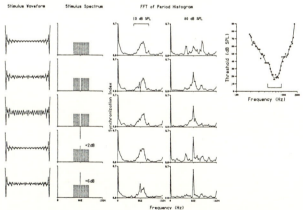

Figure 5. Waveforms (column 1), spectra (column 2), PHs (columns 3 and 5) and normalized Fourier spectra (columns 4 and 6) obtained at low and high intensities using harmonic complexes and varying single components. Neuron 84-H06-35 (CF=662 Hz, Thr=18 dB SPL, Q10=2.2, SR=80 spikes/s.) The tuning curve is also shown.

243

Response spectra obtained from the same fiber at high intensities, however, were very different. For example, removing one component caused that component to become highly emphasized in the response. Phase inversion had an even bigger effect, and increasing the amplitudes of single components by small (2-6 dB) amounts generated responses that were dominated by the emphasized component. Data such as these indicate that the auditory nerve is especially sensitive to spectral contrast (i.e., the level of one of component relative to levels of surrounding components.)

The edge and component enhancement phenomena can be explained by considering the effects of the compressive input-output nonlinearity present in hair cell and auditory nerve fiber responses. It is this feature that causes response-intensity functions of hair cells and auditory nerve fibers to saturate. Consider now what the consequences of response saturation are for cosine-phase and random-phase signals presented at low and high intensities. Little compression occurs at low intensities. Hence, the temporal waveform at the hair cell output will resemble the input waveform, and the Fourier transform will exhibit no spectral anomalies. At high intensities, the compressive input-output function limits the degree to which high-amplitude peaks can be represented in the output waveform. This is not an issue for random-phase signals, which usually have a uniform envelope and waveform fine-structure peaks of relatively low amplitude. In this case response spectra would be expected to resemble filtered versions of input spectra, which is so. Compression has a dramatic effect on phase-coherent signals, however. These phase configurations produce waveforms that are maximally peaked and exhibit a prominent envelope. In these cases the compressive nonlinearity limits the degree to which high-amplitude peaks are represented at the hair cell output, producing output waveforms that are influenced disproportionately largely by fine-structure peaks in the trough of the envelope. Thus, the spectral content of the low-amplitude portion of the period becomes over-emphasized in the response. The spectrum of such a peak-clipped, center-emphasized waveform exhibits edge effects and component enhancements of the type shown in Figs. 3-5. Fig. 6 shows schematically the temporal and spectral effects of the compressive input-output nonlinearity on phase-coherent waveforms.

DISCUSSION

The three most important facets of our data are that, first, auditory nerve fibers respond to complex tones in a highly nonlinear but nonetheless systematic manner; second, the representation of stimulus frequency in synchronized responses of auditory nerve fibers to complex tones is very sensitive to intensity and starting phase; and third, the compressive input-output nonlinearity imposed by hair cells on auditory nerve fiber responses can cause small differences in signal component intensity to be greatly amplified in phase-locked responses.

Our data show that the relatively poor resolving power exhibited by human listeners for complex tones is not due to limitations in the cochlea's and auditory nerve's ability to encode frequency information in synchronized activity. Rather, limitations in spectral resolving power are likely to be consequences of mechanisms that operate more centrally than the auditory nerve and cochlear nuclei. One mechanism that possibly underlies poor perceptual resolution in the face of excellent retention in the auditory nerve is the gradual loss of neural phase-locking in the ascending auditory pathway (see Brugge and Geisler, 1978). That is, upper limits for synchronization decline from 4-5 kHz in the auditory nerve to 1-2 kHz in the lateral superior olive and inferior colliculus to <1 kHz in the medial geniculate and primary auditory cortex. The low-pass filtering introduced by synaptic jitter may limit the CNS's ability to obtain frequency information from phase-locked activity.

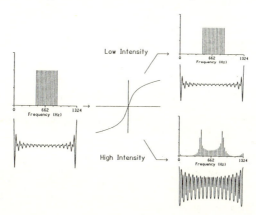

Figure 6. Schematic diagram of the effects of the hair cell compressive nonlinearity on waveforms and spectra of low- and high-intensity harmonic complexes. The compressive function is linear at intensities producing less than half-maximal response and follows a square-root function at higher intensities.

Another way that perception of phase and amplitude can be compromised by processes operating in the CNS involves differences in response spectra signaled by neurons tuned to different frequencies. Although neurons in lower auditory nuclei can temporally encode a complex tone's amplitude and relative phase spectrum, neurons with different CFs signal different waveforms. For example, in response to the same periodic wideband stimulus (a vowel, for example), neurons tuned to 2 kHz will signal a different set of amplitudes and phase angles than neurons tuned to 1 kHz. Although the CNS can integrate activity across neurons to extract information about amplitudes, integration of phase will fail unless the signal is exceptionally phase-coherent. Thus, it is not surprising that monaural phase perception is as poor as it is.

REFERENCES

Brugge, J.F., and Geisler, C.D. (1978). "Auditory mechanisms of the lower brainstem," in: Annual Review of Physiology, Annual Reviews, New York.

Buus, S. (1985). "Release from masking caused by envelope fluctuations," J. Acoust. Soc. Am., 78, 1958-1965.

Delgutte, B. (1984). "Speech coding in the auditory nerve: II. Processing schemes for vowel-like sounds," J. Acoust. Soc. Am., 75, 879-886.

Fastl, H. (1977). "Roughness and temporal masking patterns of sinusoidally amplitude modulated broadband noise," in: Psychophysics and Physiology of Hearing, E.F. Evans and J.P. Wilson, eds., Academic Press, New York.

Goldstein, J.L., and Srulovicz, P. (1977). "Auditory-nerve spike intervals as an adequate basis for aural frequency measurement," in: Psychophysics and Physiology of Hearing, E.F. Evans and J.P. Wilson, eds., Academic Press, New York.

Houtgast, T. (1974). Lateral Suppression in Hearing. Ph.D. thesis, Free University of Amsterdam.

Hudspeth, A.J. (1985). "The cellular basis of hearing: The biophysics of hair cells," Science, 230, 745-752.

Johnson, D.H. (1980). "The relationship between spike rate and synchrony in responses of auditory-nerve fibers to single tones," J. Acoust. Soc. Am., 68, 1115-1122.

Plomp, R. (1976). Aspects of Tone Sensation. Academic Press, New York.

Zwicker, E. (1970). "Masking and psychological excitation as consequences of the ear's frequency analysis," in: Frequency Analysis and Periodicity Detection in Hearing, R. Plomp and G.F. Smoorenburg, eds., A.W. Sijthoff, Leiden, The Netherlands.

Zwicker, E. (1976). "Masking period patterns of harmonic complex tones," J. Acoust. Soc. Am., 60, 429-439.

Auditory Perception of Complex Sounds:
Some Comparisons of Speech vs. Nonspeech Signals

David B. Pisoni
Speech Research Laboratory
Department of Psychology
Indiana University
Bloomington, Indiana 47405 USA

     For many years, speech researchers have been
interested in the differences in perception between
speech and nonspeech signals. Early studies revealed
marked differences in the manner in which speech sounds
were discriminated suggesting two very different modes
of response, a speech mode and a nonspeech mode. Recent
studies using nonspeech control patterns have raised
questions about these earlier interpretations and have
provided the basis for explaining several phenomena in
speech perception by means of more general principles of
complex auditory pattern perception. This paper
summarizes the philosophy behind these nonspeech
comparisons and describes two recent studies, one on
temporal order perception and the other on the
perception of the duration of rapid spectrum changes.
Both show commonalities between speech perception and
the perception of complex nonspeech patterns.

INTRODUCTION

     The study of speech perception differs in several
very important ways from the study of general auditory
perception. First, the signals typically used to study
the functioning of the auditory system have been simple,
discrete and well defined mathematically. Moreover,
they typically vary along only one perceptually relevant
dimension. In contrast, speech sounds involve very
complex spectral relations that typically vary quite
rapidly as a function of time. Changes that occur in a
single perceptual dimension almost always affect the
perception of other attributes of the signal. Second,
most of the basic research on auditory perception over
the last four decades has been concerned with problems
surrounding the discriminative capacities of the sensory
transducer and the functioning of the peripheral
auditory mechanisms. In the perception of complex sound
patterns such as speech, the relevant mechanisms are,
for the most part, quite centrally located. Moreover,
while many experiments in auditory perception and
sensory psychophysics have commonly focused on

experimental tasks involving discrimination of both spectral and temporal properties of auditory signals, such tasks are often inappropriate for the study of more complex signals including speech. Indeed, in the case of speech perception and probably the perception of other complex auditory patterns, the relevant task for the observer is more nearly one of absolute identification rather than differential discrimination. Listeners almost always try to identify, on an absolute basis, a particular stretch of speech or try to assign some label or sequence of labels to a complex auditory pattern. Rarely, if ever, are listeners required to make fine discriminations that approach the limits of their sensory capacities.

Given the published literature on the perception of simple auditory signals, it is generally believed, at least among researchers in the field of speech perception, that a good deal of what we have learned from traditional auditory psychophysics using simple sinusoids is only marginally relevant to the study of speech perception. Perhaps some of what is currently known about speech perception might be relevant to the perception of other complex auditory patterns which have properties that are similar to speech. At the present time, there are substantial gaps in our knowledge about the perception of complex signals which contain very rapid spectral changes such as those found in speech. And, there is little if any research on the perception of complex patterns that have the typical spectral peaks and valleys that speech signals have. Finally, our knowledge and understanding of patterns containing amplitude variations like the complex temporal patterns found in speech is also quite meager at this point in time. Obviously, there is a lot of basic research to do.

As Pollack (1952) demonstrated over thirty years ago, speech sounds represent a class of signals that are able to transmit relatively high levels of information with only gross variations in perceptually distinctive acoustic attributes. In other words, speech is an efficient signaling system because of its ability to exploit fundamental processing strategies of the auditory system. This theme has been taken up and expanded recently by Stevens (1980) who argues that speech signals display a certain set of general properties that set them apart from other signals in the listener's auditory environment. According to Stevens, all speech signals have three general properties or attributes in common. First, the short-term power spectrum sampled at specific points in time always has

"peaks" and "valleys." That is, speech signals display
up and down alternations in spectrum amplitude with
frequency. These peaks in the power spectrum arise from
the peaks observed in the vocal tract transfer function
and correspond to the formants or vocal resonances that
are so prominent in vowel and vowel-like sounds. The
second general property tht speech sounds display is the
presence of up and down fluctuations in amplitude as a
function of time. These variations in amplitude
correspond to the alternation of consonants and vowels
occurring in syllabic-like units roughly every 200-300
msec. Finally, the third general property that speech
signals display is that the short-term spectrum changes
over time. The peaks and valleys of the power spectrum
change; some changes occur rapidly -- like the formant
transitions of stop consonants, whereas other changes
are more gradual like the formant motions of semi-vowels
and diphthongs. According to Stevens (1980), speech
sounds have these three general attributes and other
sounds do not and it is these attributes that
distinguish speech sounds from other complex nonspeech
sounds.

It should also be mentioned here that in addition
to some of the differences in the signal characteristics
between speech and nonspeech noted above, there are also
very marked differences in the manner in which speech
and nonspeech signals are processed (i.e., encoded,
recognized and identified) by human listeners. For the
most part, research over the last thirty-five years has
demonstrated that when human observers are presented
with speech signals they typically respond to them as
linguistic entities rather than simply as random
auditory events in their environment. The set of labels
used in responding to speech are intimately associated
with the function of speech as a signalling system in
spoken language. Thus, speech signals are categorized
and labeled almost immediately with reference to the
listener's linguistic background and experience. And, a
listener's performance in identifying and discriminating
a particular acoustic attribute is often a consequence
of the functional role this property plays in the
listener's linguistic system. It is possible to get
human listeners to respond to the auditory properties of
speech signals with some training and the use of
sensitive psychophysical procedures. But one of the
fundamental differences between speech and nonspeech
signals lies in the linguistic significance of the
patterns to the listener and the context into which
these patterns may be incorporated.

In the sections below, we briefly summarize research on the perception of complex auditory patterns that have acoustic properties that are similar to speech sounds. The results of these studies demonstrate that complex nonspeech signals may also display perceptual characteristics that were once thought to be unique to the processing of speech signals. Our findings imply, contrary to popular belief in speech perception circles, that detailed knowledge and understanding of how complex nonspeech signals are processed by the auditory system may contribute in a number of ways to a much better understanding of speech perception. The converse is also true. New knowledge concerning the acoustic correlates of speech signals and more detailed understanding of the speech perception process may also contribute to a much better understanding of the perception of complex nonspeech auditory patterns.

VOICING PERCEPTION AND VOT

Interest in categorical perception has occupied the attention of speech researchers since the late 1950s. Although early studies using nonspeech control patterns failed to find similarities with the results obtained using speech signals, several more recent studies have been more successful in demonstrating comparable categorical effects. In one study, Pisoni (1977) employed a set of nonspeech tonal patterns that differed in the relative onset time of the individual components. Examples of these signals are shown in Figure 1.

ONSET TIME STIMULI

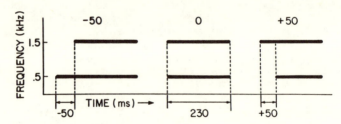

Figure 1. Schematized displays of nonspeech tone analog stimuli differing in relative onset time of individual components. [From Pisoni, 1977].

A series of experiments was carried out using these patterns to study the underlying perceptual basis of voicing perception in stop consonants that differed in voice-onset time (VOT). The results of the first experiment, shown in Figure 2, provided evidence for

categorical perception of these signals. The labeling
functions displayed steep slopes and the discrimination
functions were non-monotonic with the physical scale and
displayed peaks and valleys that corresponded to changes
in the labeling probabilities. Three additional
experiments were carried out in this study. All of them
provided additional evidence for the presence of three
distinct perceptual categories along this nonspeech
stimulus continuum which were separated by narrow
regions of high discriminability.

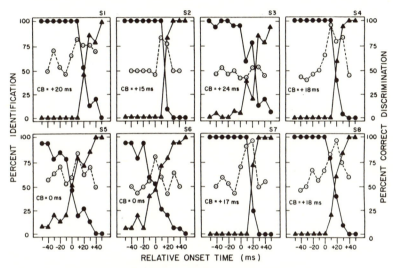

Figure 2. Identification functions (filled circles and
    triangles) and ABX discrimination functions (open
    circles) for nonspeech signals differing in tone
    onset time. [From Pisoni, 1977].

Based on these findings using nonspeech patterns
that differed in relative onset time, a general account
of the perception of voicing in initial stop consonants
was proposed in terms of the discriminability of
differences in the temporal order of the component
events at stimulus onset. At the time, we argued that
these results with nonspeech patterns as well as the
earlier data using speech signals with infants, adults
and chinchillas reflect a basic limitation of the
ability of the auditory system to process (i.e.,
identify) temporal-order information in both speech and
nonspeech signals (Hirsh, 1959). With regard to the
cues to voicing perception in word initial stops as cued
by VOT, we suggested that the time of occurrence of an
event (i.e., the onset of voicing) must be perceived in

251

relation to the temporal attributes of other events
(i.e., the release from stop closure). The fact that
these events, as well as others involved in VOT
perception, are ordered in time implies that highly
distinctive and discriminable changes will be produced
at various regions along this temporal continuum. Thus,
the discrimination of small temporal differences such as
those used here will be poor in some regions of the
stimulus continuum whereas the discrimination of
discrete attributes across perceptual categories will be
excellent. This is exactly what the previous
categorical perception experiments demonstrated and
reflects fundamental properties of the phonological
systems of natural languages. As Stevens and Klatt
(1974) observed a number of years ago, the inventory of
phonetic features used in natural languages is not a
continuous variable but rather consists of the presence
or absence of discrete sets of attributes or cues. One
of these attributes appears to be related to the
perception of simultaneity at stimulus onset.

PERCEPTION OF THE DURATION OF RAPID SPECTRUM CHANGES

    For many years speech researchers have been
interested in how one phoneme affects the perception of
other phonemes in the speech signal. This general
phenomena has been called context conditioned
variability in speech and it has been a major
theoretical issue in the field (see Miller, 1981).
Despite the variablity in the physical signal, listeners
display a form of perceptual constancy or normalization.
Several hypotheses have been proposed over the years to
account for this process. One view assumes that
listeners track changes in the talker's speaking rate.
According to Miller and Liberman (1979), the listener
interprets a particular set of acoustic cues in the
speech signal, such as the duration of a formant
transition for [ba] or [wa], in relation to the talker's
speaking rate rather than by reference to some absolute
set of context-invariant attributes in the auditory
pattern itself. In Miller and Liberman's well-known
study on the perception of [ba] and [wa] they found that
the labeling boundary for a syllable-initial [b-w]
contrast was determined by the overall duration of the
syllable containing the target phoneme. Thus, listeners
adjusted their decision criteria to compensate for the
differences in vowel length that are produced by at
different speaking rates.

We became interested in these claims concerning the perceptual basis of normalization for speaking rate and carried out a nonspeech control experiment to determine if similar changes also occur when the signals contain rapid spectrum changes but do not sound like speech (Pisoni, Carrell, & Gans, 1983). Examples of the test stimuli are shown in Figure 3.

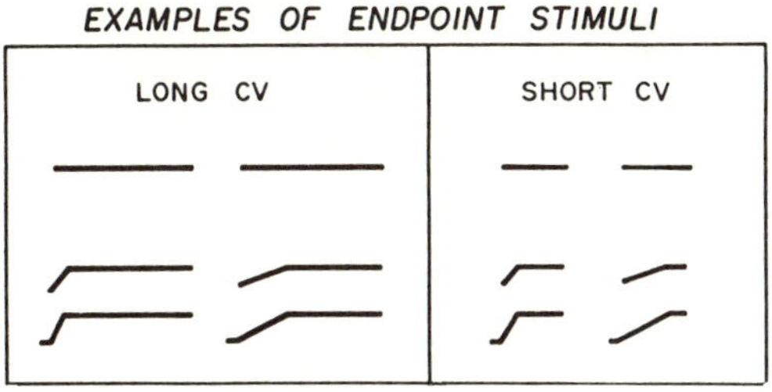

EXAMPLES OF ENDPOINT STIMULI

Figure 3.   Schematized displays of the formant motions of endpoint stimuli corresponding to [ba] and [wa]. Long duration syllables are shown on the left, short syllables are shown on the right. [From Pisoni, Carrell, & Gans, 1983].

As in the Miller and Liberman study, we varied stimulus duration of the test pattern and studied the effects of this manipulation on the identification of the duration of a rapid spectrum change at stimulus onset. Subjects were required to identify the onsets of these nonspeech patterns as either "abrupt" or "gradual." The results of our identification study are shown in Figure 4 for both speech and non-speech stimuli. We observed comparable context effects for perception of the duration of rapid spectrum changes as a function of overall duration of the stimulus with both speech and nonspeech signals. Our findings from this nonspeech control study therefore call into question the earlier claims made by Miller and Liberman that context effects such as these are specific to processing speech signals and somehow reflect the listener's normalization for speaking rate.

We suggest that context effects such as these may simply reflect general psychophysical principles that influence the perceptual categorizaton and discrimination of all auditory patterns, whether speech or nonspeech. In our experiment, the perceptual categorization of stimulus onsets as either "abrupt" or "gradual" appears to be influenced by later occurring events in the stimulus configuration as observed with speech stimuli. Thus, complex nonspeech signals may also be processed in a "relational" mode, that is, in a

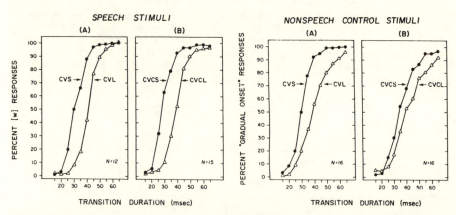

Figure 4. Labeling functions for speech stimuli (left
    panel) and nonspeech control patterns (right panel)
    that were generated from the displays shown in the
    previous figure.[From Pisoni, Carrell, & Gans, 1983]

manner comparable to that observed in the perception of
speech. Our results were particularly striking because
we replicated not only the contextual effects reported
by Miller and Liberman for syllable duration as
displayed in Figure 4 but we also found the same effects
as they did when simulated formant transition were added
to the end of the sinusoidal replicas of CV syllables,
thus changing the internal structure of the stimulus
pattern itself. In short, a relational or nonlinear
mode of processing auditory patterns is not limited
specifically to the perception of speech signals or to a
distinctive phonetic mode of response.

CONCLUSIONS

The two sets of findings summarized here taken
together with other studies using nonspeech signals
suggests that it is possible to offer alternative
accounts of specific phenomena observed in speech
perception within a somewhat larger context of what is
currently known about auditory pattern perception. In
the past, it has been very easy to explain a set of
findings in speech perception by appealing to the
existence and operation of specialized speech processing
mechanisms. As we have seen, such global explanatory
accounts are no longer satisfactory as we begin to learn
more about the psychophysical and perceptual properties
of speech and complex nonspeech signals and how the
auditory system encodes these types of acoustic
patterns. These findings make it clear to us that

theoretical accounts of speech perception can no longer
be couched in terms of vague descriptions of
articulatory mediation via specialized perceptual
mechanisms. All of the relevant nonspeech control
studies have not been carried out yet but the results of
these initial studies are very encouraging that some
rapprochement between speech and hearing scientists is
possible in the future.

ACKNOWLEDGEMENT

Preparation of this paper was supported, in part,
by NINCDS Research Grant, NS-12179 to Indiana University
and, in part, by a fellowship from the James McKeen
Cattell Fund.

REFERENCES

Hirsh, I.J.   (1959).   Auditory perception of temporal
    order. Journal of the Acoustical Society of
    America, 31, 759-767.

Miller, J.L.   (1981).   Effects of speaking rate on
    segmental distinctions, in Perspectives on the
    Study of Speech, P.D. Eimas & J.L. Miller,
    (eds.), Lawrence Erlbaum Associates, Hillsdale, NJ.

Miller, J.L. & Liberman, A.M.   (1979).   Some effects of
    later-occurring information on the perception of
    stop consonants and semi-vowels. Perception &
    Psychophysics, 25, 457-465.

Pisoni, D.B.   (1977).   Identification and discrimination
    of the relative onset time of two component tones:
    Implications for voicing perception in stops.
    Journal of the Acoustical Society of America, 61,
    1352-1361.

Pisoni, D.B., Carrell, T.D., & Gans, S.J.   (1983).
    Perception of the duration of rapid spectrum
    changes in speech and nonspeech signals.
    Perception & Psychophysics, 34, 314-322.

Pollack, I.   (1952).   The information of elementary
    auditory displays. Journal of the Acoustical
    Society of America, 24, 745-749.

Stevens, K.N.   (1980).   Acoustic correlates of some
    phonetic categories. Journal of the Acoustical
    Society of America, 68, 836-842.

255

Stevens, K.N. & Klatt, D.H. (1974). The role of formant transitions in the voiced-voiceless distinction for stops. Journal of the Acoustical Society of America, 55, 653-659.

ADDITIONAL REFERENCES

Best, C.T., Morrongiello, B., & Robson, R. (1981). Perceptual equivalence of acoustic cues in speech and nonspeech perception. Perception & Psychophysics, 29, 191-211.

Grunke, M.E. & Pisoni, D.B. (1982). Some experiments on perceptual learning of mirror-image acoustic patterns. Perception & Psychophysics, 31, 210-218.

Liberman, A.M., Delattre, P.C. & Cooper, F.S. (1958). Some cues for the distinction between voiced and voiceless stops in initial position. Language and Speech, 1, 153-167.

Liberman, A.M., Delattre, P.C., Gerstman, L.J. & Cooper, F.S. (1956). Tempo of frequency change as a cue for distinguishing classes of speech sounds. Journal of Experimental Psychology, 52, 127-137.

Liberman, A.M., Harris, K.S., Kinney, J.A. & Lane, H.L. (1961). The discrimination of relative onset time of the components of certain speech and non-speech patterns. Journal of Experimental Psychology, 61, 379-388.

Mattingly, I.G., Liberman, A.M., Syrdal, A.K. & Halwes, T.G. (1971). Discrimination in speech and non-speech modes. Cognitive Psychology, 2, 131-157.

Remez, R.E., Rubin, P.E., Pisoni, D.B. & Carrell, T.D. (1981). Speech perception without traditional speech cues. Science, 212, 947-950.

Pisoni, D.B. & Luce, P.A. (1986). Speech perception: Research, theory, and the principal issues, in Pattern Recognition by Humans and Machines, E.C. Schwab & H.C. Nusbaum, eds., Academic Press, New York.

Auditory-Perceptual Processing of Speech Waveforms

James D. Miller
Central Institute for the Deaf
St. Louis, Missouri

An account of the processes whereby the acoustic
waveform of speech is converted by the human listener to
a representation that is isomorphic with a sequence of
allophones is presented. This account is based on the
author's auditory-perceptual theory of phonetic recogni-
nition (Miller, 1984abc). Three stages of processing
are identified. In Stage I, the acoustic waveform is
converted into sensory variables that represent the
short-term spectral patterns associated with the
waveform as well as their loudnesses and goodnesses. A
key notion is that these patterns are represented as
points in an phonetically relevant auditory-perceptual
space, which is usually conceived as having three
dimensions. In Stage II, these variables are integrated
by a sensory-perceptual transformation into a single,
unitary response. This perceptual response (perceptual
pointer) can also be represented at any moment as a
point in the auditory-perceptual space, and over time a
sequence of points or a perceptual path is generated.
Stage III is the perceptual-linguistic transformation.
Here the dynamics of the perceptual pointer in relation
to perceptual target zones within the auditory-
perceptual space cause those target zones to issue
category codes or neural symbols that are isomorphic
with the allophones of the language. In a fourth stage,
not dealt with here, the sequence of category codes so
generated is converted to units isomorphic with the
language's lexicon. In this paper, the auditory-
perceptual space is described and some of the
characteristics of the preliminary estimates of the
target zones are described. Also, the hypothesized
sensory-perceptual transformation is described as is a
possible segmentation maneuver.

INTRODUCTION

Theories of speech perception treat the problem of
how the acoustic waveform produced by a talker is
transformed by the listener into linguistic units such
as phones, phonemes, morphemes, words, or other

established perceptual target zones causes the target zones to be activated and to issue neural symbols or category codes corresponding to the phones of a language.

AUDITORY-PERCEPTUAL SPACE (APS)

It is assumed that the sensory and perceptual responses to the input speech waveform can be located in a phonetically relevant auditory-perceptual space (APS) of only a few dimensions. The dimensions of this space are claimed to have characteristics similar to the variables $x=\log(P3/P2)$, $y=\log(P1/R)$, and $z=\log(P2/P1)$, where P1, P2, & P3 represent the frequency locations of the first three significant prominences in the short-term spectral envelope of the speech waveform as it is processed by the auditory sensory and perceptual systems. The variable R is a reference. Thus, the APS has the dimensions $x=\log(F3/F2)$, $y=\log(F1/R)$, and $z=\log(F2/F1)$ where R represents the sensory reference (SR) or the perceptual reference (PR), and F1, F2, and F3 represent the center frequencies of the sensory formants (SF1, SF2, SF3) or of the perceptual formants (PF1, PF2, PF3). The sensory reference (SR) is an "elastic" anchor point which is shifted from a value of about 168 Hz by the characteristics of the current talker's pitch and average spectrum such that a typical value for a male is 155 Hz and for a female is 185 Hz. In our work, the formula $SR=168(GMFO/168)^{1/3}$, where GMFO is the geometric mean of the talker's fundamental frequency or voice pitch, is often used. Of course, even though neither the particular dimensions given above nor their relations to phonetic or articulatory dimensions have been previously proposed, the general idea of such a space has been frequently stated or implied and the work of Peterson (1952), Shepard (1972), and Pols (1977) provides examples.

AUDITORY-SENSORY ANALYSES

It is hypothesized that the auditory system performs the equivalent of short-term spectral analyses based on the equivalent of a time-windowed waveform of 5-40 msec in duration. It is further hypothesized that these analyses produce the sensory equivalents of the amplitudes and frequencies of the tonal components in the input as suggested by the work of Scheffers (1983)

meaningful units. As previously noted (Miller, 1984a), such theories can be described and compared in terms of a three-stage generic model.

In Stage 1 the acoustic waveform is transformed into auditory-sensory forms expressed in auditory-sensory dimensions. Although the analyses involved in Stage 1 can be described in a variety of ways, most commonly they are likened to short-term spectral analyses with parameters chosen to emulate, to a greater or lesser degree, the characteristics of the auditory system. Because of this, it is sometimes convenient to refer to "auditory spectra" or "sensory spectra." The notion of an auditory-sensory spectrum is, of course, very familiar and has been commonly used to interpret psychoacoustic data in terms of excitation patterns, and the works of Fletcher (1940), Munson and Gardner (1950), Plomp (1970), Schroeder (1975), Zwicker and Scharf (1965), and Zwicker (1970) serve as examples.

Stage 2 involves the transformation of auditory-sensory information into perceptually relevant dimensions. In motor theories it is here that sensory input is converted to articulatory terms such as abstract motor commands (Studdert-Kennedy et al., 1970, Liberman, 1982; Kozhevnikov and Chistovich, 1965). In feature theories, such as those of Fant (1973); Stevens, and Blumstein, (1981), or Pisoni and Sawusch, (1975), the auditory-sensory forms are converted to a perceptually relevant description in terms of auditory features. In the auditory-perceptual theory the auditory-sensory representation is converted to a higher-level, auditory-perceptual representation which serves an integrative-predictive function thought to be analogous to those visual-perceptual functions involved in perception of apparent motion, figure completion, and so on.

The final stage, Stage 3, involves the conversion of perceptual information into linguistic form. Here the perceptual information is converted to a form isomorphic with linguistic units. In motor theories, the motor commands or articulatory descriptions are converted to speech sounds such as phones or phonemes. In feature theories, the acoustic features are converted to phonetic features and then to phones or phonemes. In the auditory-perceptual theory, the dynamics of the perceptual response in relation to previously

and at the same time these analyses separately produce
the sensory equivalent of the continuous power spectrum
of any significant aperiodic energy or other unresolved
high-frequency components in the input waveform.   This
information is used to distinguish aperiodic, periodic,
and mixed segments and to establish the effective pitch
(F0) and "pitch strength" of the periodic and mixed
segments.   This same short-term spectral information
undergoes further processing and, in this way, is used
to generate auditory-spectral patterns that are
variously referred to as sensory-excitation patterns,
auditory-sensory spectra, or auditory-spectral
envelopes.

SENSORY POINTERS

    Glottal-source spectra (gs-spectra) have significant
first sensory formants and are localized as the glottal-
source sensory pointer (GSSP) in the APS by the terms
$x=\log(SF3/SF2)$, $y=\log(SF1/SR)$, and $z=\log(SF2/SF1)$.   In
the special case of nasalized spectra, the first formant
splits into low (SF1L) and high (SF1H) values, and the
GSSP is localized in the APS by the terms
$x=\log(SF3/SF2)$, $y=\log(SF1L/SR)$, and $z=\log(SF2/SF1H)$.

    Burst-friction spectra (bf-spectra) do not have
significant first formants and are localized as the
burst-friction sensory pointer (BFSP) in the APS by the
terms $x=\log(SF3/SF2)$, $y=\log(SR/SR)=0$, and $z=\log(SF2/SR)$.
In this case, SF1 is arbitrarily set equal to SR, and,
thus, the BFSP is always localized in the xz-plane of
the APS.

GOODNESS AND LOUDNESS

    Each sensory spectrum and, thus, each sensory
pointer, is said to have a goodness and a loudness.   The
goodness is to be a measure of the "speech-likeness" of
a sensory spectrum.   The notion is that for each
combination of SR, SF1, SF2, & SF3 an ideal speech-like
spectrum can be defined.   An appropriately weighted
cross-correlation between the ideal and the input
spectrum is to serve as a goodness index [see discussion
of Klatt (1982) in Miller (1984a)].   The goodness index
would be low for pure tones placed at the locations of
the sensory formants, would be low for broad-band
spectra with tiny bumps at the locations of the sensory
formants, but would be high for carefully produced

natural speech of high fidelity. A variety of schemes
will produce adequate estimates of the loudness of a
spectrum. For example, one could look up the loudnesses
of each of the formants and sum them with appropriate
rules. A loudness index is defined to vary from 0.0 for
below threshold spectra to nearly 1.0 for for spectra
that are comfortably loud as moderate loudness levels
are known to produce near perfect intelligibility.
Thus, for each momemt in time that a sensory pointer is
above threshold it has a location in the auditory-
perceptual space, a goodness (or speech-likeness), and a
loudness.

SENSORY PATHS

As the incoming speech is analyzed, the glottal-
source sensory pointer (GSSP) materializes whenever a
gs-spectrum is above the auditory threshold. As the
values of SR, SF1, SF2, & SF3 change, the GSSP traces a
sensory path through the auditory-perceptual space. The
path of the GSSP is interrupted by silences and when the
GSSP is replaced by the burst-friction sensory pointer
(BFSP). One must imagine the GSSP moving through the
space as the gs-spectrum changes shape and sometimes
this movement is nearly continuous as in the case of the
sentence, "Where were you a year ago?", where the only
interruption would occur during the friction burst of
/g/. In contrast, the burst-friction sensory pointer
(BFSP) will usually appear and disappear as friction
sounds are inserted in the speech stream. As bf-spectra
are unstable, the BFSP may exhibit considerable jitter,
but it usually will not trace out a meaningful sensory
path. In most cases where the BFSP replaces the GSSP,
the BFSP will appear to "fill in" or "continue" the path
of the GSSP as there are transitions in the path of GSSP
to and away from the location of the BFSP. In the case
of voiced fricatives, both sensory pointers are
simultaneously present as one is associated with the
gs-spectrum of the voiced part of the sound and the
other is associated with the bf-spectrum of the friction
part of the sound.

PERCEPTUAL POINTER

The perceptual pointer is conceived as being the
locus of the perceptual response in the APS. Its
location is given by the terms $x=\log(PF3/PF2)$,
$y=\log(PF1/PR)$, and $z=\log(PF2/PF1)$. When the perceptual

response is nasalized, the PF1 splits into PF1L and PF1H and the locus of the PP is given by x=log(PF3/PF2), y=log(PF1L/PR), and z=log(PF2/PF1H). The perceptual pointer also has a loudness and states. Its loudness is the integrated loudnesses of the sensory pointers and, of course, this loudness decays slowly, over 100-250 msec, when the sensory pointers disappear. The perceptual pointer also has feature-like states such as glottal-source, burst-friction, periodic, aperiodic, and nasal.

SENSORY-PERCEPTUAL TRANSFORMATION

The sensory pointers are conceived as being dense with very high masses, and they are connected to the perceptual pointer by springs. Since the perceptual pointer is assumed to have unity mass, it does not significantly "act back" on the sensory pointers. The APS is assumed to be a viscous medium, and thus, the PP encounters resistance that is proportional to its velocity. The springs have stiffnesses that are reduced when either the loudness index or the goodness index of a sensory pointer is reduced. These indices are intended to vary between 0 and 1.

When the sensory pointers disappear, the perceptual pointer begins to migrate to a "neutral point" that is appropriate to its auditory state. For example, if the perceptual pointer is in the burst-friction state when the sensory pointers disappear, it will begin to migrate to the burst-friction neutral point (BFNP), which is centered in the region of the auditory-perceptual space occupied by burst-friction spectra. Similarly, if the perceptual pointer is in the gs-state when the sensory pointers disappear, then it will migrate to the glottal-source neutral point (GSNP), which is centered in the region of the auditory-perceptual space occupied by gs-spectra. When the sensory pointers disappear, the perceptual pointer maintains its current state for 100-200 msec. Then it reverts to the gs-state. Therefore, in the case of a long silence, the perceptual pointer always returns to the glottal-source neutral point. The neutral points have the potential to play an important role in explaining the results of cue integration experiments and are essential for the segmentation of phones that are preceded or followed by long silences.

Further discussion of the sensory-perceptual transformation and a preliminary mathematical formulation can be found in Miller and Chang (In press). Finally, it is noted that the idea of a perceptual system tracking and integrating sensory inputs is familiar as in the case of apparent motion in vision. In the case of speech, this notion has been frequently alluded to or implied as in the work of Joos (1948).

SEGMENTATION

The auditory-perceptual space is assumed to be divided into perceptual target zones. When activated, such target zones are capable of issuing distinct neural symbols or category codes. A perceptual target zone is activated when a segmentation maneuver occurs within its boundaries. As the perceptual pointer moves through the APS, it is nearly always inside a perceptual target zone (PTZ). Only when the perceptual pointer performs a segmentation maneuver inside of a PTZ is a category code corresponding to an allophone activated. Candidates for segmentation maneuvers include (a) a period of low velocity, (b) a sharp deceleration, and (c) high curvature in the perceptual path. Preliminary evidence favors possiblity (c) as the most frequent mechanism even though possibilities (b) and (a) both seem to operate on occasion.

PERCEPTUAL TARGET ZONES

Preliminary estimates of the sizes, shapes, and locations of some forty-four allophones of American English (Miller and Hawks, 1986) indicate the these zones are large, irregularly shaped, and have abutting boundries. The simple vowels fall in a vowel slab near the plane $x + y + z = 1.18$. Retroflex sounds and nasals fall below the vowel slab while laterals fall in and above it. Other nonretroflex approximates are located in the vowel slab. Stops and fricatives are appropriately located on or near the xz-plane of the APS.

Three slightly different types of perceptual target zones are being considered. The first and simplest type is one which defines a portion of the auditory-perceptual space which is uniquely associated with a single phone-like element. In this case, whenever a segmentation maneuver occurs within that zone, a category code or neural symbol associated with that

263

symbol is issued by the target zone. In the second type
of perceptual target zone, the category code issued by
the perceptual target zone is contingent on the auditory
state of the perceptual pointer at the time of the
segmentation maneuver. For example, it may be that the
perceptual target zones for the aspirated p, [p^h]; the
unaspirated p, [p]; and the voiced cognate b, [b] may
show a substantial common area. In this case, the
category code issued by the common area would depend on
the auditory state of the perceptual pointer at the time
of the event. A third type of target zone might be
particularly appropriate for glides and diphthongs.
Here the target zone could be a unidirectional pipe that
would be activated whenever the perceptual pointer
enters one end of the pipe and exits the other within
certain time limits, thus objectively defining quite
literally a "perceptual glide." Preference for
parsimony causes one to utilize the first and simplest
type of perceptual target zone insofar as possible with
glides and diphthongs defined as sequences of phone-like
events. However, it is not unlikely that all three
types of target zones will be required. In any case the
basic nature of the proposed perceptual-phonetic
transformation is clear. When the perceptual pointer
performs a segmenting maneuver within a target zone,
then the target zone issues a neural symbol or category
code that corresponds to a phonetic element of the
language.

REPRISE

The three stage process whereby the acoustic
waveform of speech is converted into a string of
category codes that correspond to a string of phonetic
elements has now been presented. A brief reprise
follows. At each moment the spectral envelope patterns
of glottal-source sounds and burst-friction sounds are
represented as sensory responses or sensory pointers in
a phonetically relevant auditory-perceptual space.
These sensory responses are converted to a unitary
perceptual response by sensory-perceptual transformations that rely heavily on the histories, trajector-
ies, and dynamics of the sensory responses. Finally,
segmentation and categorization mechanisms that depend
on the dynamics of the perceptual pointer in relation to
perceptual target zones result in a string of neural

symbols or category codes that correspond to the speech sounds of a language.

ACKNOWLEDGEMENT

Supported by NINCDS grants NSØ3856 and NS21994.

REFERENCES

Fant, G. (1973). Speech Sounds and Features. MIT Press, Cambridge.
Fletcher, H. (194Ø). "Auditory patterns." Rev. Mod. Phys. 12, 47-65.
Joos, M. (1948). Acoustic Phonetics. Ling. Soc. Amer., Baltimore, MD.
Klatt, D.H. (1982). "Prediction of perceived phonetic distance from critical-band spectra: A first step." Proc. Int'l. Congress Acoust, Speech, Signal Processing, Paris, 1278-1281.
Kozhevnikov, V.A., and L.A. Chistovich. (1965) Speech: Articulation and Perception. [Rech: Artikulyatsiya i Vospriyatiye, Moscow-Lenigrad.] Translated by the Joint Publications Research Service. Clearinghouse for Federal Scientific and Technical Information, U.S. Department of Commerce, Washington, D.C. 20043. (Publication nos. JPRS: 30,543; TT: 65-31233.) Cited in: The Sounds of Speech Communication by J.M. Pickett. (1980) (University Park Press, MD).
Liberman, A.M. (1982). "On finding that speech is special," Am. Psychol. 38, 148-167.
Miller, J.D. (1984a). "Auditory processing of the acoustic patterns of speech." Arch. Otolaryngol. 110, 154-159.
Miller, J.D. (1984b). "Implications of the auditory-auditory-perceptual theory of phonetic perception for speech recognition by the hearing impaired." ASHA Reports 14, 45-48.
Miller, J.D. (1984c). "Auditory-perceptual correlates of the vowel." J. Acoust. Soc. Am. 76(S1), p. S79.
Miller, J.D. and Hawks, J.W. (1986). "Spectral envelopes and perceptual target zones of consonants and vowels: Preliminary estimates." J. Acoust. Soc. Am. 79(S1), p. S66.
Miller, J.D. and Chang, H.M. (In press). Sensory-perceptual dynamics in speech perception. In: Psychophysics and Speech Perception, M.E.F. Schouten, Ed.

Munson, W.A. and Gardner, M.B. (1950). "Loudness patterns--a new approach. J. Acoust. Soc. Am. 22, 177-190.

Peterson, G.E. (1952). "The information bearing elements of speech." J. Acoust. Soc. Am. 24, 629-637.

Pisoni, D.B. and J.R. Sawusch (1975). "Some stages of processing in speech perception." In: Structure and Process in Speech Perception, A. Cohen and S.G. Nootebaum (Eds.) (Springer-Verlag, New York), 16-35.

Plomp, R. (1970). "Timbre as a multidimensional attribute of complex tones," In: Frequency Analysis and Periodicity Detection in Hearing. Edited by R. Plomp & G.F. Smoorenburg. (A.W. Sijthoff, Leiden), 397-414.

Pols, L.C.W. (1977). Spectral Analysis and Identification of Dutch Vowels in Monosyllabic Words. (Institute for Perception TND, Soesterberg, the Netherlands)

Scheffers, M.T.M. (1983). "Simulation of auditory analysis of pitch: An elaboration of the DWS pitch meter." J. Acoust. Soc. Am. 74, 1716-25.

Schroeder, M.R. (1975). "Models of hearing," Proc. IEEE, 63(9), 1332-1350.

Shepard, R.N. (1972). "Psychological representation of speech sounds." In: Human Communication: A Unified View, E.E. David and P. Denis, Eds., (McGraw Hill, New York), 67-113.

Stevens, K.N. and Blumstein, S.E. (1981). "The search for invariant acoustic correlates of phonetic features." In: Perspectives on the Study of Speech, P.D. Eimas and J.L. Miller (Eds.) (Erlbaum, Hillsdale, NJ), 1-38.

Studdert-Kennedy, M., Liberman, A.M., and K.S. Harris (1970). "Motor theory of speech perception: A reply to Lane's critical review," Psychol. Rev. 77, 234-249.

Zwicker, E. and B. Scharf (1965). "A model of loudness summation," Psych. Rev. 72(1), 3-26.

Zwicker, E. (1970). "Masking and psychological excitation as consequences of the ear's frequency analysis," In: Frequency Analysis and Periodicity Detection in Hearing. Edited by R. Plomp & C.F. Smoorenburg. (A.W. Sijthoff, Leiden), (376-394).

Uncertainty, informational masking, and the capacity of immediate auditory memory.

Charles S. Watson
Department of Speech and Hearing Sciences
Indiana University, Bloomington, Indiana 47405

Early studies of the effects of stimulus un-certainty (varying stimulus parameters from trial to trial) showed that knowing what to listen for has only minor effects (1-2 dB) on thresholds for the detection of single tones, or for the discrimination of tones by frequency (3-5 Hz) (Harris, 1952; Green, 1961; Creelman, 1973). One interpretation of these "non-effects" is that the central mechanisms of selective attention and memory play little or no role in auditory tasks....you hear whatever happens into your ear canal, so long as it is within the range of your (peripherally-determined) sensitivity and resolving power. An alternative possibility, addressed in this paper, is that auditory processing of complex sounds might be greatly influenced by cognitive mechanisms (or "psychological", or "central", ones, depending on your age), even though simple sounds are not; and that this difference is a consequence of the limited informational capacity of immediate auditory memory.

INTRODUCTION

Over the past dozen or so years we have reported a series of experiments that suggest that the more com-plex the stimulus, the more its processing is deter-mined by central rather than peripheral mechanisms of the auditory system. At present the simplest inter-pretation of these experiments seems to be that there really is a first-stage buffer of some sort in the system, and that its capacity is limited in infor-mational rather than stimulus-parameter terms (i.e., specific physical units). Having arrived at that notion from a purely empirical path, we find ourselves agreeing with cognitive psychologists like Shiffrin and Schneider (1977), who have been saying for some time, about the visual system, that short-term memory is a major limitation on the processing of complex stimuli, but also that those limits can be effectively increased by overtraining on individual complex stimuli or on portions of those stimuli. This article reviews some experimental work that suggests that this same reasoning is applicable to auditory processing.

TONAL PATTERN EXPERIMENTS

Two very general questions were mainly reponsible for this line of research: 1) Can we predict how we hear complex sounds from the way we hear simpler ones into which the complex sounds could be decomposed, especially pure tones? 2) We had been told that listeners could discriminate subtle changes in a complex sound more accurately if that sound was recognized as speech than if it was not, and we wondered whether parsimony had actually been so rudely violated by this hypothesized "fact" of evolution. (There didn't seem to be much of a data-base to support the non-speech side of that claim.) With these broad questions in mind we selected tonal sequences as test stimuli, with total durations, frequency ranges, and durations of individual tonal components chosen to be in the same general range as those of speech [we neglected spectral complexity, anticipating that Green would later invent "profile analysis" to deal with that difficult problem and, of course, he did (1983)].

Individual 75-dB, SPL components in the ten-tone patterns were typically 40 msec in duration, about the length of the briefest phonemes in the most rapid intelligible speech. Total pattern duration was about one-half second, close to that of an average word, and the frequency range covered the major portion of the speech spectrum, about 300 to 3000 Hz. A brief period of quieting occurs between successive components in these patterns, accomplished by 2.5-msec rise-decay gating.

We first measured trained listeners' abilities to detect changes in the frequency, intensity, or duration of individual components (Watson, et al, 1975; 1976). In order to study pattern discrimination, and not merely the ability of listeners to ignore everything but a target tone within a given pattern, we varied the patterns from trial to trial. In a typical experiment we used fifty different random sequences of a ten-frequency catalog, and then designated as the "target" tones (one tone subject to change on a given trial, in each pattern) components with various frequencies and temporal postitions, so that on a given trial the listeners did not know what pattern to expect, nor where in the pattern the "target tone" might occur. We tried a number of testing

268

procedures. In general, the more complex the psychophysical method, in terms of the amount of information
presented to the listener on each trial and the number
of comparisons it forced them to make, the worse their
performance. Most accurate performance was generally
found using a same-different procedure. Listeners
were trained until their performance approached
asymptotic levels. One major finding of those early
studies is illustrated in Fig.1.

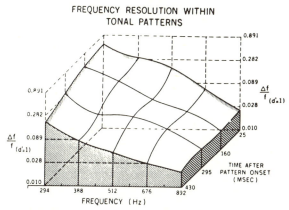

Figure 1. Detectability of changes in the frequency
of 40-ms components of ten-tone patterns, as a
function of the frequency and temporal position of
the target tones, under conditions of high
stimulus uncertainty (Watson et al., 1976).

Some portions of the patterns were resolved much
more accurately than others, especially the later-
occurring and higher-frequency components. The poorer
performance on earlier and lower-frequency components
was reflected in thresholds that were unprecedented...
50-60 percent changes were required to notice a change
in target-tone frequency, for example. It looked as
though masking were spreading in the wrong direction,
with the very salient higher frequencies masking the
lower ones. The poor performance on the early components seemed somewhat more understandable assuming
that the task required that the patterns be stored in
a limited-capacity buffer. Cognitive psychologists
have theorized a good deal about early stages of
memory in which later-arriving elements of a
complex stimulus might "overwrite", or otherwise
obscure portions that had been received earlier
(e.g.,Crowder, 1978).

269

Before accepting the notion that listeners were condemned to exceedingly degraded resolution of some portions of the tonal patterns, however, we decided to replicate the same experiments without the trial-to-trial changes of the patterns. What we learned was that after sufficient training under minimal-uncertainty listening conditions, normal listeners can hear out changes of frequency, intensity, or duration in single 40-msec components of 1/2-sec patterns that are close to their thresholds for the same components presented in isolation (Watson, et al, 1976; Watson and Kelly, 1981). While the location of the target component makes a great difference in the accuracy with which it is resolved under high uncertainty, it makes little or no difference under minimal uncertainty. The effects illustrated in Fig. 1 thus may represent listener's characteristic distribution of attention over the spectral-temporal range of a novel sound.

INFORMATIONAL MASKING

The extremes to which thresholds can be elevated as a result of trial-to-trial changes are illustrated in Table I, from a listening task we called "super-uncertainty" (Watson and Kelly, 1981). In that experiment, in addition to the previously manipulated aspects of stimulus uncertainty, the listeners didn't know which dimension of the target tone would change (intensity, frequency, or duration). While in a control experiment the signal-dimension uncertainty was shown to have little or no effect on the discrimination of isolated tones, it had severe effects when the tones were presented in a pattern context. The only terms in which the extreme threshold elevations shown in Table I seemed

Table I. Detection and Discrimination thresholds for a 554-Hz, 40-ms tone presented in a ten-tone pattern, under three levels of stimulus uncertainty (Watson and Kelly, 1981).

Uncertainty Level	ΔF(Hz)	ΔT(ms)	ΔI(dB)	Detection (dB,SPL, d'=1)
High	2400	56	9.9	58
Medium	49	27	6.8	46
Low	16	6.7	2.5	25

to make sense were that, in some manner, the listeners were almost unable to hear the individual components. That is to say, the sensation levels of the tones appeared to have been effectively reduced to very low levels. To follow that line of reasoning, we measured detection thresholds for the same target tones, again with the patterns changed from trial to trial, as were the frequency and temporal position of the target tones. The thresholds for the individual components were elevated by 40-50 dB, meaning that their effective sensation levels in the patterns were as low as -5 to 10dB.

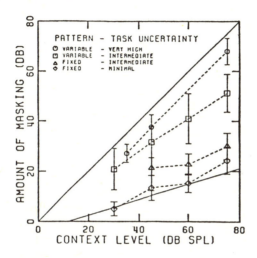

Figure 2. Amount of masking as a function of context level, under four levels of stimulus uncertainty. The lower straight line is the predicted amount of energetic masking, data above that level reflect combined energetic and informational masking. (Watson et al., 1978).

Figure 2 shows results from several experiments on component detection as a function of the level of the contextual (non-target) components in the patterns. Under high stimulus uncertainty, what we now call _informational_ _masking_, after Pollack (1975), increases approximately one dB for each dB increase in the level of the context tones. Much lower rates of increase in masking are seen as the level of stimulus uncertainty is reduced, with the very low slopes characteristic of off-frequency masking seen under minimal-stimulus-uncertainty testing.

Without providing the procedural details, here are general conclusions from some other studies of complex pattern processing:

1) It takes considerably longer to approach asymptotic performance in a pattern discrimination task than when learning to discriminate the same changes in simpler stimuli; the time course of identification tasks can be still longer, possibly requiring months or years (Watson, 1980; Leek and Watson, 1984).

2) Individual differences in pattern discrimination abilities are quite large, as shown in Table II. The tasks on a test battery varied from simple discrimination with single tones through patterns like those discussed in the preceding section. The thresholds in the table are decile values for 127 normal listeners. Notice that the thresholds for the 10th to 90th percentiles for test five...durations required to detect the presence of a middle component in a nine-tone pattern...range from 22 ms to almost 80 ms. Individual phonemes often fall between these extremes.

Table II. Population performance for 127 normal-hearing adults on a battery of auditory discrimination tests (Watson et al., 1982). Tests 1-3 are single-tone discrimination tests; Test 4 requires the discrimination of a temporal change in a six-pulse rhythmic structure; Test 5 the detection of a missing tone in a nine-tone sequence; Tests 6 and 7 the discrimination of sequences of the form "CABC" from "CBAC," for tones (6) and syllables (7); Test 8 is a modified nonsense-syllable identification test.

Test	Percentile				
	10	25	50	75	90
1.Pitch [ΔF (Hz)]	19.532	11.629	6.447	3.747	3.010
2.Intensity [ΔI (dB)]	3.154	2.132	1.223	.560	<.500
3.Duration [ΔT (msec)]	64.677	46.279	30.422	23.369	19.166
4.Rhythm [ΔT (msec)]	20.283	13.671	9.727	6.986	5.661
5.Embedded Tone [T (msec)]	77.101	57.847	39.807	32.989	22.310
6.Temporal Order (Tones) [T (msec)]	98.489	62.442	51.404	35.212	27.761
7.Temporal Order (Syllable) [T (msec)]/FA/TA/KA/PA/	>250.000	217.318	163.544	125.010	85.949
8.Syllable Identification [P(c)] (NST)	.519	.556	.611	.667	.722

3) Recently we have tried some of the uncertainty manipulations in speech discrimination tasks, with similar results to those obtained with tonal patterns (Kewley-Port, Watson, and Foyle, 1984). We replicated two experiments, Sachs and Grant's (1976) study of the categorical perception of CV stimuli (we used /pa/ and /ba/); and the nonspeech variation on that theme devised by Miller, et al (1976), in which they used a noise-buzz combination as an analog to speech stimuli. In each case non-monotonic discrimination functions were obtained, with maxima in the general vicinity of the categorical boundaries when testing was conducted with the trial-to-trial variation in the stimuli typical of VOT experiments. But a different pattern of discrimination (and much better overall performance) was obtained under minimal-uncertainty testing. In that condition discrimination functions were always monotonic; small changes in VOT were detected most accurately near VOT=0, in fact much more accurately there than near the categorical boundary. This suggests that at least some of the "perceptual boundaries" in speech are a consequence of attentional focus rather than reflecting inherent ease of discrimination in the boundary regions.

CAPACITY OF IMMEDIATE AUDITORY MEMORY

The last experiments discussed here are ones that we believe cast a little light on the origins of the uncertainty-related limitations on pattern processing, those effects we've been calling "informational masking." David Foyle and I (1985) decided that we had a lot, perhaps too much, invested in the special case of half-sec patterns with 40-50 ms components. Partly to see whether results obtained with those values were general for other pattern and component durations, we ran a series of discrimination experiments in each of which there were six different total pattern durations, randomly varied from trial to trial, 62.5 ms through 2000 ms (Watson and Foyle, 1985). In other words, we used patterns whose durations ranged from that of a spoken, "bloop", through,"Joe-took-father's-shoe-bench-out." The measure of performance was the number of independent tones that could be included in discriminably different patterns, at each of the total pattern durations. One hope for this experiment was that we might find a local maximum; listeners might be able to

extract the most information per unit time, for
patterns of some particular duration. It would have
been interesting to learn that average words are of a
duration for which the auditory system, its memory
buffers, and-so-on, are optimal. To anticipate, the
data do not seem to support that teleological
hypothesis.

An adaptive tracking procedure was used. On each
trial a pair of patterns was presented and the listener judged whether they were the same or different. The
duration of each component was $\underline{T/n}$, where $\underline{n}$ was the
current number of tones in the patterns, and $\underline{T}$ its
total duration. When the judgements were correct,
more components were added to the patterns. When the
listeners began to err, components were deleted. This
was kept up until a stable threshold was estimated, in
terms of <u>the number of components that could be presented in discriminable patterns, at each pattern
duration</u>. This experiment was repeated seven times,
for seven different types of change in the patterns.
I'll discuss the nature of those changes in relation
to Fig. 3, which shows the average results of each of
the experiments, for four listeners.

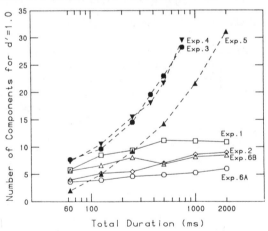

Figure 3. Threshold <u>number</u> of components for 71%
    correct discrimination, as a function of total
    pattern duration. Relatively small change in
    these thresholds when total duration is increased
    by 32 times suggests an <u>informational</u> limit on
    immediate auditory memory. Experiments 1, 2, 6A,
    6B).

274

The threshold numbers of components are shown as a function of the total pattern duration. The results clearly fall into two classes. In Experiments 3-5, the patterns had to be discriminated by the presence, or by the sequential position of a temporal gap. In the other experiments the patterns differed by a change in the frequency of one (Experiments 6A, 6B) or two (Experiments 1, 2) components, selected at random. In the four experiments requiring frequency and temporal analysis the number of components that can be included in discriminable (unfamiliar) patterns appeared to be relatively constant (i.e. was only weakly dependent on their total duration; n increases by 30-40% as T increases by 32 times).

To us, at least, this seems an unexpected result. It suggests that the degrading effects of the tonal context on the resolution of individual target components depends more strongly on the amount of information in the patterns than on any "critical values" of the physical parameters (i.e., component or pattern duration).

On the off-chance that the unusual procedure of using n as a dependent variable had somehow con-tributed to these results, Gary Kidd and I recently investigated the same basic conditions, but with fixed values of n and T, while adaptively tracking frequency discrimination thresholds. The results were essen-tially identical to those in Fig. 3, for Experiments 6A and 6B, which had used fixed values of frequency change of 20 and 40%, respectively.

Of course in these experiments all of the components of the patterns had equal durations, which might also be a very special case. As another check on just how general this "limiting-value-of-n" might be, we replicated Experiment 6A, but in a condition in which the non-target components were varied at random, by ±50% of their durations (Watson and Foyle, 1985). The patterns produced in this manner sound a great deal more different from one to the next than those with equal-duration components. The results, however, showed that this amount of temporal "jitter" has no remarkable effects; the number of components in dis-criminable anisochronous patterns is essentially the same as in the previously studied isochronous ones.

We interpret the results of these experiments to mean that the capacity of the auditory "processor" has probably not served as an evolutionary pressure to determine word or phoneme durations, although the average number of "components" per word (phonemes?) may be at least broadly consistent with the number that can be processed in non-speech patterns. There are, of course, various other consequences of informational limits on system performance, as opposed to limits expressed in terms of physical parameters, many of which should be investigated before putting great faith in this alternative view of the problem of auditory pattern discrimination.

Acknowledgments: Research described here was supported by grants from NIH and AFOSR. The collaboration of many present and past colleagues is gratefully acknowledged; in addition to those listed as co-authors, D.Kewley-Port, G.Kidd, and B.Espinoza-Varas.

REFERENCES

Creelman, C. D. (1973). Simultaneous adaptive threshold estimation with frequency uncertainty, J. Acoust. Soc. Am., 54, 316 (abstract).

Green, D. M. (1961). Detection of auditory sinusoids of uncertain frequency, J. Acoust. Soc. Am., 33, 897-903.

Green, D. M. (1983). Profile analysis, Am. Psychol., 38, 133-142.

Harris, J. D. (1952). The decline of pitch discrimination with time, J. Exp. Psychol., 43, 96-99.

Kewley-Port, D., Watson, C. S., and Foyle, D. C. (1985). Temporal acuity for speech and nonspeech sounds: The role of stimulus uncertainty. J. Acoust. Soc. Am., 77, S27.

Leek, M. R. and Watson, C. S. (1984). Learning to detect auditory pattern components, J. Acoust. Soc. Am., 76, 1037-1044.

Miller, J. D., Wier, C. C., Pastore, R. E., Kelly, W. J., and Dooling, R. J. (1976). Discrimination and labeling of noise-buzz sequences with varying noise-lead times: An example of categorical perception, J. Acoust. Soc. Am., 60, 410-417.

Pollack, I. (1975) Auditory informational masking, J. Acoust. Soc. Am. Suppl. 1, 57 S5.

Sachs, R. M. and Grant, K. W. (1976). Stimulus correlates in the perception of voice onset time (VOT):II. Discrimination of speech with high and low stimulus uncertainty, J. Acoust. Soc. Am. 60, S91.

Shiffrin, R. M. and Schneider, W. (1977). Controlled and automatic processing: II. Perceptual learning, automatic attending, and a general theory, Psychol. Rev., 84, 127-190.

Watson, C. S., Wroton, H. W., Kelly, W. J. and Benbassat, C. A. (1975). Factors in the discrimination of tonal patterns. I. Component frequency, temporal position, and silent intervals, J. Acoust. Soc. Am., 57, 1175-1185.

Watson, C. S., Kelly, W. J. and Wroton, H. W. (1976). Factors in the discrimination of tonal patterns. II. Selective attention and learning under various levels of stimulus uncertainty, J. Acoust. Soc. Am., 60, 1176-1186.

Watson, C. S., Kelly, W. J. (1978). Informational masking in auditory patterns, J. Acoust. Soc. Am., 64-S39.

Watson, C. S. (1980). Time course of auditory per- ceptual learning, Ann. Otol. Rhinol. Laryngol., Suppl. 74, 89-96-102.

Watson, C. S. and Kelly, W. J. (1981). The role of stimulus uncertainty in the discriminability of auditory patterns, in Auditory and Visual Pattern Recognition, D. J. Getty and J. H. Howard, Jr. (eds.), Lawrence Erlbaum Associates, Hillsdale, New Jersey 37-59.

Watson, C. S. and Foyle, D. C. (1985). Central factors in the discrimination and identification of complex sounds, J. Acoust. Soc. Am., 78, 375-380.

Watson, C. S. and Foyle, D. C. (1985). Memory capacity for iochronous and anisochronous patterns, J. Acoust. Soc. Am., 77, S1.

Directed Attention in Complex Sound Perception

Marjorie R. Leek
Department of Communication Disorders
University of Minnesota
Minneapolis, Minnesota 55455

Two themes frequently recur in studies of the resolution of individual components of complex sounds. Watson and Kelly (1981) have described the detrimental effects of stimulus uncertainty in the discrimination of tonal sequences. The amount of information a listener has regarding the acoustic characteristics of a sound becomes crucially important as the sound becomes more complex, and as more central processing mechanisms are involved (Watson and Foyle, 1985). Further, the magnitude of the effects of a lack of knowledge about an auditory stimulus is highly idiosyncratic across listeners. Both stimulus uncertainty effects and the large individual differences in precision of resolution of complex sounds are influenced by the distribution of auditory attention. If a listener's attention is narrowly focussed at the temporal or spectral location of a target portion of a tonal sequence, changes in that part of the sound may be detected quite precisely. Alternatively, if attention is spread throughout the sound, or is focussed inappropriately, even quite large changes in target portions may go unnoticed. Design of the stimulus or of certain aspects of the experimental situation which directs attention to a target embedded in an acoustic surround permits the listener to ignore irrelevant, contextual information and listen specifically for the component carrying the information. The result of such focussed attention is usually improved psychoacoustic performance on tasks such as detection of low intensity components of the sound or discrimination of changes in a component along various acoustic dimensions. This paper will review some experimental methods which overcome the effects of stimulus uncertainty by directing auditory attention to selected portions of complex sounds. The value of these manipulations in improving psychoacoustic performance is partially determined by the experimental task and by individual listeners' abilities to make use of attentional cues.

INTRODUCTION

The perceptual analysis of complex sounds is dependent not only on the resolving capabilities of the

278

peripheral auditory system, but also on more central processing abilities. Numerous factors influence the extraction and perceptual isolation of information-carrying portions of such sounds, including the spectral and temporal relationships of the relevant and irrelevant components of the sound, and the history, experience, and expectations of the listener. While the physical structures and functions of the peripheral auditory system may impose some absolute limitations, the manipulation of auditory attention plays a significant role in complex sound analysis.

ATTENTION DIRECTED BY PRIOR KNOWLEDGE

A listener may gain knowledge about the stimulus through experience with the sound, by knowing the probability of occurrence of specific sounds, or by the presence of a cue designed to convey information about the sound. Performance improvements resulting from training may require hundreds of hours of listening experience, with the amount of training directly related to the level of complexity of the stimulus (Watson, 1980; Watson and Foyle, 1985). Leek and Watson (1984) reported that over weeks of daily practice, listeners' detection thresholds for embedded target tones in tonal sequences improved radically, with decreases in thresholds of 40 to 50 dB. The authors surmised that through practice the listeners had learned to use the standard presentation of the pattern on each trial as a cue to where their auditory attention should be placed.

Appropriately directed attention improves psycho-acoustic performance even for simple sounds such as pure tones. Green (1961) suggested that when listeners attempt to detect a tonal signal in the presence of noise, they use an adjustable width listening band, tuned to the expected frequency of the signal. If the frequency is unknown, the listener must monitor a broad range of possible values, and detection thresholds are generally slightly elevated relative to those for a known signal (Swets, 1963). A further definition of an attentional listening band is provided by the probe signal method described by Greenberg and Larkin (1968). Listeners hear threshold-level tones at a fixed frequency over many trials. On a small percentage of trials, the frequency of the stimulus is changed, unknown to the listener. As the probe frequency was further away from the standard frequency, detection performance decreased. Sorkin et al. (1968) reported a similar result even when listeners had prior knowledge of the probabilities associated with presentation of each frequency tested. Thresholds were inversely related to the probability of occurrence of a particular tone, suggesting that listeners could make use of their knowledge of stimulus likelihood to focus attention at the most likely frequency for detection.

A logical extension of the research on detection of unknown frequency signals is the study of various kinds of cues to provide information about the most likely location of the signal. The value of a cue is heavily dependent on such aspects of the cue-signal relationship as cue intensity and phase, temporal offset from the signal, and whether the cue occurs in the same ear or the ear contralateral to the signal. Gilliom and Mills (1976) and Gilliom et al. (1977) argue that a cue must be clearly above threshold, be presented to the ear contralateral to the ear receiving the signal, and be presented with enough lead time before signal presentation so that some form of processing of the cued information can take place. Taylor and Forbes (1969) demonstrated differential effectiveness of a contralateral cue depending on its similarity to the signal to be detected. Cues presented at a high intensity actually interfere with signal detection, suggesting a form of interference at some point in the auditory system (Taylor et al., 1971; Sorkin, 1965). A poor or inappropriate cue degrades detection beyond performance observed with no cue at all (Taylor and Smith, 1975; Johnson and Hafter, 1980).

In addition to cueing a spectral location, temporal uncertainty may also be reduced by a cue to a signal to be detected. Puleo and Pastore (1980) reported reduced backward masking when the onset of a signal is indicated by the presence of a temporal cue. Pastore and Freda (1980) found no improvement in forward masking when a cue was present, suggesting that the temporal onset of the signal was already marked by the offset of the masker. When the masker and signal were so similar that temporal uncertainty about the onset of the signal was present, forward masking was reduced by a temporal cue presented either ipsilaterally or contralaterally (Moore and Glasberg, 1982).

Small but consistent improvements in detection with spectral or temporal cues are observed, but cueing as a mechanism to improve differential sensitivity has

been unimpressive. Both Chocholle (1957), studying
intensity discrimination, and Emmerich (1971) in a
frequency discrimination task, reported performance
decrements with high intensity cues, and only small and
variable improvements in response to any cues. Perhaps,
since differential sensitivity involves a change in
stimulus value along a particular dimension, a cue to
the absolute frequency does not provide relevant information aiding discrimination.

In summary, the value of a cue is strongly influenced by stimulus intensity and phase, and an ill-chosen
cue can result in significant performance decrements.
While a well-selected cue is effective in improving
detection thresholds, probably by directing attention
to the proper spectral and/or temporal locale, performance on other psychoacoustic tasks is not substantially
improved.

ATTENTION DIRECTED BY STIMULUS DESIGN

Listeners may also use information inherent in the
stimulus itself to direct attention to the location of
a target. Howard and his colleagues (Howard et al.,
1984; 1986) showed that the structure of sequential
patterns may be used by listeners as an informational
cue to attentional focus. In an experimental task
reminiscent of Greenberg and Larkin's (1968) probe signal method, listeners heard twelve-tone patterns at
levels near threshold, with the 11th component missing
on a randomly selected presentation in each 2AFC trial.
The listener's task was to discriminate the complete
pattern from the pattern with the missing component.
The frequency of the target component was fixed on 80%
of the trials but varied on the remaining trials. When
the earlier pattern components provided information
directing attention to the target sound, detection improved. This suggests a cueing mechanism similar to
that described above. In a subsequent study, the value
of frequency cues provided by early pattern elements and
of purely informational cues in the form of visual patterns was contrasted. Tone detection under these cueing
conditions was better with the auditory cues, but there
was evidence of selective attention resulting from the
use of the visual information as well (Howard et al.,
1986).

Spiegel and Watson (1981) also suggested that
listeners can use information contained in non-target

281

parts of an auditory sequence to improve resolution of
embedded target components. After training on a limited number of patterns, listeners showed evidence of
using their knowledge of the complete pattern to direct
attention to the portion to be resolved.

Auditory attention may be directed by some inherent
characteristics of sequential elements in a pattern.
The relative salience of a target component within a
tonal sequence of brief tones can be enhanced by
increased intensity or increased duration. Leek and
Colleran (1984) investigated the relationship between
target tone duration and the discrimination of changes
in the frequency of the target. In an adaptive tracking
paradigm, the duration of a target tone embedded in
rapid tonal sequences was measured for equal discrimination performance at several levels of target frequency
difference. Fig. 1 shows the durations required for
71% correct discriminations for each of 14 listeners.
While all of these listeners had previously demonstrated
frequency difference limens for isolated 46-ms tones of
10 to 20 Hz, there are obviously large individual
differences in performance when the target is part of
a sequence. Performance may be divided into two groups,
with 8 listeners requiring long duration targets for
even the largest frequency difference. The remaining
6 listeners could discriminate frequency differences at
durations similar to the durations of the remaining
pattern components.

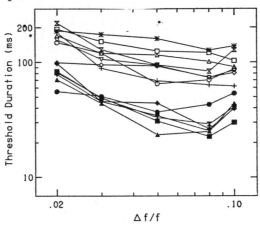

Figure 1. Duration of target tone in a tonal sequence
    required for various levels of frequency discrim-
    ination by 14 listeners.

These data reflect differences in listeners' abilities to make use of cues in the stimulus to direct attention. There were actually two types of attentional cues in this study. One was the increased loudness of the longer-duration target. This cue was used by all listeners, although as Fig. 1 shows, some listeners needed longer durations than others for equivalent target tone salience.

There may have been a second cue, however, in the experimental procedure used. The 920-Hz target tone on all trials throughout the experiment was the second component in the pattern. The tracking procedure always began at a long target tone duration, increasing or decreasing the difficulty of the task in response to listener's performance on each trial. Suppose a listener was able to use the strong loudness cue provided by the long duration at the beginning of a track to find the target, and lock attention to either its spectral or temporal location within the pattern. If attention could be maintained at that location on subsequent trials, then performance would remain good even as the duration became shorter in response to the movement of the adaptive track.

This strategy is similar to the strategy reported by Watson et al. (1976) for listeners using a method of adjustment procedure. In order to "find" a target tone embedded in a tonal sequence, listeners first would adjust the frequency difference in the target to such a large value as to make it fall outside the range of the remaining pattern components. Once the target was made to stand out from the rest of the pattern in this way, those listeners could hold it in some form of memory and continue to make finer discriminations even as they adjusted the frequency difference to levels inside the pattern range.

The factor which separates the two groups shown in Fig. 1 may have been the ability to use the additional target salience provided by the tracking procedure even when the durational/loudness cue was eliminated at shorter target durations. The "slower" listeners may have lost the target until the track was driven to longer durations by the incorrect responses. These listeners could use one of the attentional cues (target loudness) but could not use the tracking cue.

ATTENTION DIRECTED BY PERCEPTUAL ISOLATION

Rather than use loudness cues to direct attention, cues may be provided by the temporal and spectral characteristics inherent in specially designed patterns. If attention is focussed on a component which is perceptually isolated from the remaining pattern components, discrimination of small changes in the frequency of that tone should be quite precise. If, however, the component which is isolated is not the target component subject to change, discrimination performance may suffer due to an inability to ignore the highly salient but invalid cue.

The perceptual effects of isolating one or more tones in rapid auditory sequences have been described in the work of Bregman and his colleagues (e.g., Bregman and Campbell, 1971) and van Noorden (1975). Tones close together in frequency group together, producing auditory streams, segregated from other frequencies in a sequence. A component of a tonal sequence may be perceptually pulled out of a pattern if its frequency is sufficiently different from the remaining tones in the sequence. Stream segregation may also occur by virtue of the temporal characteristics of sequences. Jones et al. (1981) have demonstrated streaming effects when portions of rapid sequences have different rhythmic characteristics, with like rhythms tending to group together. An appropriate rhythmic structure within a tonal sequence might serve to isolate target portions in a manner analogous to the streaming effects observed with spectral isolation.

McBride (1986) constructed nine tonal patterns to test the attentional effects of frequency and temporal isolation of target and non-target components. Attentional focus was indirectly measured by determining frequency difference limens for target tones in each pattern. To further clarify possible individual differences across listeners in the ability to use attentional cues, the listeners in this study were divided into two groups based on their performance on a version of the Leek and Colleran (1984) study described earlier. Those listeners who required target tone durations greater than 100 ms to discriminate a frequency difference of 74 Hz were placed in the "slow" group. The remaining listeners, whose duration thresholds fell below 100 ms, were assigned to the "fast" group.

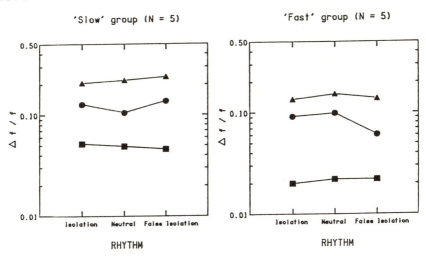

Figure 2. Frequency difference limens for target tone
   in a tonal sequence. Parameter is frequency isolation condition: ■ - target isolation; ● - no tones
   isolated; ▲ - non-target tone isolation.

   Fig. 2 shows the mean difference limens estimated
for each group. Both groups show similar effects of
spectral and temporal isolation. While the three
temporal conditions had little effect on difference
limens, the frequency conditions were clearly differ-
entially effective. As predicted, the condition in
which the target tone was in a different frequency
region from the other components ("stream") resulted in
quite precise discrimination of the target tone. The
"false stream" condition, in which the target tone was
included in the stream with the other pattern components
while a non-target component was perceptually isolated,
produced quite poor discrimination. The neutral condition, with no components segregating from the pattern,
produced performance intermediate to that of the other
two conditions.

   The data in Fig. 2 provide further evidence that
listeners differ in their ability to take advantage of
cues present in the stimulus. The center point in each
panel of the figure represents target tone discrimination when no cues are designed into the pattern. A
comparison of performance at this point suggests that
these two groups were not different in their ability to
discriminate target frequency changes when no attentional cues were present. The remaining points, however,

demonstrate that the "fast" group performed better than the "slow" group when the target was segregated by frequency.

The results of this study suggest that pattern structure along the dimensions of frequency and time may direct auditory attention, even under conditions of high stimulus uncertainty. While the temporal cues used here provided little help in frequency discrimination, it may be that the effectiveness of cues along a particular dimension is related to the dimension of the task to be performed. Jones et al. (1981) reported effects of temporal structure of patterns on a task involving temporal order. Perhaps the temporal manipulations in this study would have been useful if the task had been temporal discrimination rather than frequency discrimination.

The manipulation and control of attentional focus can significantly alter the perception of complex sounds. Poorly placed or insufficiently focussed attention results in decreased ability to resolve individual components of rapid tonal sequences. However, if attention is correctly placed along the dimensions of time and frequency, precise resolution of portions of complex sounds is possible. Attention may be placed by knowledge of the stimulus or of the probabilities associated with the occurrence of a particular stimulus. Internal characteristics of complex sounds may also serve to direct attention. The ability to use attentional cues varies considerably across listeners. The effectiveness of attentional manipulations in improving psychoacoustic performance may be related to the listening task (i.e., detection or discrimination) and to the dimension of the attentional cues.

REFERENCES

Bregman, A.S. and Campbell, J. (1971). Primary auditory stream segregation and perception of order in rapid sequences of tones. J. Exp. Psychol.,89,244-249.
Chocholle, R. (1957). La sensibilite auditive differen-tielle intensite en presence d'un son contra-lateral de meme frequence. Acustica, 7, 75-83.
Emmerich, D.S. (1971). Cueing signals in auditory detection and frequency discrimination experiments. Percept. Psychophys. 9, 129-134.

Gilliom, J.D. and Mills, W.M. (1976). Information extraction from contralateral cues in the detection of signals of uncertain frequency. J. Acoust. Soc. Am. 59, 1428-1433.

Gilliom, J.D., Taylor, D.W., and Cline, C. (1977). Should an informational cue precede or follow the signal event: results with a contralateral cue in an uncertain frequency paradigm. J. Acoust. Soc. Am. 61, S62.

Green, D.M. (1961). Detection of auditory sinusoids of uncertain frequency. J. Acoust. Soc. Am. 33, 897-903.

Greenberg, G.Z. and Larkin, W.D. (1968). Frequency-response characteristics of auditory observers detecting signals of a single frequency in noise: The probe signal method. J. Acoust. Soc. Am. 44, 1513-1523.

Howard, J.H.,Jr., O'Toole, A.J., Parasuraman, R., and Bennett, K.B. (1984). Pattern-directed attention in uncertain-frequency detection. Percept. Psychophys. 35, 256-264.

Howard, J.H., Jr., O'Toole, A.J., and Rice, S.E. (1986) The role of frequency versus informational cues in uncertain frequency detection. J. Acoust. Soc. Am. 79, 788-791.

Johnson, D.M. and Hafter, E.R. (1980). Uncertain-frequency detection: Cueing and condition of observation. Percept. Psychophys. 28, 143-149.

Jones, M.R., Kidd, G., and Wetzel, R. (1981). Evidence for rhythmic attention. J. Exp. Psychol. HP&P, 7, 1059-1073.

Leek, M.R. and Watson, C.S. (1984). Learning to detect auditory pattern components. J.Acoust. Soc. Am. 76, 1037-1044.

Leek, M.R. and Colleran, E. (1984). Individual differences in pattern discrimination by naive listeners. J. Acoust. Soc. Am. 76, S14.

McBride, D.L. (1986). Rhythm and frequency factors in the perception of tone sequences. Unpublished Master's thesis, Arizona State University.

Moore, B.C.J. and Glasberg, B.R. (1982). Contralateral and ipsilateral cueing in forward masking. J. Acoust. Soc. Am. 71, 942-945.

van Noorden, L.P.A.S. (1975). Temporal coherence in the perception of tone sequences. Doctoral thesis, Institute for Perception Research, Eindhoven, The Netherlands.

Pastore, R.E. and Freda, J.S. (1980). Contralateral cueing effects in forward masking. J. Acoust. Soc. Am. 67, 2104-2105.

Puleo, J.S. and Pastore, R.E. (1980). Contralateral cueing effects in backward masking. J. Acoust. Soc. Am. 67, 947-951.

Sorkin, R.D. (1965). Uncertain signal detection with simultaneous contralateral cues. J. Acoust. Soc. Am. 38, 207-212.

Sorkin, R.D., Pastore, R.E., and Gilliom, J.D. (1968). Signal probability and the listening band. Percept. Psychophys. 4, 10-12.

Spiegel, M.F. and Watson, C.S. (1981). Factors in the discrimination of tonal patterns. III. Frequency discrimination with components of well-learned patterns. J. Acoust. Soc. Am. 69, 223-235.

Swets, J.A. (1963). Central factors in auditory frequency selectivity. Psychol. Bull. 60, 429-440.

Taylor, M.M. and Forbes, S.M. (1969). Monaural detection with contralateral cue (MDCC). I. Better than energy detector performance by human observers. J. Acoust. Soc. Am. 46, 1519-1526.

Taylor, M.M. and Smith, S.M. (1975). Monaural detection with contralateral cue (MDCC). VI. Adding noise to the cue. J. Acoust. Soc. Am. 58, 870-874.

Taylor, M.M., Smith, S.M., and Cloarke, D.P.J. (1971). Monaural detection with contralateral cue (MDCC) IV. Psychometric functions with sinusoidal signals. J. Acoust. Soc. Am. 50, 1151-1161.

Watson, C.S. (1980). Time course of auditory perceptual learning. Ann. Otol. Rhinol. Laryngol. Suppl. 74, 96-102.

Watson, C.S. and Foyle, D.C. (1985). Central factors in the discrimination and identification of complex sounds. J. Acoust. Soc. Am. 78, 375-380.

Watson, C.S. and Kelly, W. J. (1981). The role of stimulus uncertainty in the discrimination of auditory patterns. In Auditory and Visual Pattern Recognition, D.J. Getty and J.H. Howard, eds., L. Erlbaum Associates, Hillsdale.

Watson, C.S., Kelly, W.J., and Wroton, H.W. (1976). Factors in the discrimination of tonal patterns. II. Selective attention and learning under various levels of stimulus uncertainty. J. Acoust. Soc. Am. 60, 1176-1186.

AUDITORY MEMORY: PROCEDURES TO EXAMINE TWO PHASES

Nelson Cowan
Department of Psychology
University of Missouri, Columbia, MO 65211

Cowan (1984) reviewed evidence that there are two
phases of memory for auditory sensation: one that lasts
several hundred msec and extends the duration of a
perception, and a second that contains acoustic information in a partly processed form for 10-20 sec or
more. This review is summarized, emergent issues are
discussed, and research is reported to further examine
the functioning of the first, brief memory phase. This
memory adds to a temporal integration process that
determines a sound's perceptual qualities (e.g., loudness), and it prolongs an information extraction process
that determines perceptual clarity (discriminability).

INTRODUCTION

This chapter discusses the sensory memory system.
The complexity to be considered resides in that system
rather than in the stimuli. The chapter is divided into
three parts. 1) First, research on the characteristics
of auditory memory is described. Cowan (1984) stated
the theoretical orientation in detail, and here it is
simply summarized with an emphasis on clarifications
that, in retrospect, seem helpful. 2) Next, recent data
are presented to further specify the working of auditory
sensory memory. Ways in which sensory persistence may
be used in forming the integrated percept of a sound are
examined. 3) Last, because the methods used to examine
sensory memory have differed from traditional psychoacoustics, these methodologies are briefly compared.

CHARACTERISTICS OF AUDITORY MEMORY

Cowan (1984) concluded that there are at least two
types of memory for auditory sensation, which were
simply termed "short and long auditory stores." (As
explained in that article, the term "store" is only a
convenient metaphor.) The short store entails the
sensory persistence of a sound for several hundred msec,
whereas the long store is not sensory persistence, but a
vivid recollection of the sound for 10 - 20 sec or more.

When one considers only experiments in which there was a silent period following a target sound on each trial and then a measure of memory decay during this silent period, the estimates of the duration of sensory storage cluster into a short and long set without intermediate estimates (e.g., no valid evidence that there is a 2-sec store). Intermediate estimates can be derived from some studies, but these estimates are invalid because the task included auditory interference (e.g., Treisman, 1964), because non-sensory memory may have been used (e.g., Darwin et al., 1972), or because performance was not followed to a stable asymptote (e.g., Rostron, 1974). It may seem unparsimonious to propose two auditory stores, but without two stores, investigators had to live with the disturbing conclusion that there was little consistency among auditory memory experiments.

The two-store conception also is supported by differences in the types of phenomena observed after short versus long delays. After a short delay (e.g., 100 msec), persistence of sensation can be observed. For example, Efron (1970a, b, c) found that subjects overestimated the time of offset of a brief sound by up to 130-180 msec, whereas the overestimation of onsets was much less (< 5 msec). Plomp (1964) found that a pair of clearly suprathreshold sounds presented with an interstimulus gap of up to 200 msec (depending on the relative stimulus intensities) can be perceived as a single, uninterrupted sound. In experiments with delays greater than several hundred msec, although sensory persistence is no longer observed, subjects still display a vivid recollection of the stimulus. For example, they are able to compare the acoustic properties of two slightly different tones (Kinchla & Smyzer, 1967) or vowel sounds (Pisoni, 1973) with an accuracy that is greatest with an interstimulus delay of 200-500 msec and declines with increasing delays. Further, this decay of auditory memory may occur in a structured manner. For example, Cowan and Morse (1986) found that the memory representation of the cardinal vowel /i/, as in beet, drifts closer to the neutral vowel schwa as it decays across several sec.

There are some experimental procedures that seem to permit both the short and the long auditory stores to be observed. An example is the detection of noise segment repetition (Guttman and Julesz, 1963; Pollack, 1972; Warren & Bashford, 1981). A single segment of noise is repeated continually, and what is heard depends upon the

iterated segment's duration. With segments up to several hundred msec, a repeated knocking (described as
"motorboating") can be heard, perhaps because the short
stores of successive segment onsets overlap. With
segments up to about 2 sec, subjects may detect the
repetition of the sound, although motorboating is not
heard. (This presumably reflects the long store but does
not estimate its potential duration, because auditory
interference is present.) Another procedure that may
reveal both stores is a particular modification of the
backward recognition masking procedure (Kallman & Massaro, 1979). On every trial, the target tone was to be
compared to a standard tone. When the presentation
order was "standard [pause] target-mask," an ordinary
recognition masking function was obtained, and there was
no effect of target-mask similarity. However, when the
order was "target-mask [pause] standard," with the mask
intervening between the items to be compared, there was
a substantial effect of target-mask similarity. Presumably, in the latter condition the mask interfered with
the short and long stores, with the similarity effects
occurring through interference with the long store.

Not all of the research reviewed by Cowan (1984)
was meant to serve as strong evidence for the two-store
approach. (For example, extant research does not con-
clusively link detection masking to auditory storage.)
The strategy of that literature review was to include
evidence that possibly reflects sensory storage, in
addition to more solid evidence, to sketch a possible
coherence among a wide range of data. Invalidation of
some of the more speculative evidence for the two-store
approach would not sufficiently rule out that approach.

A possible criticism of the two-store account is
that the long auditory store could be an instance of the
"short-term memory" that is part of conventional models
of information processing, which presumably applies to
all input modalities. This is possible, but if a single,
amodal store is postulated, some other mechanism must be
proposed to explain why items at the end of a word list
are remembered better when presented auditorily rather
than visually (Penney, 1975), why this auditory modality
superiority is reduced or eliminated by an interfering,
auditory item or "suffix" (Crowder & Morton, 1969), and
why the modality and suffix effects last at least 20 sec
when the subject is prevented from using verbal recoding
strategies (Watkins & Todres, 1980; Watkins & Watkins,
1980). Other researchers recently have concluded that

short-term memory cannot be regarded as a unitary concept, and must be composed of distinct subsystems (e.g.,
Crowder, 1982). Perhaps auditory storage is only a
subsystem of a more general, multimodal store, but with
modality differences in the characteristics of storage
(e.g., superior sequential recall in audition and spatial recall in vision).

Finally, some may contend that these auditory
storage mechanisms do not play a substantial role in
ordinary perception. (This criticism presumably would
be applied to the short store, because the relevance of
the long store is clear in phenomena such as memory for
unattended speech.) However, it should be remembered
that, although the effects obtained with a particular
procedure may be small, the procedures are primarily
meant to be diagnostic of underlying processes. A
subtle diagnostic effect can correspond to important
underlying processes (e.g., subtle ear advantages in
dichotic listening correspond to important hemispheric
differences.) One subtle effect is related to backward
recognition masking. Using an iso-performance measure,
Foyle and Watson (1984) found that recognition masking
effects reduce tone discrimination by at most a few Hz.
This suggests that masking effects may not be important
in ordinary perception (except, perhaps, in degraded
speech contexts in which those few Hz might make a
difference). However, according to an auditory storage
account, even this small masking effect may reflect an
auditory store that is quite important in perception.
According to this account, recognition is impaired because the mask interferes with the extraction of information from the auditory trace of the target. Only the
tail-end of an exponentially decaying trace would be
interfered with, but the earlier, more vivid portion of
the trace would be more important for perception.

SOME RECENT RESEARCH ON THE SHORT AUDITORY STORE

Cowan (in prep.-a) has conducted a series of experiments designed to examine the function of short auditory storage. Backward masking of loudness was examined, because in that phenomenon there are alternative
predictions for different possible functions of auditory
storage. In each experiment, the subjects were to judge
the loudness of one or both of two brief, 700-Hz tones
presented in rapid succession. After a 1-hour practice
session, each subject returned to the laboratory for 1,
2, or 4 test sessions, depending on the procedure.

There were three intensities of each tone (83, 85, or 87 dB(A)), or in one experiment, three tone durations (20, 30, or 40 msec). In the variable-dB experiments, all tones were 40 msec long.

There were three alternative sets of predictions for the judgment of the loudness of the first tone, which was the target tone. First, the auditory store might allow continued <u>information extraction</u> after the end of the stimulus. A recognition masking function for loudness (Moore and Massaro, 1973) suggests that the store contains loudness information that is extracted in a manner similar to pitch, spectral quality, etc. When the masking interval is short, relatively little information about the loudness of the target would be present and the subject often would have to guess the loudness of the target. These guesses would attenuate the difference between loudness judgments for tones of three intensities, whereas at longer masking intervals the three tone intensities would be more discriminable and the functions would diverge. The second possible function of the short auditory store is to extend the <u>sensory integration</u> process underlying loudness judgments (Zwislocki, 1969). At short masking intervals, the mask presumably would cut short the trace of the target. Assuming that the mask and target can be judged separately (which apparently is true except at intervals of 50 msec or less), the abbreviation of the sensory trace of the target should decrease its judged loudness, regardless of its true intensity. Therefore, judgment of the loudness of all three targets should increase across masking intervals. Finally, it is possible that <u>both processes</u> (information extraction and sensory integration) contribute to the masking functions. In that case the three functions would diverge across masking intervals, as the information extraction account predicts, but averaged across the three functions there would be a general upward trend across masking intervals, as the sensory integration account predicts.

Figure 1 presents target loudness judgments from an experiment (n=6) in which three intensities of each tone were used, with absolute magnitude estimation judgments (Zwislocki and Goodman, 1980) converted to standard scores. The results are most consistent with the third set of predictions (both processes together). Individual subject data were similar, as were the results obtained when an 8-point loudness rating scale was used (n=4) and when stimulus duration rather than intensity was manipulated (n=18). In the latter experiment, masking intervals up to 400 msec were used but little change in judgments occurred past 200 msec.

In a final experiment (n=7) with tones of three intensities, a slightly different technique was used to dissociate the information extraction and sensory integration processes. Subjects heard a standard tone, which they knew to be identical to the target on each trial, 750 msec before the target-mask tone pair. They were to judge the <u>apparent</u> loudness of the standard and target, disregarding the knowledge that these were identical. Subjects were not told what kind of difference to expect between the standard and target. It was predicted that this procedure would reduce the role of the information extraction process in the loudness judgment of the target, because the identical standard always was presented before the target. Consistent with this prediction, the experiment yielded three parallel functions for target judgments that increased across masking intervals, without the divergence between functions that would be expected on the basis of information extraction. In contrast to these target judgments, the judgments of the standard were constant across masking intervals. These results confirm that both information extraction from the sensory store and sensory integration across the target and its store ordinarily contribute to loudness judgments. Similar reasoning has been used in an examination of duration masking (Idson & Massaro, 1977; Massaro & Idson, 1978).

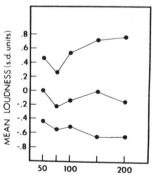

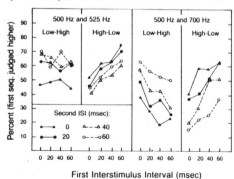

Figure 1. Judged loudness of 83-, 85-, and 87-dB target tones.

Figure 2. Percent (Sequence 1 judged higher) by tone order, Hz, & ISI.

An entirely different procedure (Cowan, in prep.-b) demonstrates that sensory persistence plays an important role in the judged pitch of rapid tone sequences. It was based on the idea that there is an overall perceived pitch of a sequence (cf. Terhardt et al., 1982). The prediction was that, because of sensory storage, tones followed by a longer silent interval would contribute to the overall pitch more heavily. Subjects (n=28) heard sequences of 20-msec-long tones separated by brief silent intervals, with 10 tones per sequence. They were to judge which of two such sequences presented on each trial sounded higher in pitch. In every sequence, two tone frequencies (L and H) were presented in alternation, with the same tone order in the two sequences. The L tone was always 500 Hz, and the H tone was in the same critical band (525 Hz) or outside of it (700 Hz). There was always a 300-msec interval between the two sequences. On each trial there were two values of a silent, interstimulus interval (ISI) between tones in a sequence (each ISI = 0, 20, 40, or 60 msec). The silent times after the L and H tones in a sequence varied independently, but silent times were reversed in the two sequences (i.e., the silent time following L tones in Sequence 1 followed H tones in Sequence 2, and vice versa). Thus, there was a First ISI value that occurred after odd-numbered tones in Sequence 1 and even-numbered tones in Sequence 2, and a Second ISI that occurred after the remaining tones. For example, with an H-L tone order, Sequence 1 followed the pattern [H, 1st ISI, L, 2nd ISI] repeated 5 times, whereas Sequence 2 was [H, 2nd ISI, L, 1st ISI] repeated 5 times. The sequence in which the longer silent interval followed the higher-pitched tone should be judged higher more often.

Generally, each 10-tone sequence was perceptible as a coherent "trill," much like a bird call, rather than as a series of separate tone pips. The results, shown in Figure 2, match the predictions (although the results were more consistent when the tones were between critical bands). Thus, the effects of the two ISIs depended on the tone order. Presumably, the sensory input for adjacent tones is integrated, and the tones followed by a longer uninterrupted trace add more to this process, which culminates in a perceptual judgment.

Notice that these experiments have used experiential rather than performance-level (e.g., discrimination) tasks (cf. Idson & Massaro, 1977), to begin to reveal how auditory storage influences the percept.

Future work may be directed toward learning the role of auditory storage in continuous stimuli (e.g., speech).

A COMPARISON OF METHODS

In most psychoacoustic methods, subjects are placed in situations designed to minimize the information to be processed (e.g., sound-attribute matching procedures). The goal of such procedures is to optimize higher-level processes so as to concentrate on the perceptual limitations caused by the peripheral nervous system (i.e., "front-end" or biologically determined mechanisms). Watson and Foyle (1985) have made this assumption more explicit by examining the large detrimental effects of stimulus uncertainty in compound stimuli, highlighting the sensitivity of performance in simpler situations. Although the present research also examines processes that are assumed to be biologically determined, they probably occur at a more central neural level (Kallman and Morris, 1984). They may not be accessible to experimentation with uncertainty minimized, and the research is guided instead by a theoretical, "working model" of information processing. Within this working model, the demands of the task are analyzed, and all stages of the model must be considered before the stage responsible for a particular phenomenon is tentatively identified.

Attempts to minimize uncertainty may inadvertently obscure a process of interest. Consider Foyle and Watson's (1984) interesting demonstration that, with an iso-performance measure of backward recognition masking, an asymptotic level of performance is reached with masking intervals close to 100 msec, not 250 msec. An implicit inference is that a sensory store lasting several hundred msec is not involved in recognition masking, but that inference may be wrong. According to the working model, information is extracted from a sensory store, and the masking process could be temporally limited either by the duration of the sensory store or the duration of the information extraction process. No masking is possible after the store has faded or after the extraction process has finished. In previous backward masking studies, the extraction process may have been relatively slow, so that the masking period reflected the duration of auditory storage. In Foyle and Watson's procedure, though, the effective speed of information extraction may have been increased to the point where it, not auditory storage, limited the duration of masking. Stated in terms of a mathematical model (Massaro & Idson, 1978), the procedure might affect only the growth parameter θ.

Future research to compare psychoacoustic and information-processing interpretations of auditory temporal phenomena should be exciting.

REFERENCES

Cowan, N. (1984). On short and long auditory stores. Psychol. Bull., 96, 341-370.

Cowan, N. (In preparation-a). Auditory sensory storage in relation to temporal integration and acoustic information extraction.

Cowan, N. (In preparation-b). Auditory sensory storage and the perceived pitch of rapid tone sequences.

Cowan, N., & Morse, P.A. (1986). The use of auditory and phonetic memory in vowel discrimination. J. Acoust. Soc. Am., 79, 500-507.

Crowder, R.G. (1982). The demise of short-term memory. Acta Psychologica, 50, 291-323.

Crowder, R. G., & Morton, J. (1969). Precategorical acoustic storage. Percept. Psychophys., 5, 365-373.

Darwin, C.J., Turvey, M.T., & Crowder, R.G. (1972). An auditory analogue of the Sperling partial report procedure: Evidence for brief auditory storage. Cognitive Psychol., 3, 255-267.

Efron, R. (1970a). The relationship between the duration of a stimulus and the duration of a perception. Neuropsychologia, 8, 37-55.

Efron, R. (1970b). The minimum duration of a perception. Neuropsychologia, 8, 57-63.

Efron, R. (1970c). Effects of stimulus duration on perceptual onset and offset latencies. Percept. Psychophys., 8, 231-234.

Foyle, D.C., & Watson, C.S. (1984). Stimulus-based versus performance-based measurement of auditory backward recognition masking. Percept. Psychophys., 36, 515-522.

Guttman, N., & Julesz, B. (1963). Lower limits of auditory periodicity analysis. J. Acoust. Soc. Am., 35, 610.

Idson, W.L., & Massaro, D.W. (1977). Perceptual processing and experience of auditory duration. Sensory Processes, 1, 316-337.

Kallman, H.J., & Massaro, D.W. (1979). Similarity effects in backward recognition masking. J. Exp. Psychol.: Human Percept. Perform., 5, 110-128.

Kallman, H.J., & Morris, M.E. (1984). Backward recognition masking as a function of ear of mask presentation. Percept. Psychophys., 35, 379-384.

Kinchla, R.A., & Smyzer, F. (1967). A diffusion model of perceptual memory. Percept. Psychophys., 2, 219-229.

Massaro, D.W., & Idson, W.L. (1978). Target-mask similarity in backward recognition masking of perceived tone duration. Percept. Psychophys., 24, 225-236.

Moore, J.J., & Massaro, D.W. (1973). Attention and processing capacity in auditory recognition. J. Exp. Psychol., 99, 49-54.

Penney, C.G. (1975). Modality effects in short-term verbal memory. Psychol. Bull., 82, 68-84.

Pisoni, D. B. (1973). Auditory and phonetic memory codes in the discrimination of consonants and vowels. Percept. Psychophys., 253-260.

Plomp, R. (1964). Rate of decay of auditory sensation. J. Acoust. Soc. Am., 36, 277-282.

Pollack, I. (1972). Memory for auditory waveform. J. Acoust. Soc. Am., 52, 1209-1215.

Rostron, A.B. (1974). Brief auditory storage: Some further observations. Acta Psychologica, 38, 471-482.

Terhardt, E., Stoll, G., & Seewann, M. (1982). Pitch of complex signals according to virtual-pitch theory: Tests, examples, and predictions. J. Acoust. Soc. Am., 71, 671-678.

Treisman, A.M. (1964). Monitoring and storage of irrelevant messages in selective attention. J. Verb. Learn. Verb. Behav., 3, 449-459.

Warren, R.M., & Bashford, J.A., Jr. (1981). Perception of acoustic iterance: Pitch and infrapitch. Percept. Psychophys., 29, 395-402.

Watkins, M. J., & Todres, A. K. (1980). Suffix effects manifest and concealed: Further evidence for a 20-sec echo. J. Verb. Learn. Verb. Behav., 19, 46-53.

Watkins, O. C., & Watkins, M. J. (1980). The modality effect and echoic persistence. J. Exp. Psychol.: General, 109, 251-278.

Watson, C.S., & Foyle, D.C. (1985). Central factors in the discrimination and identification of complex sounds. J. Acoust. Soc. Am., 78, 375-380.

Zwislocki, J.J. (1969). Temporal summation of loudness: An analysis. J. Acoust. Soc. Am., 46, 431-440.

Zwislocki, J.J., & Goodman, D.A. (1980). Absolute scaling of sensory magnitudes: A validation. Percept. Psychophys., 28, 28-38.

CONCURRENT PITCH SEGREGATION

Michael Kubovy
Department of Psychology
Rutgers--The State University of New Jersey
New Brunswick, NJ 08901

The following topics are reviewed: (1) The recent resurgence of interest in perceptual organization. (2) The types of research on auditory perceptual organization: stream segregation and concurrent pitch segregation (CPS). An introduction to the techniques of CPS. (3) The structure of Gestalts; their decomposition into parts, operations, a medium, and a perceptual outcome. Analogies between vision and audition with respect to perceptual organization and the concept of Indispensable Attributes: the organizational medium of pitch in audition is roughly analogous to the medium of space in vision. (4) Research in auditory perceptual organization introduces new concepts to psychoacoustics: Segregation by inter-aural time disparity as an example of successive-difference and concurrent-difference segregation cues and techniques for unconfounding them. (5) A review of Treisman s feature integration theory. The auditory system is shown to behave similarly to the visual system in this respect: concurrent pitch segregation cannot be caused by conjunctions of segregation cues.

INTRODUCTION

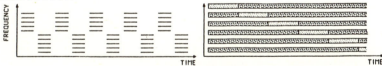

Figure 1.   LEFT: Stream segregation.   RIGHT: Concurrent pitch segregation.

There has been, over the past decade, a resurgence of interest in the Gestalt laws (Kubovy, 1986, for an overview of this resurgence). The Gestalt theorists did not provide us with a model of rigorous theorizing: their physiological theories have been refuted (Pomerantz & Kubovy, 1981) and their simplicity principle is under attack (Kanizsa & Luccio, 1985, Pomerantz & Kubovy, 1986, Rock, 1986). That is why this resurgence does not represent a resuscitation of the Gestalt theory, but rather an appreciation of the importance of the phenomena of perceptual organization. This renewed interest, which has been most intense in visual perception, has not been confined to psychologists: machine vision programs now incorporate Gestalt laws (Ballard & Brown, 1982, Barrow & Tenenbaum, 1986, Marr, 1982).

In audition, work (Deutsch, 1986) has proceeded along two main lines: The first was stream segregation (Bregman, 1981, van Noorden, 1971, van Noorden, 1975, who called the phenomenon fission) in which sounds are played in alternation. [Pioneering work had been done much earlier in Italy (Bozzi & Vicario, 1960, Petter, 1957, Vicario, 1960a, Vicario, 1960b), but was not known in this country till the 80s.] When fission occurs, two coherent streams of sound are heard, and it is difficult to tell the temporal relation between events in the two streams (see Figure 1). The second line of work to emerge was concurrent pitch segregation (CPS) (Kubovy, 1981, Kubovy & Daniel, 1983, McAdams, 1984): a set of concurrent tones is played continuously. One or more features of one of the sounds (called the target) is changed, making it the odd-man-out among the remaining sounds (called the background). In a typical experiment subjects are asked to detect whether an ascending or a descending scale was played. If the target is perceptually segregated, the feature difference between target and background is called a difference cue for concurrent pitch segregation (see Figure 1).

PERCEPTUAL ORGANIZATION AND INDISPENSABLE ATTRIBUTES

The following observations are a considerably modified version of Palmer (1982, 1983). Perceptual organization requires four elements: a set of parts, an operation, a medium, and a perceptual outcome. For instance, the figure pq conceived as a gestalt consists of a part (p or q), an operation (mirror reflection), the medium over which the elements are distributed (the xy plane), and a perceptual outcome (the perception of mirror symmetry). Another example. Look at two classic demonstrations of perceptual organization, grouping by proximity:

[1]   o+   +o   o+   +o,

and grouping by similarity:

[2]   + + + o o o + + + o o o + + +.

In both cases we speak of

<u>elements</u>   i.e., in [1] the forms o and + , or in
                   [2] the locations

                   . . . .,
                   where each . represents a place-marker.

<u>operations</u>   i.e., in [1] relative spacing, or in [2]
                   form differences,

<u>a medium</u>   implicitly, the xy plane,

<u>perceptual outcomes</u>
                   in [1] grouping of dissimilar forms by
                   spatial proximity in the plane, or in [2]
                   grouping of homogeneously spaced loca-
                   tions by similarity of form in the plane.
                   (Note that space can serve three
                   functions in a gestalt: space as a part
                   in [1], space as operation in [2], space
                   as medium in [1] and in [2].)

Thus the general pattern of a gestalt is: organization of E by O in M. Although in some cases, it is difficult to identify the elements or the operation, there always is a medium over which at least two perceptually distinct but perceptually inter-related elements are distributed.

I called these media "indispensable attributes" (Kubovy, 1981), because only physical stimulus dimensions that are indispensable for the preservation of perceptual numerosity can serve as media for gestalts. Perceptual numerosity is used as a criterion for such media because without perceptual numerosity the elements of the set E cannot preserve their perceptual individuality, and therefore cannot be perceived as having been operated upon by operator $\underline{O}$. As Figure 2 shows, spatial differences but not color differences control perceptual numerosity in vision. In contrast, pitch differences but not spatial differences control perceptual numerosity in audition. That is why I expect perceptual organization in the pitch domain to dominate any kind of perceptual organization in the spatial domain. What is the value of the theory of indispensable attributes? First of all, it provides a rational basis for downplaying the role of space in auditory perceptual organization. Secondly, it suggests that perceptual organization in audition is not confined to organization in time, as was commonly claimed, but exists in pitch as well. I have found the following thought-experiment useful in giving an intuitive interpretation to the dominance of pitch over spatial location in determining the perceptual organiza- tion of a sound. Consider two rooms in which we have hidden 6 loudspeakers: in one they form a pentagon with one loudspeaker at its center, in the other they form two concentric triangles. Over these loudspeakers we play a sextet. Will a listener who enters these rooms spontaneously form a spatial image of the disposition of the loudspeakers? If listeners are given the task of describing the spatial configuration, they will proceed by resolving the message coming from each source. The auditory system s spatial localization function is not designed to be exercised on spatial configurations of sounds: the minimal audible angle (MAA) for concurrent sounds is much higher than the MAA for successive sounds (Perrott, 1984). I do not wish to imply that spatial location is not an important function of the auditory system, but that it plays a minor role (if any) in auditory form perception. Indeed, there is some reason to believe (Auerbach & Sperling, 1974, Platt & Warren, 1972, Warren, 1970) that the localization function of the auditory system is directly connected to the orienting function of the visual system, as has been demonstrated in the owl (Konishi et al., 1985) but not yet in other species (Brugge, 1985). Nor am I claiming that the

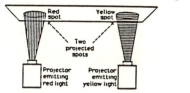 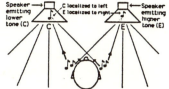

Color Difference Not Indispensable for Spatial Difference Pitch Difference Indispensable for Spatial Difference

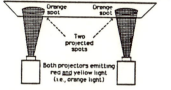 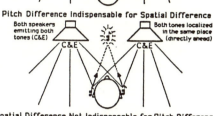

Spatial Difference Indispensable for Color Difference Spatial Difference Not Indispensable for Pitch Difference

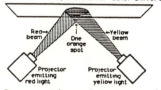 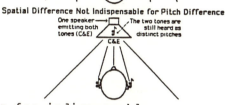

Figure 2.   Thought experiments for indispensable attributes. LEFT: Spatial difference vs. color difference. RIGHT: Spatial difference vs. pitch difference. TOP: One location per color (or pitch); one color (or pitch) per location. Two colors (or pitches) and two locations perceived. MIDDLE: Two locations per color (or pitch); two colors [or pitches] per location. One color and two locations perceived but two pitches and two locations perceived. BOTTOM: One location per color (or pitch); two colors (or pitches) per location. One color and one location perceived but two pitches and one location perceived. [Figures drawn by R. N. Shepard, reproduced with permission.]

notion of indispensable attributes rule out the existence of a contrived sound (such as white noise with interaural phase inversion) that seems to stem from more than one source even though it does not have two pitches. The thought experiment on which the concept is based applies only to the acoustic ecology in which hearing evolved, and in which such contrived sounds do not occur.

FROM ANALOGIES WITH VISION TO NEW PROBLEMS IN AUDITION

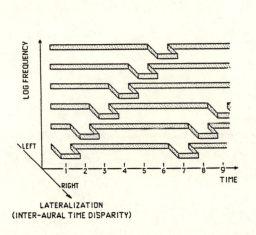
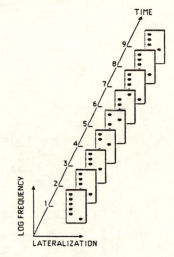

Figure 3.   Two representations of the discrete version of Huggins pitch. LEFT: A chord of six non-harmonically related pure tones is made to play an ascending scale by changing the inter-aural time disparity of one component at a time. This representation emphasizes the pattern of segregated tones. RIGHT: The same stimulus in a representation that emphasizes the differences and similarities between successive events.

The first work I did on CPS (Kubovy et al., 1974) was an attempt to create an auditory analog of the Julesz stereogram (Julesz, 1971). [It is actually a discrete version of the Huggins pitch (Cramer & Huggins, 1958). W. M. Hartmann has suggested that binaural edge pitch (Klein & Hartmann, 1981) is more closely analogous to the Julesz stereogram.] Figure 3 shows two representations of this type of stimulus. To approach this type of

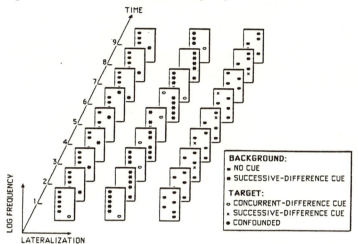

Figure 4.   Three stimuli in which the difference cue for
    segregation is inter-aural time disparity. LEFT:
    Concurrent and successive difference cues are
    confounded. CENTER: Pure concurrent difference cue
    applied to target; successive difference cue applied
    to background. RIGHT: Pure successive difference
    cue applied to target.

segregation from an organizational point of view is to
become aware of two potential segregation cues present in
the stimulus described in Figure 3.   In the left-hand
diagram of Figure 4 I have repeated the right-hand
diagram of Figure 3, but I have indicated in it that the
targets that have been lateralized to the right could be
segregated by a concurrent difference cue (represented by
empty circle) or by a successive difference cue
(represented by an X).   A concurrent difference cue is
said to apply to a target if and only if the target is
the odd-man-out with respect to that feature.   A
successive difference cue is said to apply to a target if
and only if the target has changed with respect to that
feature in a way that the background components haven t.
The other two diagrams show how one may unconfound these

305

two types of cues. Although a number of models of
binaural interaction (Colburn & Durlach, 1978) can
account for segregation by concurrent difference cues, it
is not known whether they can deal with successive
difference cues.

Two further techniques have been successfully used
to eliminate successive difference cues (Lenoble, 1986).
The stimuli we have described up to this point formed a
train of several (on the order of six) chords. In
two-chord stimuli scale direction can be heard only if
the target segregates in both chords (see, e.g., the
first two chords in the left-hand diagram of Figure 4).
If only a successive difference cue is operating, the
target will only segregate in the second chord. With
three-chord stimuli the task can be made into an
identification task, if the subjects are musically
experienced. Instead of playing only three-note
ascending (e.g., A, D, G) or descending (G, D, A) scales,
one can also play G, D, G or A, D, A, which will not be
distinguishable from the ascending and the descending
scales unless the target is segregated from the first
chord (by, necessarily, a concurrent difference cue).

CONJUNCTIONS ARE NOT CONCURRENT PITCH SEGREGATION CUES

Treisman has established (Treisman et al., 1977,
Treisman & Gelade, 1980, Treisman & Souther, 1985) that
effortless visual texture segregation cannot be based on
conjunctions (see Figure 5). She demonstrated that when
the segregation cue is simple (Figure 6), such as a
filled triangle among unfilled ones, the time it takes to
detect the presence of the target in a texture field is
independent of the number of background elements,
suggesting that the popout is due to parallel processing
of the texture field. When the odd man out is different
by virtue of a conjunction, search time is a function of
set size, suggesting a serial search through the texture
field.

According to Treisman certain feature differences

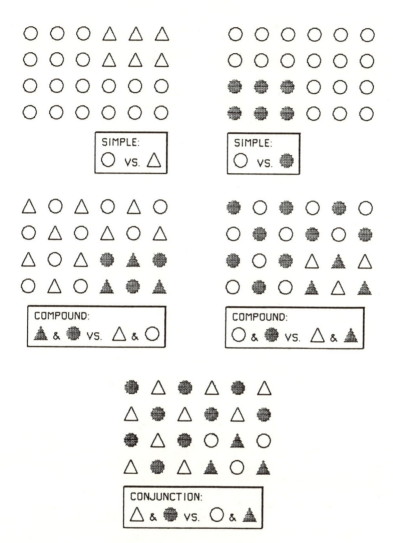

Figure 5.   Texture segregation.

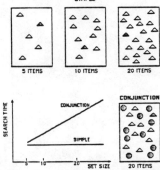

Figure 6.   Treisman s technique for demonstrating than an odd man out target will spontaneously pop out when it differs from the background by a single feature, but must be deliberately searched for when it differs from the background by a conjunction of features.

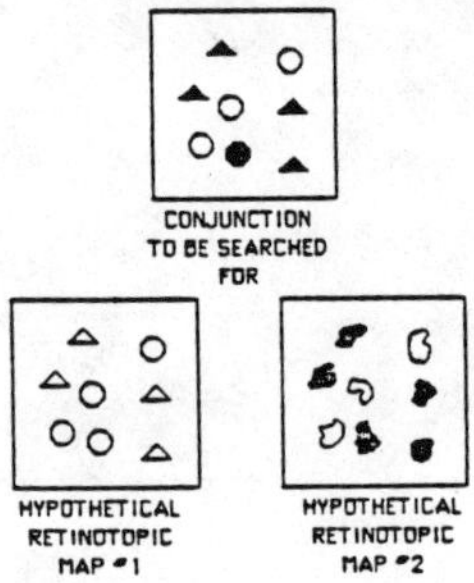

Figure 7.   Conjecture regarding why conjunctions do not pop out.

are detectable in parallel because they are subserved by specialized systems, which are sometimes identified with the multiple, seemingly redundant, cortical regions that contain a one-to-one map of the retina and are called retinotopic maps (see Figure 7).   When a conjunction characterizes the target, each retinotopic map is oblivious to the odd man out, forcing the observer to combine the two features of each item in the field in order to find the desired target.

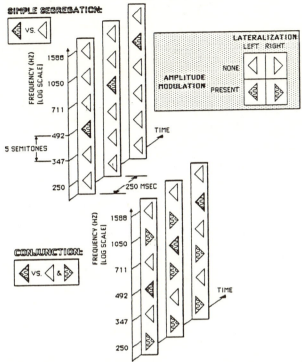

Figure 8.   Simple segregation compared to a target that
    differs from the background by a conjunction
    (Lenoble, 1986).

    The techniques developed for the study of CPS are
ideal for the study of conjuctions as segregation cues
(Lenoble, 1986).   Consider the triple of chords shown in
the upper part of Figure 8: The tones in the chords are 5
semitones apart; the target (shown with the heavy
outline) is amplitude-modulated, whereas the background
components are not.   The lower part of Figure 8 shows a
target that differs from the background by a conjunction.
A detailed report on the results of this research is
beyond the scope of the present survey, so I will confine
myself to a description of a fragment of the method and

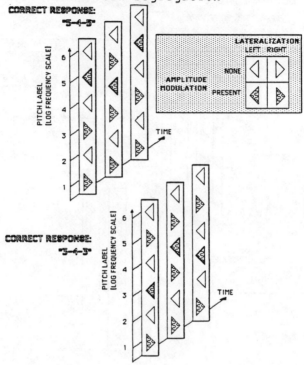

Figure 9.   Musically trained subjects were required to
    label the pitch profile defined by the targets (here
    conjunctions, drawn with heavy border).

the results. Consider the two stimuli shown in Figure 9.
Only if the target is heard in each chord can the subject
tell the difference between a 5-4-5 profile and a 3-4-3,
a 3-4-5, or a 5-4-3 profile.

    As may be seen from Figure 10, when the target
differs from the background by a single feature
(amplitude modulation or lateralization) the pitch
profile it forms over the three chords is identified
correctly much more often than expected by chance (10%).
When the target differs by a conjunction profile

310

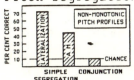

Figure 10.   Results (Lenoble, 1986): Per cent correct
    profile identification as a function of difference
    between target and background for non-monotonic
    profiles (as shown in Figure 9). Left and center:
    results for single feature. Right: results for
    conjunction.

identification is no better than chance performance.
This result, although entirely consistent with Treisman s
results in vision does not allow us to say anything about
the way in which conjunctions might be perceived in
audition. This is because no experimental technique is
available to allow us to study auditory search processes
and differentiate parallel from serial searches.

ACKNOWLEDGMENT

    The research reported in this chapter was supported
by: NSF grants BNS 76-21018 (to Yale University) and BNS
82-10578 (to Rutgers University), and USPHS grant MH
35137 (to Rutgers University). I thank Jill Lenoble for
her helpful comments on a draft of this chapter.

REFERENCES

Auerbach, C. and Sperling, P. A.   (1974).   A common
    visual-auditory space: Evidence for its reality.
    Perception & Psychophysics, 16, 129-135.
Ballard, D. H. and Brown, C. M.   (1982). Computer vision.
    Englewood Cliffs, NJ: Prentice-Hall.
Barrow, H. G. and Tenenbaum, J. M.   (1986).
    Computational approaches to vision. In Boff, K. R.,
    Kaufman, L. and Thomas, J. P. (Eds.), Handbook of
    perception and human performance. New York: Wiley.
Bozzi, P. and Vicario, G.   (1960). Due fattori di
    unificazione fra note musicali: la vicinanza

Kubovy, M. and Daniel, J. E. (1983). Pitch segregation by interaural phase, by momentary amplitude disparity, and by monaural phase. Journal of the Audio Engineering Society, 31(9), 630-635.

Kubovy, M., Cutting, J. E., and McGuire, R. M. (1974). Hearing with the third ear: Dichotic perception of a melody without monaural familiarity cues. Science, 186, 272-274.

Lenoble, J. S. (1986). Feature conjunctions and the perceptual grouping of concurrent tones. Doctoral dissertation, Rutgers University,

Marr, D. (1982). Vision: A computational investigation into the human representation and processing of visual information. San Francisco: Freeman.

McAdams, S. (1984). Spectral fusion, spectral parsing and the formation of auditory images. Doctoral dissertation, Stanford University, Program in Hearing and Speech Sciences.

Palmer, S. E. (1982). Symmetry, transformation, and the structure of perceptual systems. In Beck, J. (Ed.), Organization and representation in perception. Hillsdale, NJ: Lawrence Erlbaum.

Palmer, S. E. (1983). The psychology of perceptual organization. A transformational approach. In Rosenfeld, A. and Beck, J. (Eds.), Human and machine vision. New York: Academic press.

Perrott, D. R. (1984). Concurrent minimum audible angle: A reexamination of the concept of auditory spatial acuity. Journal of the Acoustical Society of America, 75(4), 1201-1206.

Petter, G. (1957). Osservazioni sperimentali sulla natura dell effetto tunnel. Rivista di Psicologia, 51(3), 1-15.

Platt, B. B. and Warren, D. H. (1972). Auditory localization: The importance of eye movements and a textured visual environment. Perception & Psychophysics, 12, 245-248.

Pomerantz, J. R. and Kubovy, M. (1981). Perceptual organization: an overview. In Kubovy, M. and Pomerantz, J. R. (Eds.), Perceptual organization. Hillsdale, NJ: Lawrence Erlbaum.

Pomerantz, J. R. and Kubovy, M. (1986). Theoretical approaches to perceptual organization. In Boff, K. R., Kaufman, L. and Thomas, J. P. (Eds.), Handbook of perception and human performance. New York: Wiley.

Rock, I. (1986). The description and analysis of object and event perception. In Boff, K. R., Kaufman, L., and Thomas, J. P. (Ed.), Handbook of perception and human performance. New York: Wiley.

Treisman, A. & Gelade, G. (1980). A feature-integration theory of attention. Cognitive Psychology, 12, 97-136.

Treisman, A. and Souther, J. (1985). Search asymmetry: A diagnostic for preattentive processing of separable features. Journal of Experimental Psychology: General, 114, 285-310.

Treisman, A. M., Sykes, M. and Gelade, G. (1977). Selective attention and stimulus integration. In Dornic, S. (Ed.), Attention and Performance. Hillsdale, NJ: Lawrence Erlbaum.

van Noorden, L. P. A. S. (1971). Rhythmic fission as a function of tone rate. IPO Annual Progress Report, 6, 9-12.

van Noorden, L. P. A. S. (1975). Temporal coherence in the perception of tone sequences. Doctoral dissertation, Technical University, Eindhoven,

Vicario, G. (1960). L effetto tunnel acustico. Rivista di psicologia, 54(2), 41-52.

Vicario, G. (1960). Analisi sperimentale di un caso di dipendenza fenomenica tra eventi sonori. Rivista di Psicologia, 54(3), 83-106.

Warren, D. H. (1970). Intermodality interactions in spatial localization. Cognitive Psychology, 1, 114-133.

temporale e la vicinanza tonale. Rivista di psicologia, 54(4), 235-58.

Bregman, A. S. (1981). Asking the what for question in auditory perception. In Kubovy, M. and Pomerantz, J. R. (Eds.), Perceptual organization. Hillsdale, NJ: Lawrence Erlbaum.

Brugge, J. F. (1985). Patterns of organization in auditory cortex. Journal of the Acoustical Society of America, 78(1), 353-359.

Colburn, H. S. and Durlach, N. I. (1978). Models of binaural interaction. In Carterette, E. C. and Friedman, M. P. (Eds.), Handbook of perception. Volume 4: Hearing. New York: Academic Press.

Cramer, E. M. and Huggins, W. H. (1958). Creation of pitch through binaural interaction. Journal of the Acoustical Society of America, 30, 413-417.

Deutsch, D. (1986). Auditory pattern recognition. In Boff, K. R., Kaufman, L., and Thomas, J. P. (Eds.), Handbook of perception and human performance. New York: Wiley.

Julesz, B. (1971). Foundations of cyclopean perception. Chicago: University of Chicago Press.

Kanizsa, G. and Luccio, R. (1985). La pregnanza e le sue ambiguita [praegnanz and its ambiguities]. Psicologia Italiana, 7(1-2), 11-39.

Klein, M. A. and Hartmann, W. M. (1981). Binaural edge pitch. Journal of the Acoustical Society of America, (1), pp. 51-61.

Konishi, M., Sullivan, W. E., and Takahashi, T. (1985). The owl s cochlear nuclei process different sound localization cues. Journal of the Acoustical Society of America, 78(1), 360-364.

Kubovy, M. (1981). Concurrent pitch-segregation and the theory of indispensable attributes. In Kubovy, M. and Pomerantz, J. R. (Eds.), Perceptual organization. Hillsdale, NJ: Lawrence Erlbaum.

Kubovy, M. (1986). Overview of Section VI: Perceptual organization and cognition. In Boff, K. R., Kaufman, L., and Thomas, J. P. (Eds.), Handbook of perception and human performance, Vol. II. New York: Wiley.

SUBJECT INDEX

The Chapters in which the term is described or discussed are listed after the term. "I" indicates the introductory chapter. The terms were chosen by the author as those which were most important in his or her chapter.

A

absolute pitch - 19
absolute pitch range - 19
absolute features - 19
abstraction - 15
acoustic ecology - 28
adaptation and recovery - 9
adaptive procedure - 11,25
adaptor - 7
aftereffects - 15
allophones - 24
ambiguity - 15
ametrical - 9
amplitude modulated -
     8,13,28
amplitude-modulated
     noise - 13
analytic signal - 8,12
anisochronous patterns - 25
arrhythmic - 19
articulatory mediation - 23
asymptotic performance - 25
attention - 25,26
auditory form
     perception - 28
auditory sensation - 27
auditory
     physiology - I,9,20,
     21,22
auditory space - 14
auditory memory - 25,27
auditory streaming - 6,28
auditory temporal pattern
     perception - 9,10
auditory nerve
     fibers - 20,21,22
auditory-perceptual theory
     of phonetic
     recognition - 24
auditory-perceptual
     space - 24

auditory-perceptual
     theory - 24
autocorrelation - 12,21
azimuth - 14

B

background noise - 20
background - 28
backward recognition
     masking - 27
bandwidth - 8
behavioral thresholds - 20
behavioral masked
     thresholds - 20
binary sequences - 9
binaural interaction - 14
binaural signal
     processing - 14
binaural patterns - 14
binaural masking-level
     differences
     (BMLD) - 18
biologically determined
     mechanisms - 27
broadband noise - 20
burst-friction neutral
     point - 24
burst-friction sensory
     pointer - 24

C

categorical
     perception - 14,23
categorization - I,15,24
category codes - 24
Central Spectrum - 18
central mechanisms I,7
central processing - I,26
Central Activation Pattern
     (CAP) model - 18
chopper cell - 20,21
chords - 15,28

315

Subject Index

CMR - I,6,7
COCB stimulation - 20
cochlear nerve - 21
coding - 22
cognition - I,15
cognitive mechanisms - I,25
cognitive psychology - 15
comodulation masking
    release
    (CMR) - I,6,7
comodulation - 6,7
comparing information - 3
comparison process - 3
complex - I,21
complex nonspeech - 23
component matching - 17
compound psychometric
    functions - 8
compound stimulus - 11
compressive input-output
    functions - 22
computational models - 10
concurrent pitch
    segregation
    (CPS) - 28
consonances - 5
context conditioned
    variability - 23
context-invariant - 23
contextual effects - 23
continuous
    random noise - 7,12
contour - 15,19
contourization - 15
cowbirds - 19
Cramer-Huggins - 18
critical
    band - I,1,3,4,7,11,12
critical bandwidth - 8
crossed olivocochlear
    bundle - 20
cyclic pattern - 9

D
decision variable - 3
dendritic tree - 20
detectability - 25
detection - I,13

detection theories - 11
dichotic - 14,18
dichotic pitch - 18
difference cue - 28
difference limen (DL) - 8
diphthongs - 24
discretization - 15
discrimination - I,1,2,8,
    10,13,23
discrimination
    training - 19
discrimination of musical
    intervals - 5
distortion - 15
dominant harmonics - 17
Duplex perception - 17
dynamic range - 20
Duplex Theory of
    Localization - 18

E
EC model - 18
echo suppression - I,14
efferent innervation - 20
efferents - 20
electrical stimulation - 20
electrical analog model - 3
empirical and
    critical ratio - 8
energetic masking - 25
energy detection - 3
ensemble average - 12
envelope - 6,8
envelope encoders - 21
envelope - 12
envelope function - 8
envelope-weighted average
    of instantaneous
    frequency (EWAIF) - 8
Equalization/Cancellation
    (EC) model - 18
ergodic - 12
evoked potentials - 9
evoked brain stem
    responses - 9
EWAIF Model - 8
excitation patterns - 14
excitatory synapses - 20

Subject Index

existence region
    for dichotic
    pitch - 18

F
feature - 28
fifth and fourth
    similarity - 15
figure - I,28
filter model - 9
fine-structure
    encoders - 21
fission - 28
fixed-amplitude
    random-phase
    noise - 1,4,12
fixed-phase - 1
fluctuations - 12
formants - 23,24
forward masking - 7,14
Fourier transforms - 22
Fourier series - 8
Fourier analysis - 15
frequency DL - 13
frequency discrimination
    (DL) - 5,7,8,17,20
frequency resolving
    power - 8,22
frequency fluctuations - 8
frequency modulated - 8
frequency ratios - 5
frequency pattern - 10
frequency analysis - 4
frequency uncertainty - 5
frequency fluctuation - 8
frequency-time domain - 11
fricatives - 24
frozen noise - 3,12

G
gap variability - 10
Gaussian envelopes - 11
Gaussian
    distribution - 3,12
Geometric illusions - 15
Gestalt - I,15,28
glides - 24
glottal-source spectra - 24

glottal-source neutral
    point - 24
glottal-source pointer - 24
GO/NOGO procedure - 19
goodness index - 24

H
Haas effect - 14
hair cells - 20,21,22
harmonic sieve - 17
harmonic complexes - 22
harmonies - 15
hearing impaired - 13
hierarchical rhythmic
    structure 9
hierarchical pattern - 19
high SR fibers - 20
Hilbert transform - 8
HPC - 15
HPC concept: Hierarchical
    Processing of
    Categories - 15
HPC Concept of Gestalt
    Perception - 15

I
identification - 23
illusory contour - 15
immediate auditory
    memory - 25
indispensable
    attributes - 28
individual
    differences - 25,26
information processing - 27
information - 15
information extraction - 27
informational masking - 25
informational capacity - 25
inharmonic signals - 21
inhibition - 20
inhibitory synapses - 20
instantaneous frequency - 8
instantaneous frequency
    functions - 8
integration theory - 28
integrator - 3

317

Subject Index

VOT - 23,25
vowels - I,24,27

W
waveform periodicity - 21
waveform synchrony - 5
weighted average
      algorithm - 10

AUTHOR INDEX

The Chapters in which the authors are cited follow the author's name. 'P' is for the Preface and 'I' is for the introductory chapter.

A
Abbas, P.J. - 1,9,20
Abramson, J. - 9
Ahumada, A. - 3
Aitkin, L.M. - 9
Akerboom, S. - 9
Alford, B.- 20
Anderson, D.J. - 21
Arthur, R.M. - 21
Atler, E. - 20
Auerbach, C. - 28

B
Bacon, S.P. - 7,13
Ballard, D.H. - 28
Barron, M. - 14
Barrow, H.G. - 28
Barta, P. - 20
Bashford, J.A., Jr. - 27
Beauvillain, C. - 9
Bechtereva, N.P. - 9
Benbassat, C.A. - 25
Bennett, K.B. - 26
Berliner, J.E. - 2
Bernstein, L.R. - 1
Best, C.T. - 23
Biddulph, G.R. - 8
Bilsen, F.A. - 18
Blackburn, C. - 20
Blauert, J. - 14
Blumstein, S.E. - 24
Bock, D.E. - 7
Boer, E. de - 21
Boggs, G.J. - 2,9,10
Boomsliter, P. - 5
Boring, E. - 21
Boulez, P. - 12
Bower, G. - 19
Bozzi, P. - 28
Brachman, M. - 20
Bradley, R.A. - 10
Bradley, D.W. - 10
Brady, S.L. - 2,9,10
Braida, L.D. - 10

Bregman, A.S. - 6,9,26,28
Broadbent, D.E. - 9
Brocaar, M.P. - 13
Brown, M. - 20
Brown, P. - 21
Brown, C.M. - 28
Brown, E.L. - 9
Brugge, J.E. - 21,22,28
Buell, T.N. - 14
Buffardi, L. - 9
Bundzen, P.V. - 9
Burns, E.M. - 5,13
Buus, S.- 4,6,22

C
Callaghan, B.P. - 4
Calvert, D.R. - 13
Campbell, J. - 9,26
Capranica, R.R. - 9
Carlyon, R.P. - 6,7
Carrell, T.D. - 23
Chang, H.M. - 24
Chiang, C. - 9
Chistovich, L.A. - 24
Chocholle, R. - 26
Clark, W.W. - 13
Cline, C. - 26
Cloarke, D.P.J. - 26
Cohen, M.F. - 6
Cokely, J.A. - 6
Colburn, H.S. - 18,28
Colleran, E. - 26
Coombs, S.L. - 20
Cooper, L.A. - 9
Cooper, F.S. - 23
Costalupes, J.A. - 20
Cowan, N. - 27
Cramer, E.M. - 18,28
Cranford, J. - 20
Creel, W. - 5
Creelman, C.D. - 2,9,25
Crowder, R.G. - 27
Cutting, J.E. - 18,28
Cynx, I. - 19

323

Author Index

D
Dallos, P. - 7,9
Daniel, J.W. - 28
Dannebring, G.L. - 6,9
Danner, W.F. - 9
Darwin, C.J. - 9,27
David, E.- 9
de Ribaupierre, F. - 9
de Boer, E. - 12
Delattre, P.C. - 23
Delgutte, B. - 9,20,22
Deutsch, D. - 9,15,19,28
Dewson, J.H. - 20
Divenyi, P.L. - 9,14
Doehring, P. - 9
Dolan, T.R. - P
Dooling, R. - 13,15,19,25
Duifhuis, H - 17
Dunlop, C.W. - 9
Durlach, N.I. - 2,10,18,28
Dye, R.H. - 18,20

E
Ebata, M. - 14
Efron, R. - 27
Eggemont, J.J. - 9
Ehrenfels, C. - 15
Elfuer, L.F. - 9
Elliot, D. - 20
Elliot, L.L. - 7,9
Emmerich, D.S. - 26
Erber, N.P. - 13
Essens, P.J. - 9
Evans, E.F. - 1,9,20,21

F
Fant, G. - 24
Fantini, D.A. - 5
Farley G.R. - 9,22
Farmer, R.M. - 9
Fastl, H. - 22
Faulkner, A. - 17
Fay, R.R. - 13,20
Fernandes, M.A. - 3,4,6
Feroe, J. - 19
Feth, L.L. - 8
Fitzgibbons, P.J. - 9

Fletcher, H. - 3,6,24
Florentine, M. - 14
Flottorp, G. - 7
Forbes, S.M. - 26
Formby, C. - 13
Forrest, T.G. - 1
Foster, J. - 15
Foyle, D.C. - 9,25,26,27
Fraisse, P. - 9
Frankish, C. - 15
Freda, J.S. - 26
Frijns, J.H.M. - 18
Frisina, R.F. - 21
Frisshkopf, L.S. - 9
Fruhstrofer, H. - 9
Fujitani, D.A. - 15

G
Galambos, R. - 9
Gans, S.J. - 23
Gardner, M.B. - 24
Garner, W.R. - 9,19
Gaskell, H. - 14
Geisler, C.D. - 21,22
Gelade, G. - 28
Gerson, J. - 21
Gerstman, L.J. - 23
Gerzso, A. - 12
Gibson, D.J. - 20
Gilkey, R.H. - 3
Gilliom, J.D. - 26
Glasberg, B.R. - 7,16,17,26
Glaser, E. - 21
Glass, I. - 9
Goldberg, J. - 21
Goldberg, I.A. - 12
Goldstein, M.H. - 9,13
Goldstein, J.L. - 6,17,
    21,22
Goodman, D.A. - 27
Gordon, W. - 20
Gorga, M.P. - 9
Gorta, A. - 9
Gottwald, R.L. - 9
Grant, K.W. - 25
Gray, S. - 15

Author Index

Green, D.M. - 1,2,3,4,5,6,
    7,8,11,12,18,
    20,25,26
Greenberg, G.Z. - 26
Greenberg, S. - 21
Gruhn, J.J. - 9
Grunke, M.E. - 23
Guinan, J. - 20
Guttman, N. - 7,27

H
Haas, H. - 14
Hafter, E.R. - 14,20,26
Haggard, M.P. - 3,4,6,15
Hall, J.W. - 3,4,6
Halpern, A.R. - 9
Halwes, T.G. - 23
Hamernik, R. - 13
Handel, S. - 9
Hanna, T.E. - 2,3,8,12
Harder, P.J. - 18
Harmuth, H.F. - 8
Harris, K.S. - 23,24
Harris, J.D. - 2,25
Harris, D.M. - 7,9
Hartmann, W.M. - 12,18,28
Harvey, A.D.G. - 6
Hawkins, J.E. - 9
Hawks, J.W. - 24
Heinbach, W. - 15
Henderson, D. - 13
Hibi, S. - 9
Hiese, G.A. - 9
Hillgard, S.A. - 9
Hind, J.E. - 21
Hirsh, I.J. - 8,9,23
Horst, E. - 22
House, J.F. - 9
Houtgast, T. - 3,11,22
Houtsma, A.J.M. - 5
Howard, J.H. - 26
Hudspeth, A.J. - 22
Huggins, W.H. - 18,28
Hulse, S.H. - 19
Humpal, J. - 19

I
Idson, W.L. - 27

Igarashi, M. - 20
Iwamiya, S. - 8

J
Jausfeld, S. - 9
Javel, E. - 21,22
Jeffress, L.A. - 3
Jesteadt, W.- 2,5,7,9,20
Johnson, D.H. - 22
Johnson, D.M. - 26
Johnson, L.L. - 9
Jones, M.R. - 9,19,26
Joos, M. - 24
Julesz, B. - 27,28

K
Kallert, S. - 9
Kallman, H.J. - 27
Kanizsa, G. - 28
Karlovich, R.S. - 9
Keidel, W.D. - 9
Kelly, W.J.- 2,4,5,10,25,26
Kewley-Port, D. - 25
Kiang, N.Y.S. - 1,20
Kidd, G., Jr. - 1,2,4,6,
    8,26
Kim, D.O. - 20,21
Kinchla, R.A. - 27
Kinney, J.A. - 23
Kitamura, O. - 8
Klatt, D.H. - 23,24
Klein, M.A. - 18,28
Kniazuk, M. - 9
Koch, C. - 20
Kohler, W. - 15
Kohlmann, M. - 15
Konishi, M. - 28
Kotovsky, K. - 19
Kozhevnikov,V.A. - 24
Kruskal, J.B. - 10
Kubovy, M. - 9,18,28

L
Ladefoged, P. - 9
Lamore, P.J.J. - 13
Lane, H.L. - 23
Langford, T.L. - 18
Larkin, W.D. - 26

325

Author Index

326

Author Index

Sykes, M. - 28
Syrdal, A.K. - 23

T
Takahashi, T. - 28
Taylor, W.G. - 13
Taylor, D.W. - 26
Taylor, M.M. - 26
ten Hoopen, G. - 9
Tenenbaum, J.M. - 28
Terhardt, E. - 15,17,21,27
Thomas, I.B. - 9
Thurlow,W.R. - 9
Tiffin, J. - 8
Todres, A.K. - 27
Torre, V. - 20
Townsend, R.E. - 9
Trahiotis, C. - 3,20
Treisman, A.M. - 27,28
Turvey, M.T. - 27

V
van Zanten, G.A. - 13
van Meurs, G. - 9
van Noorden, L.P.A.S. -
     26,28
Verweij, C. - 13
Vicario, G. - 28
Viemeister, N. - 6,7,9,
     15,20
Voelcker, H. - 8
Voight, H.F. - 20
von Bekesy, G. - 6
Vos, J. - 9

W
Wallach, H. - 14
Walsh, E.J. - 9
Ward, W.D. - 5
Warr, W.B. - 20
Warren, D.H. - 28
Warren, R.M. - 9,27
Watkins, M.J. - 27
Watkins, O.C. - 27
Watson, C.S. - 2,4,5,9,
     10,11,25,26,27
Weaver, M.S. - 9
Weber, D.L. - 3,11,16
Wetzel, R. - 26
Whitfield, I.C. - 9
Wiederhold, M. - 20
Wier, C.C. - 5,20,25
Wightman, F.L. - 21
Wilkens, H. - 14
Willems, L.F. - 17
Wilson, J.P. - 7
Winslow, R.L. - 20
Winzenz, D. - 19
Wollberg, Z. - 9
Wroton, H.W. - 4,10,25,26

Y
Yeni-Komshian, G. - 9
Yoder, D. - 9
Yost, W.A. - P,18
Young, E.D. - 1,20
Yoyer F.L. - 9

Z
Zurek, P.M. - 14
Zwicker, E. - 7,15,22,24
Zwislocki, J.J. - 7,27